READING THE WEB

Reading the Web

Strategies for Internet Inquiry

second edition

ELIZABETH DOBLER
MAYA B. EAGLETON

Foreword by Donald J. Leu

THE GUILFORD PRESS
New York   London

Library of Congress Cataloging-in-Publication Data

Dobler, Elizabeth, 1963–
   Reading the Web : strategies for Internet inquiry / Elizabeth Dobler, Maya B. Eagleton ;
foreword by Donald J. Leu. — Second edition.
      pages cm
   Includes bibliographical references and index.
   ISBN 978-1-4625-2087-9 (paperback)
   1. Internet in education.   2. Computers and literacy.   I. Eagleton, Maya B.
II. Title.
   LC149.5.E16 2015
   371.33′44678—dc23
                                                                        2015003997

To my husband,
who has an engineer's mind and an educator's heart
—E. D.

To my father,
who always said that I could accomplish
anything I set out to do
—M. B. E.

ABOUT THE AUTHORS

Elizabeth Dobler, PhD, is Professor of Literacy at Emporia State University in Kansas. She teaches undergraduate and graduate courses in information literacy, children's literature, and language arts, and supervises student interns in the Topeka Professional Development School program. A former classroom teacher, Dr. Dobler's research interests include Web literacies and reading comprehension.

Maya B. Eagleton, PhD, is Department Chair of the Teacher Education Program at Pima Community College in Arizona. She designs and teaches online and hybrid courses with a focus on elementary and middle school language arts, 21st-century literacies, and exceptional learners. Dr. Eagleton has extensive K–12 classroom experience as a Title I coordinator, reading interventionist, instructional coach, and learning supports coordinator. She has also worked as a research scientist, instructional software designer, and educational consultant.

FOREWORD

Seldom has a book appeared that is timelier, more important, and more appropriate to our work today in literacy classrooms than the second edition of *Reading the Web: Strategies for Internet Inquiry*. Elizabeth Dobler and Maya B. Eagleton address a central question: How do we best integrate the Internet into our classrooms? They also explain instruction clearly, with both feet planted firmly in classroom contexts. Finally, they push us to reconceptualize reading and learning in today's online world.

The Internet has profoundly disrupted many aspects of education (Christensen, Horn, & Johnson, 2008), none more important than literacy. At the current rate of adoption, half of the world's population will have access to the Internet in 2017 and nearly everyone will have access by 2025 (UNESCO, 2014). Thus, by the time today's second graders graduate from high school, over seven billion people in the world will be reading, writing, and learning together with online information. Moreover, additional reading skills are required to use online information effectively. The Internet and the new literacy skills that it requires are clearly a cornerstone for literacy, learning, and life in an online age of information.

This highly readable book has already become a classic. As you read this second edition, the authors will become your new friends and instructional mentors. They will take you on a journey that opens new doors to learning, substantially improving opportunities for each student in your classroom.

The second edition has been thoroughly updated with many new elements. Most important is the wonderful focus on inquiry learning. The ability to conduct online research, comprehend it, and learn from it will enable students to read the Web and develop rich and complex understanding of the world around us. The skills and social practices of online reading that are the focus of this book are now reflected in new standards in the United States, Canada, Australia, and many other nations. Successful online inquiry skills will define our students' future, enabling them to work and live together successfully with others around the world.

Surprisingly, our students' online reading skills are quite limited. They lack many skills associated with locating information online (Bilal, 2000; Kuiper & Volman, 2008). They also are relatively unskilled at critically evaluating online sources (Walraven, Brand-Gruwel, & Boshuizen, 2008). Many find it difficult to judge the accuracy, reliability, and bias of information that they encounter during online reading and research (Bennett, Maton, & Kervin, 2008). And many students believe that they can read online information more successfully than they do (Kuiper & Volman, 2008). This book shows you how to support our students' development with online information skills.

There is also an important issue of social justice. Recent work by Reardon (2011) shows that the "offline" reading gap, based on income inequality, is large and growing. This, however, does not take into account an additional online reading achievement gap that has recently been reported (Leu et al., 2015). These growing achievement gaps for reading, including online reading, limit in important ways any attempt to achieve greater equity and opportunity in any nation. This book will provide important direction for helping us to close these gaps.

Finally, this volume will increase the number of educators who understand that the challenge of the Internet has less to do with technology than with new forms of reading and learning. In this book, the authors show us how to make an important difference in the lives of our students, preparing them for these new forms of reading and writing that now define college and career readiness in an online age of information.

We change the world when we teach a child to read online. Every page of the book you are reading will help you accomplish this.

DONALD J. LEU, PhD
Neag Endowed Chair in Literacy and Technology
University of Connecticut

REFERENCES

Bennett, S., Maton, K., & Kervin, L. (2008). The "digital natives" debate: A critical review of the evidence. *British Journal of Educational Technology, 39*(5), 775–786.

Bilal, D. (2000). Children's use of the Yahooligans! Web search engine: Cognitive, physical, and affective behaviors on fact-based search tasks. *Journal of the American Society for Information Science, 51*(7), 646–665.

Christensen, C. M., Horn, M. B., & Johnson, C. W. (2008). *Disrupting class: How disruptive innovation will change the way the world learns.* New York: McGraw-Hill.

Kuiper, E., & Volman, M. (2008). The Web as a source of information for students in K–12 education. In J. Coiro, M. Knobel, C. Lankshear, & D. J. Leu (Eds.), *Handbook of research on new literacies* (pp. 241–246). Mahwah, NJ: Erlbaum.

Leu, D. J., Forzani, E., Rhoads, C., Maykel, C., Kennedy, C., & Timbrell, N. (2015). The new literacies of online research and comprehension: Rethinking the reading achievement gap. *Reading Research Quarterly, 50*(1), 1–23.

Reardon, S. F. (2011). The widening academic achievement gap between the rich and the poor: New evidence and possible explanations. In R. Murnane & G. Duncan (Eds.), *Whither opportunity? Rising inequality and the uncertain life chances of low-income children*. Retrieved from *http://cepa. stanford.edu/content/widening-academic-achievement-gap-between-rich-and-poor-new-evidence-and-possible#sthash.LHo2QIev.dpuf*.

UNESCO. (2014). *The state of broadband 2014: Broadband for all*. Geneva, Switzerland: United Nations.

Walraven, A., Brand-Gruwel, S., & Boshuizen, H. P. A. (2008). Information-problem solving: A review of problems students encounter and instructional solutions. *Computers in Human Behavior, 24*(3), 623–648.

ACKNOWLEDGMENTS

We owe a special debt of gratitude to the students, teachers, and library-media specialists who have shared their thoughts and experiences with us. We would specifically like to thank Gennifer Birk, Sue Bower, Donna Charbarneau, Erin Fitzpatrick, Sandi Herrington, Karen Langlais, Ginger Lewman, Judi Moreillon, and Scott Ritter for generously sharing both their teaching insights and their classrooms. We also wish to thank our colleagues Don Leu, Julie Coiro, Kathleen Guinee, Colin Lankshear, Michele Knobel, Colin Harrison, Bernadette Dwyer, Jill Castek, and Laurie Henry for their forward-thinking research in the field of Web literacies.

We owe a huge thank you to the brilliant researchers, educators, and instructional designers at CAST, Inc., who envisioned and supported some of the research that went into this text. We would especially like to acknowledge David Rose, Anne Meyer, Ada Sullivan, Grace Meo, and Bridget Dalton.

We thank the U.S. Department of Education Office of Special Education Programs for funding portions of the research that informed this work.

To our families, we thank you for your endless patience and understanding. We'd like to give a special shout out to Maya's brother, Stephen B. Eagleton (*www.eagletondesign.net*), for designing the QUEST logo and other original images that appear in the text.

To Craig Thomas, William Meyer, Elaine Kehoe, Paul Gordon, Marian Robinson, Seymour Weingarten, and everyone else at The Guilford Press, thank you for believing in us.

PREFACE

In 2005, we began the process of writing the first edition of *Reading the Web: Strategies for Internet Inquiry*. Prior to this endeavor, both of us had spent extensive time observing and working with students during the process of Internet inquiry. Maya's research had focused on middle school students and their processes for searching the Web and creating products to share their learning. Beth's had entailed working with fifth and sixth graders, watching and listening as they thought aloud during their Internet search for information. We had also worked with classroom teachers and librarians who had made teaching about online reading part of their instruction. Our goal with the first edition was to build a bridge between the processes of print reading and online reading, drawing from insights and examples we gleaned from our classroom experiences.

A decade later, it's time to update *Reading the Web*, not because the needs of Web readers have changed but because the Web itself has changed. Readers are still in need of effective strategies for locating, understanding, evaluating, and using information; the Internet, on the other hand, has changed tremendously. Over the past 5 years, Maya has been working as a K–8 reading specialist and instructional coach, and her daily interactions with students and teachers have given her opportunities to promote effective literacy practices. Beth spent time in four elementary and middle school classrooms observing and interacting with students and teachers on various inquiry projects. Both of us continue to teach classes for educators at the university level. These experiences have convinced us that now, more than ever, all educators must teach the process of Web reading and give students guided instructional activities for practicing this important real-world skill.

During one of our early collaborative writing sessions, we generated a list of aspects of Web reading that have changed since the publication of the first edition of this book and also aspects that have remained the same. Both lists are telling signs of the complexities surrounding the Web reading process.

Aspects of Web Reading That Have Changed

- Information searching can occur anytime and anywhere. Mobile devices (e.g., smartphones, tablets) are like miniature libraries in the palms of our hands.
- Information found on the Internet can easily be collected and organized. Students can save and sort the information they deem important using curation tools such as Pinterest, Scoop.it, Symbaloo, and Diigo.
- Images and multimedia have become more prominent sources of information. Sites such as YouTube, Flickr, and Google Images let students explore and tag visual displays of information. Visual literacy skills have become crucial for understanding and critically evaluating online information.
- Information travels faster than ever. Social networking promotes the sharing of information in the form of text, images, and links to websites. Through the use of such tools as Twitter, Instagram, and Facebook, information travels in fractions of a second, and misinformation can spread like a wildfire. The need to be a critical evaluator of information is imperative.
- The Internet is a collaborative space. Information is being created and shared through virtual communities and user-generated content. Ordinary people are creating ebooks, blogs, wikis, and other Web resources. Again, the need for strong evaluation skills has multiplied exponentially.
- The Internet has become more intuitive. Browsers and search tools analyze phrases and user actions and use these data to tailor the information that is presented to each user. Although there are many advantages to this development, it can also limit the types of information found during Internet searching.

Aspects of Web Reading That Have Not Changed

- Curriculum is narrowing because of high-stakes testing, mandates, rules, and regulations.
- Obstacles to technology integration still exist (e.g., lack of funding, time, technical support, wireless access, training for teachers).
- The socioeconomic digital divide is still with us, thus preventing some students from gaining essential Web literacies both in and out of school.
- Teacher training programs tend to focus on print literacies or technology tools that support outdated pedagogical outcomes.
- Technology use in some classrooms is still limited to tutorial games or a reward for completing work.

Although these lists are not meant to be exhaustive, they illustrate that Web reading has become even more complex in the past decade and that our education system has not resolved issues that could promote success with Internet reading. In our experience with teachers, librarians, and students, knowledge about effective Web reading practices has not kept pace with this increased complexity. Children and adults still benefit greatly from learning strategies that can make their Web reading more effective and efficient. One influential change since the publication of the first edition of this book is the Common Core State Standards (CCSS; National Governors Association [NGA] Center for Best Practices & Council of Chief State School Officers [CCSSO], 2010), which promote the process of gathering information from a variety of sources and presenting this information using various formats. Another trend that is gaining in popularity is the "flipped classroom" model, in which the typical lecture and homework elements of a class are reversed. For instance, students might view a podcast or digital slide show outside of class, then use class time to do exercises, projects, or discussions.

Our goal in the second edition of this book is to continue strengthening the bridge between online and offline reading while building a case for *the importance of developing and implementing a systematic K–12 Web literacy curriculum.* In the decade between the two editions of this book, students of all ages continue to lack strategies for reading the Web. The situation is urgent. As a field, we now know much more about what it takes to be an effective Web reader because research on Internet reading has seen a tremendous increase in the past decade. Yet, at the same time, technology continues to outpace what research and practice help us to understand, and students continue to enter college and the workforce without essential 21st-century literacies. The purpose of this book is to provide a rationale and framework for teaching the most important 21st-century skill of all: Web literacy. Web literacy means locating, comprehending, evaluating, and using online information efficiently and effectively.

In the first edition of *Reading the Web*, we made a statement that still holds true: The heart and soul of this book is our belief in the importance of providing our students with the skills and strategies needed to be successful in their current role as students as well as in their future role as productive citizens. We have both made it our professional mission to carry the torch to promote the need for effective instruction about the Internet inquiry process. We hope you will join us in this endeavor.

About This Book

Reading the Web offers a balanced mix of theory, research, and practice. The theory and research provide a foundation for the instructional practices we describe. The practice guides us, and educators, toward creating a systematic way to provide students with the skills and strategies needed to become Web literate.

In Chapter 1, "Opportunities and Challenges," we focus on some of the reasons learners struggle with reading on the Web. We describe a Web literacy curriculum and explore some of the challenges in implementing Web literacy practices in the classroom. The overarching message in this chapter is that *Internet inquiry is the pedagogical "sweet spot"* where teachers can engage students while also promoting Web literacies and addressing numerous learning standards.

In Chapter 2, "Learning How to Learn," we seek to answer the questions "What is learning?" and "What are some effective ways to promote learning?" Toward that end, we outline three time-tested theories of learning—constructivism (learning by doing), socioculturalism (learning with others), and semiotics (learning through symbols)—that guide our work in the classroom and help us interpret the research data we collect. We present Universal Design for Learning (UDL) as a research-based framework for ensuring that instruction is differentiated to meet the needs of diverse learners. Next, we describe four components of instruction—modeling, scaffolding, practice, and feedback—that compose a robust model for effective teaching in any subject. Finally, we describe the optimal outcomes of Internet inquiry and the educator's role in developing students' ability to learn about, with, and from technology. The overriding message in this chapter is that *teaching students transferable strategies for learning how to learn* will serve students not only while learning on the Web but also throughout their school careers, personal lives, and beyond.

In Chapter 3, "Becoming Literate," we provide answers to the questions "What does it mean to become literate?" and "What are Web literacies?" We begin with a listing of the varying, and often overlapping, terms used to describe what it means to be literate in a digital world. Next, we apply two influential reading theories—cueing systems theory and transactional theory—to the reading process, both in print and on the Web, noting that digital texts are similar to but more complex than print texts. Next, we describe how reading comprehension strategies and foundational reading skills are challenged when applied to online reading. Then we describe features of informational text structures found in print and on the Web. Finally, we take a look at the reciprocal nature of literacy learning and the ways online literacy practices benefit offline literacy practices and vice versa. The theme for this chapter is that *reading is a very complex cognitive and metacognitive process*. Therefore, although some students become proficient readers without adult guidance, many others benefit from reading strategy instruction, both in print and on the Web.

The first three chapters serve as a solid, research-based foundation for exploring what it means to be "Web literate," which is the central aim of this book. Literacy gives individuals access to power, and people who are not fluent with culturally valued literacy practices are disadvantaged. This has consequences for what constitutes literacy and how literacy is taught in schools. The remaining chapters, 4 through 10, focus on classroom instructional practices that can promote and nourish Web literacy. These chapters include numerous handouts that can immediately be used as activities and informal assessments to guide instruction and promote Web literacy.

What's New in This Edition?

For those of you who have read the first edition of *Reading the Web* and have returned for another visit, welcome back. Here are some new features you will find in the second edition:

- A brand-new chapter (Chapter 1) that focuses on the opportunities and challenges in becoming Web literate.
- Description of how the Web has evolved from Web 1.0 to Web 2.0 to Web 3.0.
- Connections to the CCSS.

- Stronger focus on UDL and differentiated instruction.
- An emphasis on informal and formal assessment of Web literacy skills.
- Updated Web tools, searching techniques, and a Web literacy curriculum.
- Updated classroom examples, instructional handouts, and lesson plans.
- Updated references reflecting the plethora of research and professional writing that has occurred in recent years across the fields of literacy, librarianship, and technology.

Getting Started

We'd like to point out some logistics that govern the style and organization of this book. First, we alternate gender pronouns throughout the chapters. Second, whenever we give examples of keywords, we place them in angle brackets, because quotation marks have a specific purpose in keyword construction. For example, we might suggest key-word combinations such as <basketball + history> or <hurricane + "disaster relief">; however, when you are searching the Web, the brackets should not be included. Third, although we have provided numerous activities and handouts, you should not attempt to use all of them in one lesson, unit, or semester. Fourth, the learning standards that are sprinkled throughout the book were derived from the CCSS (NGA & CCSSO, 2010), the American Association of School Librarians (AASL, 2007), and the Next Generation Science Standards (NGSS, 2011).

Finally, we provide definitions for some terms that are used in this book. Although the Internet and the Web (World Wide Web, or WWW) are technically different, they have merged to the point where the terms are often used interchangeably. The *Internet*, which is a global network of computers that includes features such as email, messaging, apps, and websites, is accessed via an *Internet service provider* such as AT&T or Comcast using a phone line, cable, or wireless connection. The *Web*, which is actually a subset of the Internet, is accessed through *Web browser* software such as Safari or Firefox. The Web is a massive interconnected set of *websites* that use standardized coding languages (html, XML, flash, etc.) so that everyone's devices can interpret them. People typically locate web pages by typing the *URL* (uniform resource locator) directly into the address field or by using a *search engine* such as Google or Bing.

We define *literacy* as the ability to encode or decode meaning in any of the forms of representation used in a culture to convey or express meaning, which includes being able to create and interpret print but also could encompass art, dance, music, multi-media, and other areas of expressive language. We are particularly interested in defining what it means to be *Web literate*, that is, making meaning out of texts typically found on the Web. The word *text* should be broadly interpreted as any unified chunk of meaning in any format that can be shared with others. Therefore, when we talk about *Internet texts*, *Web texts*, or *web pages*, we mean documents found on the Web that may contain a variety of features, including type, images, links, icons, multimedia, and so on. Similarly, a *reader* is someone who is actively constructing meaning from any of these media forms, not just from print.

We earnestly hope you find this information easy to understand and immediately applicable to your teaching situation, whether you are a preservice teaching candidate, an English language arts teacher, a science teacher, a library media specialist, or a university professor. More and more of us are using the Internet to satisfy our information needs at home, in school, and in the workplace; however, we cannot assume that our students automatically know how to effectively locate, evaluate, and synthesize online information. It is our job as educators to help students become more strategic and flexible readers on the Web.

CONTENTS

Purchasers of this book can
download and print the handouts from
www.guilford.com/dobler-forms

1 Opportunities and Challenges

● ●

- There are many reasons why learners of all ages struggle with reading on the Web.

- The Web is a complex system because it is *massive*, *mutable*, *nonlinear*, *multimodal*, *unfiltered*, and *unbounded*.

- Today's students may be fluent with some technologies, but it is a myth that they are skilled at efficiently finding online information.

- Barriers to technology integration include access, technical issues, time, professional development, preservice teacher and librarian preparation, standards and high-stakes assessment, and systemic resistance to change.

- The research process can be challenging whether it is carried out offline or online, but Internet inquiry has the potential to engage students while addressing numerous learning objectives across content areas.

- We advocate a systematic Web literacy curriculum that spans K–12 and beyond.

> We need to think of a child who is about to click on an Internet link as a person standing inside a room that has 25 billion doors and having absolutely no idea of where a door may lead or what is behind it.
>
> —Harrison (2011, p. 113)

Have you ever noticed just how many people use technology in their everyday lives? While traveling recently, Beth was struck by the proliferation of digital devices. At the airport, she could see a child playing a video game, an adolescent watching a movie, a woman reading an ebook, a man with limited vision using the speech-to-text feature to compose an email, two people talking on the phone, and three people who appeared to be surfing the Web. With all of this screen time, we should be skilled with technology, right? The truth is, for the electronic tasks we do frequently, we develop habits and patterns that may help us accomplish what we want to do, but we aren't necessarily as efficient or effective as we could be. Nowhere is this point more obvious than in our reading on the Web. The Web is not a movie, an ebook, or a text message to be comprehended. It's a complex system of text, multimedia, and hyperlinks with unfettered changes occurring constantly.

Research helps us understand that Web reading is a complex, multidimensional process, and many people think they are more skilled at it than is really the case. This discrepancy between reality and self-perception presents a serious problem, because much of the information we use for solving problems and answering daily questions is a result of searching the Internet. People use the Internet inquiry process to make big and small decisions every day. This text sets out to explore what we know about Internet reading complexities and how readers can apply effective strategies to make this process a success.

The question that guides this chapter is "What are the opportunities and challenges of reading on the Web?" We begin by describing the nature of the Web, students' dispositions, barriers to technology integration, and the research process. We present *Internet inquiry as the pedagogical sweet spot* for addressing multiple learning objectives across content areas (Bruce & Casey, 2012). We use the terms *Web reading* and *online reading* synonymously with *online research and inquiry* because online reading usually takes place within a research and problem-solving task on the Internet. Unless students are using class time to surf online for pleasure, the purpose of online reading is to answer a question or solve a problem. In essence, Web reading *is* research (Leu, Forzani, et al., 2013); therefore, Web literacy is the ability to use the Internet to locate, read, understand, and communicate information (Zhang & Duke, 2008). When we describe the opportunities and challenges of online reading, it is within the context of Internet inquiry. Technically, the Web is a subset of the Internet, but the terms are close enough to be used interchangeably. Two other terms that are often used interchangeably are *Web literacy* and *information literacy*. Both terms refer to the process of locating, understanding, evaluating, and using information, but information literacy encompasses both print and Web texts. In Chapter 3, we explore these and other types of literacies in greater detail.

There are countless new technologies and literacy practices that have the potential to engage students, such as blogging, podcasting, social networking, writing fan fiction, and crafting game scripts. Out of all of these options, *there is one literacy practice that is absolutely crucial to success in today's society, and that is locating and comprehending information on the Web*. Once considered ancillary, this skill is now essential in school, at home, and in the workplace, as people use online information to

> When educators ask students to search and find information on the Internet . . . it is not to just get the answer. It is to learn an important process.
>
> —November (2012, p. 62)

learn, solve problems, answer questions, and participate in a digital society. As a result, countries around the world are incorporating Web literacy into their learning standards. Two notable examples are the Australian Curriculum Assessment and Reporting Authority (ACARA, 2012) and the U.S. Common Core State Standards (CCSS). The CCSS explicitly require students to engage in online inquiry:

> To be ready for college, workforce training, and life in a technological society, students need the ability to gather, comprehend, evaluate, synthesize, and report on information and ideas, to conduct original research in order to answer questions or solve problems, and to analyze and create a high volume and extensive range of print and nonprint texts in media forms old and new. The need to conduct research and to produce and consume media is embedded into every aspect of today's curriculum. (National Governors Association [NGA] Center for Best Practices & Council of Chief State School Officers [CCSSO], 2010)

Despite the facts that standards call for 21st-century literacies and that many of today's youth appear fluent with them, it is well documented that learners of all ages *lack strategies for locating online information* (Castek, Zawilinski, McVerry, O'Byrne, & Leu, 2011; Coiro & Dobler, 2007; Dwyer & Harrison, 2008; Kuhlthau, 2010; Rouet, Ros, Goumi, Macedo-Rouet, & Dinet, 2011). Evaluating online information is particularly challenging (Coiro, 2012; Colwell, Hunt-Barron, & Reinking, 2013; Fabos, 2008; Goldman, Braasch, Wiley, Graesser, & Brodowinska, 2012; Macedo-Rouet, Braasch, Britt, & Rouet, 2013; Walraven, Brand-Gruwel, & Boshuizen, 2009). In fact, learners struggle with every stage of the Internet inquiry process, including:

- Formulating a plan (Harrison, Dwyer, & Castek, 2014)
- Asking questions (Rothstein & Santana, 2011)
- Analyzing search engine results (Miller & Bartlett, 2012)
- Scanning websites (Leu, Zawilinski, Forzani, & Timbrell, 2014)
- Synthesizing ideas (Todd & Gordon, 2011)
- Citing sources (Ladbrook & Probert, 2011)
- Transforming information into knowledge (Guinee & Eagleton, 2006).

One reason children struggle with online reading is that they haven't been taught how to manage the inquiry process. Unlike traditional print resources, the Web is not a text nor even an organized collection of texts—it is a highly complex system that requires specialized knowledge to access and use effectively. Sending students to the Internet to find, evaluate, and use information without teaching specific strategies is akin to sending a person out in the wilderness without proper training, supplies, and gear.

Oh, What a Tangled Web We Weave

The Web is a multidimensional system that bears little resemblance to a print-based text. Web readers find themselves challenged by too much access to too much information.

Although it has unparalleled potential to connect learners with knowledge, there are at least six characteristics of the Web that can impede learning. The Web is:

1. *Massive.* The sheer size of the Web forces readers to increase their pace, using a "skimming and bouncing" style of reading to manage information overload.
2. *Mutable.* Because the Web is constantly shifting and mutating, readers must keep up with constantly evolving tools and practices.
3. *Nonlinear.* The inherent nonlinearity of the Web means that readers must create mental maps to navigate pathways of their own construction.
4. *Multimodal.* The variety of multimedia requires Web readers to make meaning from multiple media formats.
5. *Unfiltered.* In the absence of gatekeepers, readers must ignore distractions and critically evaluate information.
6. *Unbounded.* Because the Web is nearly infinite and valuable content is often hidden from view, readers must be familiar with search engine technologies.

Massive

One aspect of the Web that can cause difficulty for readers is its incomprehensible size. The Web's greatest attribute is also its greatest flaw. The sheer volume of information on the Web is sometimes referred to as *data smog*. This metaphor conjures an image of a child wandering through a littered dystopian landscape without a compass or GPS (global positioning system). In addition, the Web has its own architecture, with its own grammar, punctuation, and syntax. The Web is not designed for children, nor is it designed for educational settings; as a result, it is filled with "inconsiderate texts" with unpredictable structures, cues, and features. One way that readers cope with the magnitude of the Web is to proceed at breakneck speeds, as if it were actually possible to find everything there is to find on any given topic in one sitting. Web readers are often impatient and tend to make choices before thinking, which rarely results in efficient searching.

When working individually, Web readers spend much of their time trying to find their way around and only a small amount of time actually viewing or processing information (Walraven et al., 2009). Instead of reading, they tend to skim, scan, and squirrel (hoard) information to be processed later (Rowlands & Nichols, 2008). The terms *lateral reading* and *power browsing* have been used to describe the way Web readers rapidly skim across search results and sites, only occasionally dipping into content and then bouncing back out again (Miller & Bartlett, 2012). Power browsing is a style that is in direct contrast to *power searching*, which experienced Web readers utilize to locate information. We describe power search strategies in Chapter 6.

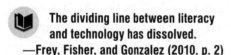 **The dividing line between literacy and technology has dissolved.**
—Frey, Fisher, and Gonzalez (2010, p. 2)

The Internet is also filled with countless forms of representation, or genres (e.g., blogs, email, text messages, social networking, multiuser gaming), with new genres cropping up daily to fulfill the functions of communicating, collaborating, curating, networking, and sharing. Not only do these genres have their own sets of cues and features, but each also has its own set of grammatical structures, such as using all lowercase letters, defying spelling conventions, and using abbreviations; for instance, YOLO (you only live once), TTYL (talk to you later), and f2f (face to face). New text genres have generated vocabulary that has become part of our daily lexicon (e.g., *hashtag, selfie, emoji, mashup, crowdsourcing*). Although the focus of this text is on websites, these other genres and the devices we use to access them (computers, tablets, mobile devices, wearable gear) are reshaping the way we think of literacy and literary structures (Figure 1.1). Some would even say that these genres and tools are reshaping the way we think (Carr, 2008; Cascio, 2009).

Mutable

The Web is highly mutable, meaning that it's constantly evolving and changing. The Web has gone through several mutations, referred to as Web 1.0, 2.0, and 3.0. Web 1.0 was the first generation of the Web, often referred to as the "mostly read-only web." It was somewhat like an online library, or a collection of resources for people to access. During this phase the focus was primarily on building the Web, making it accessible, and commercializing it. There was a clear distinction between producers and consumers of information, with most of us in the consumer role. Encyclopedias provide a fascinating illustration of this evolutionary process. Before the advent of technology, encyclopedias were sets of enormous hardbound books that took up a lot of shelf space and were outdated before they even went to press. When CD-ROMs became popular, the era of the printed encyclopedia ended abruptly, with printed volumes launching new careers as quaint doorstops. When the Web gained traction, encyclopedia publishers moved their content online and made it available for a fee, as in the case of *Britannica Online*. This Web 1.0 product, which still exists today, is designed and vetted by experts in the field of publishing.

Unlike Web 1.0 tools and practices, in which the distinction between producers and consumers is very clear, Web 2.0 invites collective participation, sharing, and collaboration. Web 2.0 is known as the "wildly read-write web." If we think of Web 1.0 like

FIGURE 1.1. Devices give students access to information in new ways.

a library of resources at our disposal, Web 2.0 is more like a big group of friends and acquaintances. You can still use it to passively receive information, but now you can contribute to the conversation. A classic Web 2.0 tool is Wikipedia, a free encyclopedia that can be edited anytime by anyone. Its veracity depends on the goodwill and collective intelligence of anyone who decides to participate. If an entry is updated incorrectly, it is quickly amended. A humorous incident occurred during the 2014 World Cup when an enthusiastic fan changed the Wikipedia entry for U.S. Secretary of Defense Chuck Hagel to USA goalkeeper Tim Howard after a record-setting 16 saves in one game. When the entry went viral, Wikipedia corrected the entry, locked the page, and condemned the act as vandalism but also complimented the anonymous prankster's ingenuity. Creating wikis (such as Wikipedia) is one example of a popular Web 2.0 practice; other examples are blogging, photo and video sharing, social networking (e.g., Facebook, Instagram), and social bookmarking (e.g., Diigo, Delicious). Mobile devices have been a major factor in promoting Web 2.0 practices, especially outside of the United States.

> The Web is a massive, shifting repository of human knowledge.
> —Schrock (2014, n.p.)

Web 3.0, still in its infancy, continues to blur the lines between producers and consumers, readers and writers, humans and machine, reality and virtual reality. Web 3.0 is known as the "portable, personal Web." Some changes we are beginning to see are intelligent search, personalization, behavioral advertising, and the semantic Web. Increasingly, readers can ask search engines for what they seek as if they were speaking to a real person, thus reducing the need to parse natural language into keywords. Soon, we may be able to make complex, contextual requests as we might to an acquaintance; for instance, "I'd like to visit a museum, do some shopping, and then have an affordable lunch with my friends." A Web 3.0 browser, or personal assistant, will consult its records of what you like and dislike, take into account your current location, analyze your contacts, and suggest an itinerary.

Amazon is an example of a website that has smoothly weathered each mutation of the Web. In the Web 1.0 era, Amazon was an online superstore, offering products for us to browse and purchase. During Web 2.0, Amazon also became a place for us to sell our own products, tag products we like, and comment on products for the benefit of others. Now, Amazon (and other Web 3.0 tools, including search engines) tracks and remembers our online activity so it can make informed recommendations based on our history. This has implications for the relationship between readers and texts, as the Web is now "reading" us and adapting itself to our perceived needs. In some ways, this makes the Web more intuitive and user friendly, but inexperienced readers may lack the ability to direct the process and take charge of what they want to do while searching and reading online. The mutability of the Web presents opportunities and challenges for everyone to keep up with constantly evolving tools and practices.

Nonlinear

An examination of the nature of the Web must include its inherent nonlinearity. Although nonlinear text is not historically new (e.g., encyclopedias, magazines, "choose your own adventure" stories), forging a path through an immense, hyperlinked, unlimited information space such as the Web can be taxing. Web readers engage in a lot of backtracking in order to reorient themselves, and even proficient readers of print text can exhibit characteristics associated with reading disabilities when trying to read online.

Unlike static printed texts, Web texts are dynamic, responding to the actions and perceived needs of the reader. Most online reading entails continuous decision making and physical action in order to proceed. In essence, reading strategies become navigation strategies in a hypertext environment. The term *three-dimensional* has been used to describe Web reading (Coiro & Dobler, 2007) because readers are constantly moving left to right and top to bottom on web pages, as well as forward and backward within and across websites. If the element of time is considered, we are confronted with a four-dimensional (4D) space, one in which reading pathways are ephemeral, with links changing or becoming inactive, pages being revised, and entire websites disappearing without notice. This makes is difficult to return to the "text" to recreate the reading experience once some time has passed. A 4D view of Web reading is like a futuristic transit system, which must be navigated with consideration to vehicles that are moving parallel and perpendicular to us (2D), above and below us (3D), amidst physical conditions, such as weather, natural disasters, and construction, that change over time (4D). Thus, "the new frame for online reading must be conceived in three-dimensional or n-dimensional terms and metaphorically, as the traversal of systems. This system is dynamic and evolving and simply cannot be mapped in advance" (Hartman, Morsink, & Zheng, 2010, p. 151). Let's return for a moment to our metaphor of the child drifting through the dystopian wasteland. Imagine that the child has stumbled into a gigantic city with futuristic skyscrapers, flashy billboards, and airborne vehicles speeding along multiple dimensions. Without guidance, how can a child safely navigate this dense, overwhelming, multidimensional environment?

The fact that online readers create their own paths through the Web can increase engagement, but this freedom to choose can also distract readers from their original goals. We have all seen students "wandering off into the glitter-paved, hypertext-linked pathways of the Web" (Fabos, 2008, p. 856). Just today, while Maya was searching for updated information on the semantic Web, she became interested in an article on what the Web will be like in 2050 and somehow ended up viewing a list of hilarious autocorrect mistakes. Even the important tasks of fact checking and verifying sources can lead us away from the text we originally chose to read and may not have even finished reading.

This relentless process of decision making and goal monitoring while reading online is mentally exhausting and can lead to cognitive

> **Students may be expected to attend to large amounts of information from one site, hold that information in working memory while searching and attending to information from other sites and still have cognitive resources to process it.**
> **—Kauffman, Zhao, and Yang (2011, p. 313)**

> **TEACHER: How do you know when you find good information for your inquiry project?**
>
> **STUDENT: When you find something really juicy, the people who look at your presentation will probably be surprised because they didn't know that before.**

overload (Hargittai, Neuman, & Curry, 2012). Reading on the Web depends not only on individuals' prior knowledge but also on brain power (Figure 1.2), or the ability to successfully allocate and monitor cognitive resources while navigating from one text to another. In some ways, reading on the Web can best be described as a series of "comings and goings," as there is so much traversal between and within texts. The active verbs that we use to describe movement on the Web illustrate this dynamic spatial metaphor—for example, *navigating, browsing, surfing, visiting,* and *exploring* the Web.

One secret to successful online reading is creating a temporary mental map of the information space (DeStefano & LeFevre, 2007). This is easier said than done in a 4D environment that is constantly shifting. When was the last time you were searching for something online, perhaps a lesson plan or instructional video, and found yourself proceeding at a leisurely pace? If you're like most of us, a reckless pace is the norm. Think about how you feel when trying to locate a great resource that you found previously but forgot to bookmark. Few would disagree that searching for information can sometimes be frustrating. The good news is that we *can* teach students about the architecture of the Web, thus leading to more sophisticated mental maps and greater success in reading on the Web.

Multimodal

Another feature of the Web that can both help and hinder comprehension is the fact that information is presented in multimodal formats (e.g., audio, video, animation, icons, buttons, tabs, hyperlinks). Although alternate modalities can serve as valuable learning supports for text comprehension (Dalton & Proctor, 2008), making meaning with multimedia can also present challenges because different modalities require different strategies for navigating, understanding, and remembering (Serafini, 2012; Wyatt-Smith & Elkins, 2008). "Reading a Web text makes greater demands on critical reading skills than reading printed texts, owing to the large proportion of nontextual elements,

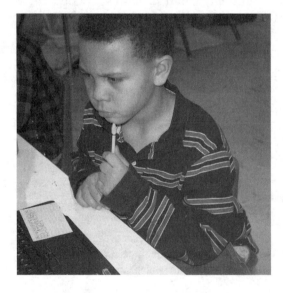

FIGURE 1.2. Internet inquiry takes brain power.

the possibilities for interactivity, and the demands the nonlinear character of the Web make on the associative ability of the student" (Kuiper & Volman, 2008, p. 249).

The CCSS (NGA & CCSSO, 2010) require students to conduct online inquiry and synthesize information from multiple media formats starting as early as third grade. Young learners are expected to "use text features and search tools (e.g., key words, sidebars, hyperlinks) to locate information relevant to a given topic efficiently" (RI.3.5); "conduct short research projects that build knowledge about a topic" (W.3.7); and "gather information from print and digital sources, take brief notes on sources, and sort evidence into provided categories" (W.3.8). Synthesizing information does not come easily to most learners, which is why we devote an entire chapter to it later in this text.

Unfiltered

One of the defining characteristics of the Web is the absence of gatekeepers to filter out "misinformation, malinformation, messed-up information, [and] mostly useless information (Kuiper & Volman, 2008, p. 247). Because Web content is unfiltered, the burden of evaluation falls on the reader (Frey, Fisher, & Gonzalez, 2010; Mackey & Jacobson, 2011). Readers must maintain a high level of metacognitive awareness in order to ignore distractions and critically evaluate information. Unfortunately, many Web readers do not automatically evaluate for authority, accuracy, or bias (Coiro, 2012; Leu, Forzani, et al., 2013; Walraven et al., 2009). Evaluation is not automatic for many readers because it is not typically emphasized when reading printed materials that have been vetted. Online readers need to adopt

 In this increasingly global world of information, students must be taught to seek diverse perspectives, gather and use information ethically, and use social tools responsibly and safely.
—American Association of School Librarians (2007)

a critical stance because "the habits of asking questions, discussing concepts, and formulating opinions are vital in an age when we are becoming our own editors" (Fisher, Frey, & Lapp, 2012, p. 2). Considering the Web's massive size and readers' lack of experience with critical evaluation, it is understandable that evaluation is a skill that requires explicit instruction, modeling, and guided practice. We return to the topic of evaluation in Chapter 7 with more in-depth explanations and instructional activities.

Unbounded

A challenge of searching for information on the Web is that it is unbounded. Unlike a printed text, which is bound between two covers, the Web is open-ended. There is no table of contents, and there will never be a single index that captures all that exists on the Web. This fact requires readers to take an active role in deciding where to go and what to read. Passive Web readers can easily become lost in a sea of information.

Despite the fact that there are online library databases that are better suited for many educational purposes, the reality is that virtually everyone uses search engines to find information, and most use Google as their search

Library Media Standard: **Display emotional resilience by persisting in information searching despite challenges.**

engine of choice (Pew Research Center, 2013). However, there are some problems with relying on today's search engines to find information. For example, search engines such as Google are driven by corporate interests, not educational ones (Figure 1.3). As a result, search engines are inherently biased. Because most Web readers tend to click on the first few links and do not look beyond the first page of search results, search engines intentionally place sponsored sites at the top of the list. Many search engines give prominence to popular, wealthy, and powerful sites at the expense of others. This is like going to a public library where "instead of nonjudgmentally serving patrons with a wide array of texts, the library's primary motive is to make money. To do this, the library accepts payments (without the patron's knowledge) from a handful of authors who pay every time their books are checked out. The public library would understandably steer its patrons toward these books, and not others" (Fabos, 2008, p. 855).

Another problem with relying on search engines is that they access a very thin layer of the Web. Much like the tip of an iceberg, the easily accessible "surface Web" represents less than 1% of Web content (Open Education Database, 2013). The other 99% (the deep Web, invisible Web, or hidden Web) represents tens of trillions of pages that are difficult to index, such as dynamically generated content, social media comments, unlinked pages, private networks, intentionally hidden content, and password-protected databases. It is difficult to fathom that you haven't found every website imaginable when a search engine returns millions of results, but the fact is that the information you seek might not show up simply because it hasn't been indexed by a search engine.

FIGURE 1.3. A student's view of the Internet as a commercial space.

Because many search engines trawling the surface Web are already using Web 3.0 technologies that personalize results for each user, we are starting to receive even more limited search results than in the past (Miller & Bartlett, 2012). For some of us, this may come as a relief, as it already seems like there's more information than anyone could possibly need in the thin layer of the surface Web. The downside of personalization is that we might not be exposed to information that challenges or broadens our preexisting worldview. Many of us unknowingly exist in information silos, or "filter bubbles," because we see only what search engines "think" we want to see based on our past actions (Pariser, 2012). These issues serve as a strong reminder of the importance of preparing students with skills and strategies needed to manage online information.

> " " One challenge I face is how to let my struggling students feel valued in the inquiry process without me or other students stepping in and doing it for them.
> —Scott Ritter, third-grade teacher

Driving without a License: Gen Zs on the Web

As stated earlier, learners of all ages struggle with reading on the Web. This is partly a result of the complex nature of the Web but is also due to the behaviors and dispositions of Web readers. Because this text is focused on students in grades 3–8 (approximately 8–15 years of age), we use the popular label "Gen Z" to refer to those who were born after the year 2000. In this section we describe some characteristics of these students that may have an impact on their development of Web reading skills.

One glaringly obvious reason that Gen Zs are unskilled with online reading is that they are inexperienced. Many are still developing foundational literacies such as decoding, fluency, skimming and scanning, comprehension, spelling, and writing. They lack prior knowledge of topics, search engines, marketing tactics, the inquiry process, and the architecture of the Web. Gen Zs may be unable to deploy advanced search techniques because they lack the metacognitive awareness and vocabulary to develop and refine search queries. They may use Google because they don't realize there are any other ways to find information on the Web. As with other Net-naïve learners, misconceptions lead to uncritical choices; for example, they may choose the first result on a search engine list because they are unaware of the distinction between paid and unpaid results and they assume that search engines rank the results according to relevance and credibility (Kiili, Laurinen, & Marttunen, 2008).

The Digital Native Myth

Regardless of socioeconomic status, ethnicity, or gender, Gen Zs are characterized as being constantly plugged in, wired, and "tethered" to their mobile devices (Turkle, 2011). Gen Zs have never known a world without Google, smartphones, and tablets. However, despite the impressive level of proficiency that many of them display while texting and downloading music, it is a myth that Gen Zs are skilled with searching the Web for information. In fact, many Gen Zs suffer from the Dunning–Kruger effect, meaning that they have an overly inflated sense of self-efficacy when it comes to online searching. One problem with this rampant overconfidence is that students are unlikely to seek help, even when their attempts at finding information fail or result in low-quality or incomplete information (Gross & Latham, 2012).

Gen Zs are stereotyped in the literature both positively and negatively. Sometimes they are portrayed as active, independent, and creative multimedia producers (November, 2012). Although some Gen Zs do enjoy sharing content such as photos, less than 10% of youth actively "geek out," lending support to the 1% rule, which says that 1% produce material, 10% comment on what they find, and 89% are consumers, not producers (Harrison et al., 2014). Sometimes Gen Zs are described as emotionally disconnected, passive, risk aversive, struggling with intimacy and identity, and *less* creative than their predecessors (Gardner & Davis, 2013). It is imprudent to present a homogeneous profile of an entire generation of diverse learners; suffice it to say that many are comfortable with mobile devices, but the fact remains that most struggle with online reading.

 Encourage students to stop seeing research/assignments as a process of collecting information and instead to see in terms of forming their own perspectives and creating new insights.
—**Spiranec and Zorica (2010, p. 148).**

The Principle of Least Effort

One reason that Gen Zs tend to be so confident about their searching ability is that search engines such as Google are so easy to use. A lack of understanding about the architecture of the Web and the limitations of search engines combined with the near certainty of results can lull information seekers into a false sense of security that they have found what there is to be found (Mackey & Jacobson, 2011). It is axiomatic that we don't know what we don't know. Even when introduced to library databases and other useful online resources, many Gen Zs still prefer to use Google. Years of Googling create idiosyncratic habits and dispositions that are hard to break, even after instruction and practice (Colwell et al., 2013). Online reading strategies should be systematically introduced early in students' lives, before they develop poor habits and unwavering brand loyalty.

Math Standard: **Make sense of problems and persevere in solving them.**

A substantial number of researchers (too many to cite) have found that online search behavior tends to follow the path of least resistance, also known as the principle of least effort. It is easy to blame this tendency on the seemingly overstimulated, hyperpaced world in which Gen Zs live, but the principle applies to learners of all ages. Recently, when Maya commented that students seem to want all the answers on a silver platter, Beth quipped, "Don't we all?" How true! One would hope that, with instruction and maturity, Gen Zs will come to understand that the answers to important questions do not always arrive on a magical platter, as much as we would all like for this to be the case.

Roadblocks on the Information Superhighway

In addition to the complex nature of the Web and the dispositions of young Gen Zs, some students struggle with online reading because they simply haven't been taught. There are a host of reasons that Web practices and tools have been slow to be integrated into the curriculum. Obstacles can be attributed to issues of access, curricular demands, and systemic resistance to change.

The Digital Divide

Despite intensive efforts over the past 20 years, issues of access and digital divide persist. Although 100% of U.S. public schools have had "Internet access" since 2003 (Nation-Master, 2014), there is a substantive difference between enjoying a 1:1 ratio of students to Web-enabled devices in a classroom and moving children to a separate location for access. There are also disparities in access to peripherals such as document cameras, smartboards, projectors, and printers. We know this all too well from personal experience. Recently, Maya went back into the classroom to teach at-risk sixth graders. Her classroom had one teacher computer with one Internet connec-

 Reading Standard: Integrate and evaluate information presented in diverse media and formats, including visually, quantitatively, and orally.

tion, and although there was a digital whiteboard, she was unable to use it because the projector was too old and the smartboard features wouldn't calibrate properly. There was no document camera, wireless Internet, or convenient access to a printer. To meet essential learning objectives, Maya transferred her class across campus to the library or computer lab, losing valuable learning time along the way. Once in the lab, more time was lost getting situated and logging in. Neither the library nor the lab had a document camera, projector, or digital whiteboard for modeling, instruction, feedback, and sharing student thinking and work. When the bell rang, the class had to vacate the lab to make room for the next group. Although managing this situation was not impossible, it was far from ideal.

Clearly, an obstacle to technology integration is time. Deep learning takes time, authentic inquiry takes time, and Web exploration takes time. Unfortunately, schedules, transitions, behavior problems, fire drills, assemblies, and other interruptions reduce the time available for learning, retention, and transfer. Just as no one would expect a student to become a proficient reader, mathematician, or dancer after one or two lessons, semesters, or years, it is unrealistic to expect learners to become instantly proficient with all the complexities of finding and using information on the Web. This is why we advocate an Internet inquiry curriculum that spans K–12 and beyond. Learners need time to discover, make mistakes, self-regulate, and integrate new knowledge with what they already know.

Other barriers include technical problems, lack of quality software, weak funding for repairs and upgrades, and poor administrative support (Bingimlas, 2009). Furthermore, despite the

 TEACHER: What have you learned about inquiry?

STUDENT: I have learned that it's not easy for kids like me.

clichéd image of Gen Z kids with mobile devices more or less permanently attached to their bodies, many students do not have Internet access outside of school. In Maya's class of 26 sixth graders, there were 5 students who did not have technology access at home; therefore, it would not have been fair to assign Internet-dependent homework.

Preservice Preparation and Professional Development

Teachers and other educational professionals also need time to explore new technologies, preferably with an emphasis on pedagogical practices rather than on specific tools that quickly become obsolete. Preservice programs need to better prepare teachers and library educators to integrate technology into their work with learners (Branch-Mueller & deGroot, 2011). Although 1:1 and bring-your-own-device (BYOD) initiatives are becoming more common in schools, all too often the focus remains on teaching in traditional ways with new gadgets. Online programs for teachers may provide flexible learning opportunities, but some still fall victim to the sit-and-get delivery method, rather than actively engaging teachers with a variety of Web practices. Change is neither quick nor easy. It is well established that professional development with technology integration takes longer than do other areas of classroom instruction, as much as two to three times longer (Leu, Kinzer, Coiro, Castek, & Henry, 2013). Just like their students, educators need modeling, scaffolding, practice, and feedback to learn new skills.

Standards and High-Stakes Assessments

One reason Web literacies haven't been taught is that core curriculum standards and high-stakes assessments have not addressed them until very recently (Coiro, 2014). The instructional paradigm in any given setting will determine whether or not technology will be fully integrated into the curriculum. If the focus is on teaching foundational print literacies or basic computer skills, students will not become Web literate (Eisenberg, 2008). Similarly, if the focus is on using technology to replicate existing instructional activities rather than addressing modern practices such as finding information on the Web, students will not be prepared for the future. Successful technology integration is more complex than simply providing students with access to computers. We have to teach students to use technology to "innovate, solve problems, create, and be globally connected" (November, 2012, p. 14).

It is well known that high-stakes assessments drive curricular decisions. Assessments that measure traditional print literacies often determine what is taught during literacy instruction, especially in economically challenged schools that are under the greatest pressure to raise test scores (Coiro, Knobel, Lankshear, & Leu, 2008). It will be interesting to see whether things change now that most states have adopted the CCSS (NGA & CCSSO, 2010). States and districts that decide to use the Partnership for Assessment of Readiness for College and Careers (PARCC) assessment in its current iteration (PARCC,

> As students develop skills across grades, the Common Core State Standards expect that their writing should appear more and more like an expert discussing a topic.
>
> —Lehman (2012, p. 33)

2014) will need to ensure that students are skilled with keyboarding, word processing, dragging and dropping, and manipulating drop-down menus. For logistical reasons, PARCC does not require students to search the open Web or use "technology, including the Internet, to produce and publish writing as well as to interact and collaborate with others" (W.6). Instead, PARCC has created a research simulation task that requires students to integrate information from preselected text and multimedia. It is unclear at this time whether PARCC, Smarter Balanced (Smarter Balanced Assessment Consortium, 2014), and other state-designed assessments will demand more than just basic computing skills. We return to the topic of assessment in Chapter 4.

Resistance Is Futile

Historically, educational systems tend to resist change. For instance, Socrates warned against writing letters because he feared they would promote forgetfulness, and "when books started rolling off Gutenberg's press, people thought they would be confusing and harmful, overwhelming young people with data" (Bartlett & Miller, 2011, p. 10). Even chalkboards were once demonized as a tool that would make teachers lazy. Similar concerns have been triggered by newspapers, comic books, radio, TV, and video games. Today, some worry about detrimental long-term health effects of online reading, such as data asphyxiation, information fatigue, cognitive overload, and time famine (Bartlett & Miller, 2011). Other people worry that ebooks will displace printed books. Although there may be kernels of truth in these fears, we cannot sidestep our obligation to prepare students for tomorrow, not just for today. As Mahatma Gandhi observed, "A principle is a principle, and in no case can it be watered down because of our incapacity to live it in practice. We have to strive to achieve it, and the striving should be conscious, deliberate, and hard" (cited in Frey et al., 2010, p. 121).

Resistance to systemic change often occurs because there is a tendency among elders to look critically at younger generations (Gardner & Davis, 2013) and to distrust out-of-school literacy practices (Wyatt-Smith & Elkins, 2008). However, the generational divide in technology use between teachers and students is not as wide as some believe. Aside from game use, teachers and students engage in highly similar online literacy practices (Burn, Buckingham, Parry, & Powell, 2010). According to Rowlands and Nichols (2008), "we are all the Google generation now . . . the young may have been early adopters but older users are fast catching up—the so-called Silver Surfers" (p. 21). The strongest predictors of technology integration are teacher attitudes and access (Branch-Mueller & deGroot, 2011), not age or years of teaching experience (Chandler-Olcott & Lewis, 2010).

Teacher attitudes may include the perception that Gen Zs are constantly immersed in new media and therefore do not need to spend additional time on the Web during school hours (Lewis & Fabos, 2005). But, as we've noted, most Gen Zs are not skilled in locating information online, regardless of the amount of time they spend immersed in technology outside of school. It is imperative that we teach Web literacies and, while we're at it,

> Showing students the pool and then shoving them into the deep end is more likely to foster despair than self-reliance. —Kolowich (2011, n.p.)

we may as well engage students by leveraging "turn-around pedagogies" that "address their interests in text messaging, music, videos, comics, graphic novels, games, personal web pages, podcasts, and virtual environments that foster social networking" (Alvermann, Hutchins, & McDevitt, 2012, p. 41).

Research Is Not a Four-Letter Word

It is important to recognize that the research process has never been easy for learners, whether the information is being gathered from books, library databases, or the Web. Information literacy requires a reader to find, understand, and use information, and library media specialists especially recognize the elements of this process that may serve as roadblocks for learners. Survey data compiled from 11,000 students from 57 universities showed that 80% of college students reported having "overwhelming difficulties with getting started on research assignments," and half reported "nagging uncertainties

 Science Standard: Define the system under study, specifying its boundaries and making explicit a model of that system.

with concluding and assessing the quality of their research efforts" (Head, 2013). If college students feel this way, imagine how our elementary and middle school students feel. Some learners associate research with a feeling of dread and distress. This is one of the reasons we prefer to use the term *inquiry* instead of *research*. Along with other educators, we have found that kids get really excited and engaged when inquiry is introduced as an opportunity for students to become experts on a topic of personal interest (Figure 1.4).

The purpose and level of task difficulty are also factors, as it is easier for most people to find an answer to a simple question than it is to synthesize information from multiple sources. It is no surprise that Web readers are subject to the "serendipity effect," in which they tend to visit the first site on a search result list and grab the first bit of information they find, even switching topics if they don't immediately find something. If the purpose of an inquiry task is unclear, readers often endeavor to find "the right answer" in as short a time as possible (Ladbrook & Probert, 2011). U.S. employers report that "most college hires rarely [go] beyond a Google search and the first page of results looking for 'the' answer to a workplace problem" (Head, 2013, p. 476). This behavior fits with a consumerist stance rather than a learning stance (Harrison et al., 2014). One way to counteract this tendency is to insist that students consult more than one source so that they understand that authentic inquiry often goes beyond simple fact finding.

Despite the fact that 99% of students in grades 3 through 12 (ages 8–18) believe that school libraries and their services help them become better learners (Todd & Gordon, 2011), research consistently shows that Web readers do not consult librarians for help with clarifying tasks, defining purposes, or searching for information (Head, 2013). Perhaps

 Writing Standard: Use technology, including the Internet, to produce and publish writing and present the relationships between information and ideas clearly and efficiently.

related to increasing cuts in school library positions, more than 70% of American teens ages 12–17 teach themselves or rely on peers to show them how to locate information on the Web for

FIGURE 1.4. Internet inquiry promotes engagement.

school assignments (Zhang, 2013). A danger of having students teach one another is that they can propagate misinformation. It is imperative that schools take on the task of teaching strategies for understanding today's information resources so that students develop strategic rather than haphazard research habits early in their school careers.

Internet Inquiry: The Sweet Spot

Given what we know about the challenges and affordances of online reading, Internet inquiry emerges as the pedagogical "sweet spot" (Bruce & Casey, 2012). Not only does inquiry fulfill a wide variety of instructional objectives across content areas, but it also enhances student engagement and promotes independent, self-regulated learning (Guccione, 2011). Inquiry also provides an opportunity for teaching and learning to occur around real-world issues that encourage critical thinking and that focus on those questions that matter to students. An atmosphere of acceptance for asking questions and wondering about the unknown brings learners and teachers together as explorers and creators of knowledge. Inquiry is more than just a teaching method; it is a *stance* that underlies our lives as learners, both inside and outside of school (Short, 2009) based on the following premises:

- Online research and comprehension is a self-directed process of text construction and knowledge construction.
- Five practices appear to define online research and comprehension processing: (1) identifying a problem and then (2) locating, (3) evaluating, (4) synthesizing, and (5) communicating information.

- Online research and comprehension is not isomorphic [identical] with offline reading comprehension; additional skills and strategies appear to be required.
- Students are not always skilled with online research and comprehension.
- Online contexts may be supportive for some struggling readers.
- Collaborative online reading and writing practices appear to increase comprehension and learning. (Leu, Kinzer, et al., 2013, p. 1164)

Providing opportunities for students to engage in inquiry early in their schooling helps learners to develop favorable attitudes toward learning and to improve their ability to develop research questions, formulate queries, browse search results, navigate links, evaluate sources, and comprehend online information (Macedo-Rouet et al., 2013). In a series of studies on scaffolding the development of effective search strategies conducted by Dwyer and Harrison (2008), upper elementary-age children demonstrated growth in keyword selection, navigation, flexible strategy use, self-monitoring, and confidence. Improvement was especially noticeable when collaborative groups were given specific roles, such as Navigator, Questioner, and Summarizer. The Web may be complex, but it is well within reach to teach young learners how to navigate this multidimensional system (Figure 1.5).

A Web Literacy Curriculum

Although challenges do exist in preparing students to be Web literate, these challenges also present opportunities. To meet these challenges, we advocate the development of a systematic K–12 Web literacy curriculum that focuses on three phases within and across grade levels:

FIGURE 1.5. Third graders work as an inquiry team.

- Phase I: basic computer and Internet use.
- Phase II: problem-solving activities using the Internet.
- Phase III: independent inquiry (Henry, Castek, O'Byrne, & Zawilinski, 2012).

Educators must collaborate to create a seamless continuum of literacy and technology skills while providing various levels of support as students are able to become more independent in their learning. It is crucial that we move beyond the current *tabula rasa* approach, in which teachers at every grade level are forced to review basic computing skills before being able to engage students with problem-solving activities and independent Internet inquiry.

A Web literacy curriculum should start as soon as children begin their literacy education programs. A useful first step to introduce young children to the Internet is to use *online* resources to teach foundational *offline* reading skills in the primary grades (Leu et al., 2014). Foundational reading skills, such as phonics

> When learning is driven by students' own questions and connects to their own understandings of the world, motivation is natural and intrinsic.
> —Kuhlthau, Maniotes, and Caspari (2007, p. 30)

and sight word recognition, can be taught online using quality educational websites such as Starfall (*starfall.com*). Students in the primary grades should also learn basic computer skills and engage in restricted Web exploration (e.g., teacher-designed portals, library databases, online encyclopedias). The CCSS require first graders to "locate key facts or information in a text" using features such as "electronic menus" (RI.1.5) and "use a variety of digital tools to produce and publish writing, including in collaboration with peers" (W.1.6). Third graders must be proficient with keyboarding in order to take the PARCC and Smarter Balanced exams, and by fourth grade they are expected to "demonstrate sufficient command of keyboarding skills to type a minimum of one page in a single sitting" (W.4.6). Most students do not gain skill, speed, and stamina with keyboarding outside of school, especially given the fact that children may access the Web using touchscreen mobile devices equipped with speech recognition technology.

In the upper elementary grades (ages 8–11), we recommend that children learn how to locate and comprehend information using a combination of closed- and open-information spaces. The decision to engage in restricted versus unrestricted Web inquiry should be governed by the teacher's objective. For example, if a fifth-grade teacher's objective is for students to "analyze how visual and multimedia elements contribute to the meaning, tone, or beauty of a text" (RL.5.7), she may wish to restrict her students to a set of preselected texts or websites. In contrast, if the teacher's objective is for students to "analyze multiple accounts of the same event or topic, noting important similarities and differences in the point of view they represent" (RI.5.6), she may want to provide unrestricted access to the Web so students can practice locating and evaluating online information. By the time students reach middle school, they should be armed with the strategies and dispositions to be successful readers in the vast, unrestricted universe of the Web (Castek, 2012). However, adolescents continue to need modeling and guided practice as their Internet inquiry tasks become more sophisticated. The need for a Web literacy curriculum that prepares students for these high-level expectations is urgent. We cannot afford to wait to teach students how to become Web literate.

SUMMARY ●

Learners struggle with Web reading for a number of reasons. One is that the Web is a very complex system. Another is that there are many obstacles to technology integration in schools. Yet another is that the research process itself can be challenging. The overarching message in this chapter is that *Internet inquiry is the pedagogical "sweet spot"* where teachers can engage students while also promoting Web literacies and addressing numerous learning standards.

Considering the multidimensional nature of the Web, the Gen Zs in our classrooms, the barriers to technology integration, and the task of doing research, we suggest that online reading is far more complex than offline reading, requiring higher levels of thinking and self-regulation. The good news is that today's students are highly motivated to engage with new technologies and can learn strategies to work with them efficiently and effectively. Therefore, we advocate a systematic Web literacy curriculum that spans K–12 and beyond.

Next, Chapter 2 provides a theoretical foundation for understanding how humans learn. In addition to constructivism, socioculturalism, and semiotics, we present Universal Design for Learning (UDL) as a research-based framework for ensuring that instruction is differentiated to meets the needs of diverse learners. We describe the essential elements of instruction, the outcomes of Internet inquiry, and the educator's role in promoting Web literacies.

2 Learning How to Learn

- Because there is no single method of teaching that works with all learners, it is important that students *learn how to learn*.

- Constructivism, socioculturalism, and semiotics are three compatible theories that guide our understanding of the learning process and are easily applicable to Web-based learning.

- Universal Design for Learning is a research-based framework for ensuring that instruction is differentiated to meets the needs of diverse learners.

- Four elements of effective instruction in any context are modeling, scaffolding, practice, and feedback.

- The educator's role during Internet inquiry is one of curriculum designer, guide, and coach.

> Every effort must be made in childhood to teach the young to use their minds. For one thing is certain: If they don't make up their own minds, someone will do it for them.
> —Eleanor Roosevelt, cited in Harvey and Goudvis (2013, p. 439)

The questions that guide this chapter are "How do people learn?" and "What are some effective ways to promote learning?" Because we believe that there is no single method of teaching that will reach all learners at all times in all places, it is imperative that we help children *learn how to learn* so that they can adapt and extend their knowledge and strategies when they encounter new tasks in new contexts. Our philosophy of learning merges three highly compatible theories (Figure 2.1): constructivism (learning by doing), socioculturalism (learning with others), and semiotics (learning through symbols). This combination leads to a definition of learning that reads: *Humans construct and deconstruct meaning in socially situated contexts using multiple sign systems.* Put simply, we try to make sense of the world by communicating with others for authentic purposes. In this way, babies learn to talk, children learn to read, and people learn to navigate and comprehend on the Web.

This chapter focuses on three effective theories for teaching and learning that can set students on the path of self-regulation in many areas of learning, but we apply these specifically to developing Web literacies. For each theory, a brief description is illustrated, with an example of how the theory is typically applied in the classroom and the ways in which reading on the Web affects teaching from each of these perspectives. We also present four elements of effective instruction that are consistent with these theories and easily applicable to learning in any context, noting that effective instruction must be differentiated to reach all learners.

Learning by Doing: Constructivism

Constructivism's basic premise is that learning is an active process in which students construct new ideas or concepts based on their current knowledge (Bruner, 1986). In constructivist classrooms, teachers encourage students to make their own discoveries

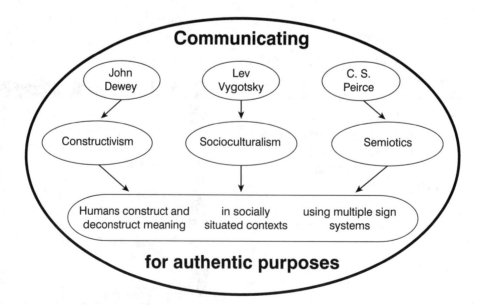

FIGURE 2.1. A holistic view of learning theories.

rather than always relying on the teacher to tell them what to think. The constructivist teacher is often described as the "guide on the side" rather than the "sage on a stage," as in more traditional classrooms in which the teacher is viewed as an authority figure whose primary job is to dispense knowledge.

Teachers who are guided by constructivist principles view the cup as being half full rather than half empty; in other words, our job is not to transmit knowledge by pouring information into our students' heads but rather to set up active learning opportunities that allow students to create their own personal meanings and associations. From this stance, many aspects of the curriculum are negotiated between the students and the teachers, so that students are empowered and engaged in the learning process (Harste, 1994; Short et al., 1996).

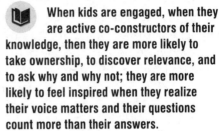 When kids are engaged, when they are active co-constructors of their knowledge, then they are more likely to take ownership, to discover relevance, and to ask why and why not; they are more likely to feel inspired when they realize their voice matters and their questions count more than their answers.
—Fisher, Frey, and Lapp (2012, p. 27)

Strategy Instruction

A classic example of a teaching approach used by constructivist-oriented teachers is metacognitive strategy instruction, or teaching students to become aware of the patterns of thinking they use to learn and read. Strategies are the in-the-head processes students use to develop an understanding of a concept. Although some students develop flexible strategies on their own, most benefit from explicit instruction in this area.

When students are given multiple opportunities to practice certain strategies—for example, predicting what will happen next in a text—the goal is for them to be able not only to apply those strategies independently in similar contexts but also to generalize and transfer them to other texts or new learning situations. Ideally, the strategies that are used by proficient learners are assimilated by novices and eventually become automatic, unconscious habits. Strategy instruction and modeling are major frameworks for the ideas and teaching activities presented in this text, subjects to which we return frequently.

Constructivism on the Web

In constructivist classrooms, the Web can be used as a powerful tool for exploration and discovery. Although it is a complex learning environment, it allows learners to engage in authentic, meaningful experiences that they might otherwise be unable to access, such as virtual field trips to museums, zoos, and parks in other states or countries. Expanding on Dewey's (1938) belief that "a philosophy of education [should be] based upon a philosophy of experience" (p. 29), one of the most promising applications of the Web in the classroom is to help students visualize and understand concepts they have never directly experienced, such as the Doppler effect or the water cycle. Websites that use multimedia to illustrate complex ideas can help activate children's prior knowledge, promote new knowledge, and highlight connections between difficult concepts. As Eisner so eloquently stated, "Through imagination—the creation of mental images—we are able to conceive what we have never experienced in the empirical world" (1994, p. 25).

Further, multimedia technology has the potential to level the playing field between learners with high prior knowledge and those with low prior knowledge by providing a group of learners with a common experience at the outset of a lesson or unit. This type of input is helpful for young children, English language learners, and students with disabilities because it gives all learners an opportunity to discuss what they observe using similar language. Multimedia can serve as a jumping-off point to trigger the inquiry process or inspire ideas when presenting information (May & Downey, 2009). For example, one can find a video clip on YouTube to learn how to do just about anything from changing a tire to crocheting a scarf to drying out a cell phone that fell in a toilet (all of which have been viewed at Beth's house). Multimedia demonstrations (e.g., videos, apps, podcasts, online simulations) can bridge gaps in learning and provide a common experience and a shared vocabulary for all students to draw upon as they embark on a unit of study.

A combination of constructivist theory and technology naturally leads many teachers across all content areas to invite students to create multimedia (e.g., websites, podcasts, wikis, electronic slide shows) in their classrooms. The students with whom we've worked have published their research on incredibly diverse topics, everything from Arnold Schwarzenegger to wheelchair-accessible vacations. Although some children have dabbled in multimedia design outside of school, most still benefit from instruction. Fortunately for educators, with today's software, composing with multimedia has become as easy as word processing, and we will share several examples later in this text, especially in Chapter 9.

> It is school's mission, particularly when colored by constructive hues, to enable students to think and to acquire skills of intelligently handling information, not to drown them in it.
>
> —Kiili et al. (2008, pp. 92–93)

Learning with Others: Socioculturalism

Whereas constructivism emphasizes the individual learner's construction of meaning through active learning experiences, socioculturalism is primarily focused on the social benefits of learning with others. However, the two theories are not incompatible. Each offers a slightly different lens to understand how people learn, and each helps us create effective curricula and make instructional decisions in our classrooms.

Current understanding of the sociocultural perspective on learning is based on the assumption that "human learning presupposes a specific social nature and a process by which children grow into the intellectual life of those around them" (Vygotsky, 1978, p. 88). From this perspective, two primary aims of schooling are for students to learn to communicate their understandings effectively to others and for teachers to provide experiences for students that promote purposeful interactions with others. The zone of proximal development (ZPD) is "the distance between the actual developmental level as determined by independent problem solving and the level of potential development as determined through

> Education researchers working within the sociocultural tradition have asserted that the most effective means of constructing knowledge is through dialogue arising from cooperative inquiry.
>
> —Guccione (2011, p. 568)

problem solving under adult guidance or in collaboration with more capable peers" (Vygotsky, 1978, p. 86). As Dewey (1938) states, "all human experience is ultimately social . . . it involves contact and communication" (p. 38).

A sociocultural perspective views all learning as socially situated; that is, it takes place in a certain setting at a certain time, whether it is school sanctioned or outside of school. This means that the context that surrounds the learning activity should not be overlooked. All learners filter new ideas through their own personal views of the world based on sociocultural influences, such as culture, religion, family, and community.

Collaborative Learning

A classroom teacher with a sociocultural perspective creates multiple opportunities for students to collaborate. Collaboration is not easy and does not come naturally to all learners, so the mediating role of the teacher remains important. Most students need to be taught how to collaborate productively. There are numerous educational benefits of collaboration. The old adage "two heads are better than one" is certainly applicable in the classroom. In fact, working in groups of three or four can help children improve their communication skills, design more creative solutions to problems, and gain a sense of what it is like to manage real problems in the workplace (Figure 2.2). As society becomes more complex, finding ways to share our knowledge and skills is essential.

Socioculturalism on the Web

Despite concerns that computers might promote social isolation in the classroom (it is interesting to recall that there were once critics who feared that books would hamper children's social development because they were considered to be an isolationist medium!), in many classrooms the computer center can more accurately be described as a "social center" that expands communication close to home and far away. Researchers have noted that social media and other new technologies invite purposeful communication among students and promote collaborative efforts to solve problems (Dresang, 2005; Leu, Kinzer, et al., 2013).

In addition to the social interactions inside the classroom, technology promotes social interaction with students in other classrooms, neighborhoods, cities, states, and countries. Online communication serves to break down classroom walls and lessen

FIGURE 2.2. Student collaboration.

community isolation as students from different geographic regions, with different worldviews and resources, communicate with each other. Although it is possible to utilize more traditional forms of communication, such as pen pals, for these kinds of exchanges, the Internet is more immediate and can provide a wider range of audiences and purposes for reading, writing, talking, listening, viewing, and researching.

Internet technologies also provide powerful tools for helping children with special needs to engage in meaningful communication with others. For example, multilingual students can make contact with children in other locations with a shared first language; children in a cultural minority group can communicate with people from the same cultural group in other communities; and students with physical disabilities can interact with other students who may be unaware of their disabilities and can respond without any preconceived images of disability (Garner & Gillingham, 1998; Reinking, 1997).

Learning through Symbols: Semiotics

We have defined *constructivist learning theory* as learning by doing and *socioculturalism* as learning with others. Now we add just one more lens through which to view the learning process and guide our classroom decisions: *semiotics* (learning through symbols). Semiotic theory is highly compatible with the previous two theories because it describes the symbolic forms we use to communicate with others in our efforts to construct meaning.

Humans use signs (defined as anything we use to convey meaning, such as pictures, letters, words, gestures, and/or objects) to describe the world. Our capacity to create and interpret signs, symbols, and sign systems is a major distinguishing feature between humans and animals (Gardner, 1983; Siegel, 1995; Suhor, 1984). Whereas signs can have significance to just one person (such as a personal shorthand style), symbols are conventionalized (such as the fairly universal symbols for women's or men's restrooms). A sign system is a conventionalized set of symbols that is commonly understood by people versed in certain disciplines, such as art, music, dance, language, science, and mathematics. The phrase *forms of representation* refers to how we symbolically communicate our private conceptions about the world, and it is often used synonymously with the phrase *sign systems*.

> The birth of writing did not destroy human memory. . . . The birth of printing did not destroy beautifully wrought graphic works, nor did it undermine all hierarchically organized religions. And the birth of apps need not destroy the human capacities to generate new issues and new solutions.
>
> —Gardner and Davis (2013, p. 192)

It is important to expose children to different sign systems because each is uniquely capable of addressing different aspects of the world around them (Labbo, 1996; Kozma, 1991; Salomon, 1997). Certain sign systems are better suited for representing specific concepts or ideas; therefore, one aim of education is to teach students which symbols to apply at which times. For example, an algebraic concept is best represented using mathematical symbols, whereas a poetic concept might be well represented using art, song, dance, or writing but would be hard to express through a mathematical equation.

Multiple Literacies

From a semiotic perspective, the goal of instruction is to teach children how to understand and orchestrate a variety of sign systems. Many semioticians recommend a multiple-literacies approach to learning, in which students are taught to move freely between sign systems. The following is an example of a multiple-literacies approach: A social studies teacher invites his students to conduct a cross-curricular inquiry project on a critical social issue, and one student chooses air pollution. This student might search the Internet (information literacy), interview experts (oral literacy), read books and articles (print literacy), analyze images taken from space (multimedia literacy), and explore the current and future impact of pollution on the environment (critical literacy). Toward the end of the inquiry project, students may use a variety of formats to demonstrate what they've learned, such as poems, posters, slide shows, podcasts, wikis, word clouds, or websites.

 Science and Technical Literacy Standard: **Determine the meaning of symbols, key terms, and other domain-specific words and phrases as they are used in a specific scientific or technical context.**

In the United States, a multiple-literacies approach is easy to accomplish in the lower grades, where the separations between content areas are easily blurred; however, secondary teachers can also teach interdisciplinary units or team up with colleagues to help students explore issues from multiple perspectives, which is much closer to how inquiry is carried out in the real world outside the classroom.

Semiotics on the Web

Teaching and learning on the Web is a satisfying fit for educators with a semiotic viewpoint because the Web has the unique capacity to combine multiple sign systems. Before the advent of computers and the Internet, no medium could combine so many semiotic systems in one place at one time; for example, a website may contain print, graphics, audio, video, and animation—all on one page. When multiple sign systems are presented together, they can complement and extend the intended meaning of the message. For example, when text about the rain forest is accompanied by photographs and a multimedia clip, the information can be accessed in a variety of ways to support the reader's knowledge acquisition. The clichéd phrase "a picture is worth a thousand words" expresses how pictures can transmit large amounts of information instantly, whereas language is constrained in a linear sequence of ideas.

> Multimodal texts that combine language, imagery, sounds, performance, and the like are what students deserve and expect, coming as they are from a world rich in multimedia.
> —Alvermann, Hutchins, and McDevitt (2012, p. 40)

One of the most promising aspects of combining multiple sign systems through technology is that it provides alternate methods for communicating complex concepts and ideas other than by the use of print alone. In fact, teaching students effective skills for making meaning from multimedia has the potential to improve print literacy skills (Hobbs, 2006). The inclusion of icons, graphics, visuals, audio, and multimedia conveys information in a variety of ways, which provides greater educational equity for children who struggle with language-based delivery systems such as lectures and books (Hall, Meyer, & Rose, 2012; Novak, 2014). We mentioned earlier the capacity for multimedia to level the playing field in terms of students' prior knowledge, but it can also do so in terms of learning exclusively through language (Gordon, Proctor, & Dalton, 2012). For years, print has been the dominant sign system for learning in just about every core content area, from language arts to social studies to science (Alvermann, 2008; Hobbs & Frost, 2003). Although we still value print, we recognize the importance of offering alternative, supportive learning experiences to students who find print difficult to manage, such as struggling readers or second language learners. Some of these same students who encounter difficulty with linguistic tasks excel in other sign systems, such as those associated with musical, logical/mathematical, spatial, bodily/kinesthetic, and interpersonal intelligences (Gardner, 1983).

Universal Design for Learning

Universal Design for Learning (UDL) is a framework for curriculum design that encourages educators to find innovative ways to meet the needs of learners with different backgrounds, learning styles, and abilities (Meyer, Rose, & Gordon, 2014). With a focus on adapting the curriculum to suit the learner rather than the other way around, UDL guides us toward creating flexible materials and methods from the start, rather than trying to retrofit inflexible materials to each learner. UDL recognizes that we must endeavor to differentiate instruction to the extent possible because "one-size-fits-all curricula and pedagogy deserve to be anachronistic, if not indictable offenses" (Gardner & Davis, 2013, p. 174).

> **Whereas traditional education sets low expectations for many students and tends to see them as too disabled, too disadvantaged, or too diverse to make adequate yearly progress, UDL raises a radically different expectation: that it is our curricula that are too disabled, too disadvantaged, or too uniform to reach goals that really matter.**
> —Rose, Gravel, and Domings (2012, p. 134)

UDL is based on neuroscientific research. Brain imaging (i.e., positron emission tomography [PET] scans and magnetic resonance imaging [MRI]) is the most direct measure of how people learn. Individual differences in the brain shed light on the incredible diversity of learning styles and preferences. Perhaps the most revolutionary discovery is that the human brain displays substantial individual differences with respect to three neural networks: recognition, strategic, and affective.

The recognition network is the "what" of learning. Although human brains all share the same basic recognition architecture and recognize things in roughly the same way, our recognition networks come in many shapes, sizes, and patterns. A UDL curriculum activates diverse learners' recognition networks by offering multiple means of representation to give learners various ways of acquiring information and knowledge (Meyer et al., 2014).

The strategic network is the "how" of learning. It is through strategic networks that we plan, execute, and monitor our mental and motor patterns. Strategic brain networks vary widely between individuals. Learners differ in the ways that they can express what they know, so we need to allow for multiple means of action and expression (Meyer et al., 2014).

The affective network is the "why" of learning. The affective network determines whether a student is engaged and motivated depending on the level of challenge, excitement, and interest. Affect is a crucial element to learning, and learners differ dramatically in the ways in which they can be engaged or motivated. UDL principles call for multiple means of engagement to tap into diverse learners' interests, challenge them appropriately, and motivate them to learn (Meyer et al., 2014).

UDL on the Web

UDL recognizes the power of technology to meet the needs of individual learners because of the inherent and nearly limitless flexibility of technology itself. The UDL framework is useful and important without access to technology, but technology makes it much easier to differentiate instruction. For example, it's nearly impossible to make a printed textbook accessible to students whose first language is not English, to learners with limited vision, and to those with reading disabilities. In contrast, digital texts can be translated, fonts and images can be adjusted, and various supports can be embedded for those in need.

Internet inquiry is one of the best ways to address diverse learners' recognition networks because it automatically exposes students to multiple forms of representation. Web reading immerses students in a "multimedia symbol bath" (Mackey, 2003) while they explore ideas using different sign systems. Information that is presented in one modality (e.g., lecture or textbook) is boring for some learners and inaccessible for others. Let's face it, no one learns to think independently by listening to someone else talk all day. Educators must move away from a "tell-not-show" curriculum because "there are other modes (moving and still images, sounds, performances and the like) that are equally, if not better, suited for showing rather than simply describing conceptual relationships" (Alvermann et al., 2012, p. 35).

Internet inquiry is an ideal way to address diverse learners' strategic networks because it invites multiple means of action and expression. Through inquiry projects, learners ask questions, think critically, and construct knowledge

★ *Library Media Standard:* **Collaborate with others to exchange ideas, develop new understandings, make decisions, and solve problems.**

by "flexibly deploying a range of strategies to help them accomplish a variety of reading and learning tasks. They monitor comprehension and goal attainment and take corrective action as needed" (Dalton & Proctor, 2008, p. 313).

Internet inquiry is a powerful vehicle for addressing diverse learners' affective networks because it offers multiple means of engagement. Affect is an entry point for educators because it plays such an important role in the constructive process of inquiry (Kuhlthau, 2010). Web readers experience a range of emotions, such as "optimism at the beginning, a feeling of frustration when they cannot find any information, and satisfaction when they succeed" (Kuiper & Volman, 2008, p. 252). Researchers and educators have repeatedly found that learners are highly engaged when reading online, despite the challenges of navigating within this complex environment (Drew, 2012; Leu & Forzani, 2012).

Components of Effective Instruction

Once teachers are able to identify and articulate their own theories of learning and their comfort with particular curricular approaches, they can begin thinking about lesson planning. Theory and research drive curriculum, and curriculum drives daily practice. As beginning teachers, while trying to comply with learning standards and preparing our students for high-stakes testing, we often rely on textbooks and random lesson plans found on the Internet simply in order to survive. However, as we mature as teachers, we begin to figure out what works and what doesn't work, through experience and a better understanding and application of research. What works for me might not work for you if we don't share the same theory of learning; however, there are four key research-based instructional elements that are consistently found in the classrooms of effective teachers and that also apply to learning on the Web. These four techniques are (1) modeling; (2) scaffolding; (3) practice; and (4) feedback (Figure 2.3), all of which depend on effective, ongoing assessment.

FIGURE 2.3. Components of effective instruction.

Modeling

Anyone who has taught a young child a new skill has most likely used modeling to demonstrate proficient use of the skill, such as tying a shoe. "Let me show you" is an oft-heard refrain in this context. Similarly, after assessing learners' needs, effective teachers show students how to perform an unfamiliar set of skills or strategies before expecting them to execute these independently. An extremely powerful use of modeling is the teacher think-aloud, in which a teacher narrates his thinking as he performs a task (Figure 2.4).

Thinking aloud provides a natural opportunity for teachers to model key vocabulary appropriate to the task (Kymes, 2005); even more important, it sets up an occasion to develop a common *metalanguage*—a language for talking about language, images, texts, and meaning-making interactions (New London Group, 1996). Talking about the learning process with others stimulates students to be more metacognitive about their own learning processes, that is, to think about their own thinking. Successful teachers continually prompt learners to become more metacognitive so that students begin to monitor their own learning, adjusting and extending strategies as needed. Teachers who are effective at modeling clearly articulate the purpose of a learning objective so that students not only know *what* the strategy, process, or product looks like but also *how* to apply it, *when* and *where* to apply it, and *why* it can be useful.

Scaffolding

Another extremely effective element of instruction is scaffolding. This is analogous to Vygotsky's Zone of Proximal Development (ZPD), in which a more experienced child or adult helps a learner perform a task that is slightly beyond his ability to do independently (Vygotsky, 1978). Nudging learners along their individual ZPDs helps them extend their current levels of knowledge and ability in incremental steps.

My first thought, as I look over this website, is a feeling of being a bit overwhelmed. There are lots of elements to look at, such as the blinking red box in the upper right corner, the scrolling photos at the top of the page, and the bright green headings along the left-hand side. There seem to be so many things to look at, I am unsure where to begin. Let me think back to my question, "What was the role of children in the Civil War?" On this website, I am going to the search box and type in my key words <children + civil war> to see if I can find some more specific information. Now that I have narrowed my search within this website, I can see several topics that might be helpful and some that are not. This first heading "Civil War families split apart." Hmm, there might be information about children here, but I am not sure. When I look at this second heading, I see "Boys in Battle," and I think this is a good match to my question because it has both boys and battle in the title.

After clicking on this link, I see lots of text. I know this is the time when I need to read more carefully. As I am reading this text, I am thinking about what the words mean, but also about how I might use this information to answer my question. Here I see the statement, "Boys served as drummers, and assisted with cooking, cleaning, and care of wounded." This information fits perfectly with my question! I am going to record it on my notetaking document and copy and paste the URL for the website.

FIGURE 2.4. Think-aloud example.

In all forms of scaffolding, there is a gradual release of responsibility from the expert to the novice (Fielding & Pearson, 1994; Pearson & Gallagher, 1983). The gradual release entails a parent, teacher, librarian, coach, or expert explaining, then demonstrating, then guiding practice with learners, and finally giving the reins to the learner as he begins to independently use the skill. The more experienced learner provides scaffolding for the less experienced learner, but over time, less of the work is done by the teacher and more by the student. Think of the metaphor of a house painter's temporary scaffold—it is never intended to adhere to the house permanently but is dismantled piece by piece until the painter can reach the walls without the scaffolding. Reading teachers have long understood the need to give young learners time to build skills and strategies before expecting fledgling readers to skillfully orchestrate the reading process on their own.

> We think aloud to reveal our own reading processes, and we model what it is to be a thinking-intensive reader, one who pays attention to thinking and monitors for understanding.
> —Harvey and Goudvis (2013, p. 432)

Novice Web readers also need a lot of scaffolding. This may be as formal as students following a set of oral and written instructions prepared by the teacher or librarian in advance or as casual as the teacher looking over students' shoulders while they are on the computer and providing metacognitive prompts. Experienced teachers are masters at providing just the right amount of scaffolding so each learner can perform the task with confidence and awareness.

> Appropriate scaffolding is essential to teaching in the ZPD. Too much scaffolding undermines a student's sense of accomplishment; too little means frustration and discouragement. The right amount helps engage students in the learning process, building interest and enjoyment. The right blend of challenge, support, and meaningful feedback can put even beginning students in the state of flow described by Csikszentmihalyi, fully engaged in the learning process.
> —Meyer and Rose (1998, p. 60)

Interestingly, well-designed technology tools can also be used to scaffold learners. Although no tool or app has yet to match the sensitive and nuanced learner support provided by an experienced teacher, students can develop intellectual partnerships with programs that embed models of expert performance, strategy prompts, feedback systems, and tools to reduce cognitive load. A premiere example of this type of tool is the "UDL Editions" (*udleditions.cast.org*). These free online texts are loaded with "just-in-time" scaffolds and supports; for example, text to speech, synchronized highlighting, animated strategy coaches, vocabulary definitions, linked Web resources, and so on.

Practice

Another linchpin of effective instruction is providing adequate time for students to practice new skills and strategies. Individual and collaborative guided and independent practice is also important so that learners can confidently implement strategies on their own. Some students may need very little practice to master a new skill, whereas others may need to revisit a learning task repeatedly—in different contexts and at different times.

Whenever feasible, practice activities need to be authentic; in other words, students should be engaged in activities that have a real purpose rather than a contrived one. For example, synthesizing ideas from websites assigned by the teacher is not nearly as potent a practice as having students synthesize information gleaned from sites of their choosing. Similarly, creating a product that is never shared with others, such as a website that is never actually published on the Web, is not an authentic activity. An audience of one (i.e., the teacher) is not really an audience at all. Research has repeatedly shown that students produce higher quality work when writing for an authentic audience (Beach, 2012). In a similar vein, inquiry topics that are chosen by the teacher are much less engaging for students than those that are driven by authentic learner questions. Giving students an opportunity to select their own inquiry topics builds a sense of ownership and empowerment. Many of our students have the capacity to design creative solutions to real-world problems if we allow them to take on the mantle of the expert.

Related to the concept of authenticity is that of relevance. Unless they are highly motivated by grades and/or instructor approval, students need to perceive school-related tasks as relevant to their lives. The understanding that children have an intrinsic need to make connections with what they are learning in school has been noted throughout history by educational theorists such as Dewey (1938) and Vygotsky (1978), who believed that teaching should involve tasks that students see as connected and relevant to their lives rather than tasks that seem isolated from the real world.

Technology is a natural point of reference for today's children because they are already immersed in and familiar with media. It is fascinating to observe that the novelty of computers has not worn off; in fact, it is quite the opposite. Now, more than ever, students are eager to practice online literacies, and mobile devices have made it even easier to explore new ways to use the Web (Figure 2.5). With mobility comes the power to access the Internet just about any time and anywhere, thus the need for instruction in Web literacies. One of the best ways to help students become skilled at learning on the Web is to have them read a variety of Web texts and then reflect on their experiences together. This authentic, relevant activity can familiarize students with the features commonly found on the Web and eventually lead to independent, self-regulated learning.

Speaking and Listening Standard: **Prepare for and participate effectively in a range of conversations and collaborations with diverse partners, building on others' ideas and expressing their own clearly and persuasively.**

Feedback

Another element of effective instruction is feedback. Learners need to know how they are doing on a task so they can modify their approach if necessary and develop the confidence to continue with the task (Tovani, 2011). Feedback can be given in a variety of forms, but it is crucial that it be specific and timely. Anyone who has taken a basic teacher education course knows that generic praise such as "good job" or "great" does not offer adequate specificity to influence student performance in the future. Experienced teachers recognize that feedback must be timely in order to make a difference. There is a point of diminishing returns as feedback is delivered farther and farther away

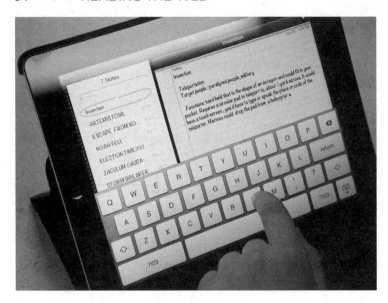

FIGURE 2.5. Web exploration supports the creation process.

from the original act. We have all met teachers who are so slow to grade tests or review their students' work that the papers end up in the "circular file" (aka the trash can) because they are no longer useful for improving student learning.

Feedback should also be ongoing, not just at the end of a chapter, unit, or semester. When students receive constructive feedback—whether it's enthusiastically positive or gently negative—on their understanding of a topic or their performance on a task *right at the moment of need*, there is a much greater chance of retention and transfer. For example, when a teacher acknowledges that a student has found useful information within a website, the student not only develops confidence in his Internet reading abilities, but he is also more likely to look for information about other topics for other purposes. The ideal time to give feedback to students is when they are immersed in a task and open to suggestion; this is often referred to as the "teachable moment."

 Library Media Standard: **Use interaction with and feedback from teachers and peers to guide own inquiry process.**

Feedback is not only useful for students but also serves as a primary formative assessment tool for teachers. Although it can be difficult with large class sizes, effective teachers are aware of their students' learning processes and can modify and adapt instruction as needed in order to reach as many learners as possible. True diagnostic instruction guides teachers toward what needs to be taught or retaught next, thus initiating a new cycle of modeling, scaffolding, practice, and feedback (Figure 2.6).

There are many instances in which teacher feedback is critical during the process of learning on the Web, as the Web itself does not typically provide feedback to learners. When possible, teachers and librarians should prescreen students' research questions and search terms. While students are online, teachers should "hover," providing specific feedback regarding students' choices of search engines, search terms, links to follow, and web pages to skim quickly or read more deeply.

FIGURE 2.6. Feedback is helpful for moving along the inquiry process.

Outcomes of Effective Instruction

We have stated that the ultimate goal of instruction is for students to learn how to learn. Specific outcomes of effective instruction include the lifelong learning goals of independence, self-regulation, metacognitive awareness, monitoring, cognitive flexibility, critical thinking, and engagement. Successful readers of print-based text are motivated, alert, observant, responsive, responsible, self-reliant, and flexible (Afflerbach, Cho, Kim, Crassas, & Doyle, 2013; Beers & Probst, 2013). Web readers must possess all of these habits of mind and dispositions plus resilience, persistence, patience, confidence, creativity, and the ability to set learner-centered goals (Coiro, 2012; Harrison et al., 2014). Internet inquiry has the potential to promote all of these outcomes and more.

Our goal with students is to guide them toward *independence*. After all, we cannot always be looking over students' shoulders to make sure they are using effective search strategies or skimming over important information on a web page when they should be reading more closely. Independent learning focuses on each person's ability to "activate, alter, and sustain specific learning practices" (Zimmerman, 2002, p. 70), such as comprehending when reading online.

Effective Web reading also depends on *self-regulation*. Web readers gain practice with self-regulation because they must pace themselves and stay focused on their goals (Rouet et al., 2011). Decisions must continually be made

 TEACHER: **What have you learned about the inquiry process?**

STUDENT: **That it's all about learning.**

about which links to access, what to read next, and whether sufficient information has been gathered. In other words, *metacognitive awareness*, or monitoring one's understanding, during the Web reading process is critical for moving forward and making effective choices about what information to access next (Goldman, Braasch, Wiley, Graesser, & Brodowinska, 2012). Web reading requires an awareness of one's learning needs, strategy use, and orientation in space. Learners rely on this awareness of their own strengths and limitations and flexibly apply this awareness to setting learning goals, adapting strategies to the learning task, and *monitoring* their progress toward their goals (Zimmerman, 2002).

Internet inquiry also promotes *cognitive flexibility* (Spiro, 2006), which is crucial to success when reading in a complex and continually changing environment. Web readers develop cognitive flexibility by applying and adapting a wide range of strategies while rapidly moving across texts and modalities (Dwyer & Harrison, 2008). Effective Web readers construct meaning by making purposeful choices about accessing information from various Web links, thus demonstrating their versatility and efficiency at traversing the Web terrain. Responding to rapid movement across multiple modes enables, and may even demand, new cognitive processes (Moje, 2009). Researchers are in the very early stages of identifying these new cognitive processes.

Educators continually seek to foster students' higher order skills, such as critical thinking. Internet inquiry provides opportunities for learners to develop "a critical thinking filter to continuously differentiate the usable from the unusable. If the filter is not already present in the medium itself, the information user must develop one as part of the search process" (Mackey & Jacobson, 2011, p. 72). A person with a critical disposition is "truth seeking, confident in reasoning, judicious, inquisitive, systematic, analytical, and open-minded" (Kiili et al., 2008, p. 77).

Humans are motivated by basic needs, as well as by the desire for autonomy, mastery, and purpose (Pink, 2009). Few individuals enjoy being controlled by others, and children are no exception. "Students love choice. Children and adolescents have little control over their lives, so they will take it wherever they can get it. Even the perceived element of choice seems to increase student buy-in" (Novak, 2014, p. 73). The beauty of Internet inquiry is that there are so many ways to engage students with choices. They can choose topics, questions, resources, navigational pathways, final products, and so on. Choice leads to ownership of the learning process and ownership leads to *engagement*.

> When teachers establish an atmosphere of inquiry, students are no longer anxious about admitting that they do not know something. Instead, they see this admission as a jumping-off place for their inquiry.
> —Fisher, Frey, and Lapp (2012, p. 77)

For most learners, the opportunity to collaborate and communicate with others increases engagement. Inquiry projects can convert classrooms and schools into communities of practice where students pursue personally relevant questions and solve important problems. "If you can evolve your class to the point where it feels like a learning community where every kid is dependent upon every other kid for their learning and they feel this reliance on each other, then good things happen" (November, 2012, p. 46). Online reading not only allows us to make text-to-self, text-to-text, and text-to-world connections, but it also enables us to make reader-to-reader connections. Today's technologies allow us to highlight, extract, annotate, curate, and share our thoughts with others about what we're reading. Now, more than ever, reading has become a social act (Beers & Probst, 2013).

Another reason inquiry-based learning is so motivating is that it provides so many options for creativity. An inquiry stance places learners at the helm of the learning process, giving them an "energized sense of agency" (Leander, 2010). Students feel inspired to create when they realize their voices are being heard and their questions count more than their answers (Fisher, Frey, & Lapp, 2012). A student who is engaged in a self-generated task is more likely to reach an unconscious state of flow (Csíkszentmihályi, 1998) than is a child listening to a droning lecture or laboring through a dense textbook. When an inquiry project leads to a creative final product chosen by students themselves, many willingly spend extra hours working on projects. They experience learning as play, not work.

For example, one group of elementary students carried out an inquiry project on the history of cartoons. They conducted interviews and surveys (speaking, listening), consulted books and websites (reading, notemaking), created a hilarious script that depicted Wile E. Coyote suing the Acme Corporation for selling him defective products (collaborative writing), and posted everything on a website, using colorful animations to illustrate cartoon characters, cartoon artists, and how cartoons are made (multimedia design). We've also worked with whole classes of elementary and middle school students who have designed inquiry projects about famous people, prospective careers, or interesting animals, representing their findings using technology tools that combined print, audio, video, and/or animation. Internet inquiry truly is the sweet spot in which even the most reluctant learners find themselves begging to work on projects beyond the time allotted in the classroom.

> **Every aspect of learning and teaching requires the gathering, processing, and communication of information.**
> —Eisenberg (2008, p. 39)

The Educator's Role

Without a doubt, the teacher's role is a significant factor in students' ability to learn about, with, and from technology. The teacher's role as curriculum designer and learning facilitator continues to be integral, even in situations in which some students appear to be more tech savvy than their teachers (Guinee, 2012). It has been repeatedly noted by researchers that the teacher's stance must shift away from a transmission-oriented philosophy toward a more constructivist approach if effective learning is going to take place on the Web. If there is a mismatch between the teacher's philosophical beliefs and an instructional activity such as Internet inquiry, students are not likely to be successful. In some cases, this will require a shift in control and pedagogy, as well as being open to the possibilities offered by Web 3.0 technologies.

Suffice it to say, many changes are occurring because of technology's proliferation into teaching and learning. One key change focuses on the role of learners, and another on the role of educators. In the past, students have primarily been seen as consumers of information. True, students often created projects and wrote reports based on their learning, but these frequently did not leave the classroom. The

> **The models we provide students allow them access to academic language and thinking as well as information about expert problem solving and understanding. Daily modeling is critical if students are going to understand complex content.**
> —Frey, Fisher, and Gonzalez (2010, p. 12)

Internet facilitates students' connecting with others beyond their classroom, out into the school, the community, and the world. Essentially this connectedness is redefining the role of the learner as contributor. The work of students can shape the opinions, learning, and actions of others when created and shared on blogs or wikis or when connected using video conferencing or podcasting. Educators may need to step out of their comfort zone to allow students to produce and share, not just consume, knowledge (Frey et al., 2010).

Integrating technology into the classroom also shifts the role of educators into those of curriculum designer, guide, and coach, leading students toward self-regulation in their location, understanding, evaluation, and use of information (Figure 2.7). In 2011, Harrison predicted that "teachers who are specialists in literacy are likely to be

- More knowledgeable and active in the area of reading development.
- More knowledgeable about the Internet information architecture.
- Information managers rather than managers of student behavior" (p. 128).

Does this ring true for you today? If not, do you see yourself moving in this direction?

Clearly, a teacher's level of computer expertise is an influential factor in students' success with technology, and this knowledge must be balanced with the gradual release of responsibility that is a hallmark of effective instruction. Just as search engines are not designed to be teaching tools, neither are most websites. It is up to the teacher to provide support but also to "strive against the often natural inclination to be a ready

FIGURE 2.7. The educator's role as guide and coach.

source of specific information for students. Instead, when students ask for specific information, a teacher might use such requests as an opportunity to query students about what strategies they have used thus far, to constructively critique those strategies, to make suggested modification in their approach, and to model appropriate strategies" (Colwell, Hunt-Barron, & Reinking, 2013, p. 22). Although bold teachers can, and do, learn alongside their students, it is certainly conducive to students' learning on the Web if teachers have at least a minimal level of comfort with hardware, operating systems, the Internet, search engines, and search strategies. The availability of experts, the amount of professional development opportunities, and sheer time spent online can greatly enhance teachers' technology expertise. However, as with students, this type of learning takes time, so teachers who have not yet begun to integrate technology into their teaching need to get started right away.

SUMMARY ●

Because there is no single method of teaching that works with all learners all the time, a more practical and far-reaching instructional objective is *teaching students transferable strategies for learning how to learn*. In this chapter we described three well-established theories of learning: constructivism, socioculturalism, and semiotics. We presented UDL as a framework for ensuring that instruction is differentiated for diverse learners. Four elements of effective instruction were presented, with the goal of guiding students toward independence. Educators can lead this charge by modeling effective Web literacy practices and encouraging their use throughout Internet inquiry activities.

In Chapter 3, we turn our attention from learning in general toward literacy in particular. Although reading on the Web is similar in many ways to reading in print, when we apply our understanding of cueing systems and transactional theories to the process, we find that the complexities of Web reading are many. We discuss the similarities and differences between print reading and Web reading with respect to comprehension strategies and foundational reading skills. Finally, we explain how knowledge of informational text can aid readers in making meaning on the Web.

3 Becoming Literate

KEY IDEAS ●

- Researchers are seeking to understand the challenge of what it means to be literate in a digital world.

- Cueing systems and transactional theories provide a useful foundation from which to view the reading process.

- Decades of reading research have consistently revealed comprehension strategies used by proficient readers that are necessary for both print and electronic texts.

- Reading on the Web bears some similarity to reading print, but online reading is more complex.

- In order to gain automaticity and comprehension, readers need to be proficient with foundational skills such as decoding, fluency, vocabulary, and spelling.

- Familiarity with informational text can aid readers in making meaning on the Web.

- The reciprocal nature of learning means that online and offline literacies are mutually beneficial.

> Much of human activity involves information seeking—a purposeful search for information in order to bridge the gap between what is known and what is unknown—and, as such, it demands cognitive processes.
> —Tabatabai and Shore (2005, p. 224)

In this chapter, we seek to answer the question "What does it mean to become literate?" by building on what we already know about the reading process in print and applying it to reading on the Web. In this chapter, we focus specifically on the ways people make meaning from text, both print and digital. We explore the term *literacy* and describe two well-established views of the reading process, applying each theory to reading on the Web. We summarize reading comprehension strategies used by strategic readers of both print and Web texts. We follow with a description of the role that foundational skills play in comprehending any type of text. Finally, we investigate the role of informational text that is ubiquitous on the Web and the reciprocal nature of reading and writing online. The theme for this chapter is that *reading is a very complex cognitive and metacognitive process.*

One of the goals of this text is to build a bridge between traditional literacy and new literacies. This concept of connecting the old with the new is important because teaching Web literacies is not about teaching completely new concepts or adding on to the currently overloaded curriculum. We view Web literacies as an extension of our traditional view of literacy, incorporating the technologies that so strongly influence the ways we access information. The main ideas in this chapter, in conjunction with the focus in Chapter 2 on the ways we learn, serve as a solid foundation for exploring what it means to be literate in today's world.

Literacy Family Tree

Scholars in the fields of education, communications and media studies, library and information science, literary theory, history, psychology, sociology, rhetoric, and linguistics are all seeking to understand the challenge of what it means to be literate in a digital world. Literacy is no longer the sole responsibility of the reading teacher or the English language arts teacher. A review of the literature across disciplines reveals a plethora of terminologies, presented here in alphabetical order: *computer literacy, critical literacy, cyberliteracy, digital literacies, information and communication technologies (ICT) literacies, information fluency, information literacy, Internet literacy, multiliteracy, multimedia literacy, multiple literacies, new literacies, 21st-century literacies,* and *Web literacy.* In addition, the terms *New Literacies, transliteracy,* and *metaliteracy* have been generated in an effort to find a comprehensive concept to unify the important work that is being done in each of these areas (Leu, Kinzer, et al., 2013; Mackey & Jacobson, 2011).

Many of these terms represent similar concepts but may differ when viewed through the lens of a specific discipline or theoretical framework. "Like the parable of the blind man and the elephant, each stakeholder group approaches the topic of multiliteracy from different perspectives, and as a result, there are numerous, differentially nuanced visions of what these skills encompass" (Hobbs, 2006, p. 16). This list of terms illustrates the difficulty of finding a single word to capture the complexities of understanding and communicating ideas in a digital world. Reading on the

 Library Media Standard: **Read, view, and listen for information presented in any format (e.g., textual, visual, media, digital) in order to make inferences and gather meaning.**

Web necessitates more than just recognizing words and comprehending text; it also requires an understanding of how information is produced and evaluating online information in all of its modalities. Although not the primary focus of this text, being literate in today's world also includes producing and sharing information using collaborative online tools. With so many options to describe such a multidimensional concept, we chose to use the term *Web literacy* because it carries meaning that can be applied to a broad audience and because it is a good fit with what we know about reading comprehension on the Web. Next, we present cueing systems and transactional theories as a foundation to help us understand what it means to be Web literate.

 It's not just fact-finding, but rather active interpretation and learning.
—Kuhlthau, Maniotes, and Caspari (2007, p. 22)

Cueing Systems Theory

In Chapter 2, we discussed sign systems from a semiotic perspective. Every major symbol system, such as dance, music, art, math, and print, uses a common set of cues or "cueing systems" to help the learner understand and create meaning in that form of representation. For example, in musical notation, there are cues for melody, rhythm, harmony, texture, form, dynamics, and timbre. A widely accepted view of the reading process suggests that there are at least three major cueing systems used by readers to make sense of text: graphophonic (letter–sound relationships), syntactic (grammar), and semantic (meaning; Goodman, 1996; Clay, 1991). Although some educators have suggested that readers of print text utilize additional cueing systems, such as lexical (word knowledge),

FIGURE 3.1.
The three-cueing-systems model.

schematic (prior knowledge), and pragmatic (knowledge of audience/purpose) systems (Keene & Zimmermann, 1997), the three-systems model provides a useful starting point for understanding the cognitive complexity of making meaning from print (Figure 3.1).

Effective readers simultaneously apply cueing systems through the use of complex mental connections. For instance, in order to understand the word *forelimbs* in a text on whales, a reader would likely consider her knowledge of compound words (syntactic), letter–sound combinations (graphophonic), and an illustration with labeled parts (semantic), all within a matter of seconds. Effortless application of cueing systems is a complex task requiring a high level of mental effort. Reading is clearly not a passive process; rather, it is a very active process, involving multiple parts of the brain as connections are made between the various cues provided by the text.

When literacy researchers talk about cueing systems, they are typically referring to print. Comprehension on the Web requires the orchestration of a daunting number of additional cueing systems, plus knowledge of informational text structures and the inclination and ability to access supports, thereby placing an even heavier cognitive load on learners. It's one thing to have three or four cues working together to help determine meaning, but now the Web reader may encounter at least a dozen cues within broad categories, such as operational cues (hardware, software, navigation), organizational cues (orientation, page layout, text structure), sign system cues (text, still image, multimedia), and relevancy cues (typographic, usefulness, truthfulness; see Figure 3.2). Reading on the Web is truly a cognitively complex endeavor, requiring continuous self-regulation and the ability to rapidly analyze and act upon multiple cueing systems.

FIGURE 3.2. Website cueing systems. From How Stuff Works (*www.howstuffworks.com*). Used with permission.

Transactional Theory

The transactional view of literacy is attributed to American literary critic Louise Rosenblatt, who first advanced the theory in 1938. Rosenblatt theorized that the meaning of the text does not merely lie within the words on the page but is created when each individual reader interacts with the text. The meaning becomes a new entity—a virtual text in one's mind—each time the text is read, based on a combination of what the reader brings and what the author created. The transactional theory of reading focuses on "the reading act as an event involving a particular individual and a particular text, happening at a particular time, under particular circumstances, in a particular social and cultural setting, and as part of the ongoing life of the individual and the group" (Rosenblatt, 1985, p. 100). What is significant about this interpretation of the reading process is that it is impossible to find "a single absolute meaning for a text because the same text can take on different meanings in transactions with different readers or even with the same reader in different contexts or times" (Rosenblatt, 1994, p. 1078).

Another key idea in transactional theory, also known as reader response theory, is that the reader's "stance" has a significant influence on how she approaches the text and on what she takes away from the text. The concept of reader stance refers to the unique combination of a reader's perspective and purpose for reading. An *aesthetic* stance focuses on a reader's sense of enjoyment and personal connections made with the text. An *efferent* stance focuses on the information or the details gathered from the text. Efferent and aesthetic stances are not mutually exclusive but rather form a continuum on which the reader moves seamlessly throughout the reading process. Rosenblatt describes this flow as a continuous, unconscious fluctuation between the two stances. The skilled reader effortlessly moves between both stances, blending information and emotions, facts and personal connections, as she progresses through the reading process. In contrast, the novice or struggling reader is less able to move effortlessly between stances and is often less aware of her purpose for reading in the first place.

> Texts are constructed by authors to be comprehended by readers. The meaning is in the author and the reader. The text has the potential to evoke meaning but has no meaning itself; meaning is not a characteristic of texts . . . meaning does not pass between writer and reader. It is represented by a writer in a text and constructed from a text by a reader.
> —Goodman (1994, p. 1103)

Like the reader of print text, the reader of Web text also brings prior knowledge and purpose to the reading task as she fluctuates between the efferent (informational) and the aesthetic (personal) stances. However, a printed text cannot literally change its characteristics as a result of being read, nor is there a direct interaction between the reader and the author of the text, so this transactional exchange is purely metaphorical. In contrast, electronic texts actually do change the fundamental relationship between the reader, the author, and the text by permitting a *literal* transaction between the reader and the text (McEneaney, 2011). Not only do texts continuously modify themselves based on user actions, but hypertext documents also allow the reader to select her own path through extensive networks of textual and multimedia information. Therefore, the idea of the act of reading being an "active process" takes on new and more literal meaning when we describe Web reading, in which the process involves engaged readers' constantly making choices about where to go and then taking

FIGURE 3.3. Web reading is an active process.

physical action by selecting links or scrolling (Figure 3.3). In addition, when reading an e-textbook, readers may move between the text and the embedded Web links and multimedia, necessitating nimble thinking about the best ways to acquire information from a variety of sources (Dobler, 2015). The physical act of navigating on the Web requires constant decision making and a high level of metacognitive awareness.

Reading Comprehension Strategies

Throughout the reading process, proficient readers orchestrate a number of comprehension strategies to support their construction of meaning (Fisher et al., 2012; Pearson, Roehler, Dole, & Duffy, 1992). Understanding the thinking

★ *Reading Standard:* **Read closely to determine what the text says explicitly and to make logical inferences from it.**

used by proficient, or strategic, readers provides teachers with insights into where readers should be headed along the path to comprehension. Strategies are those in-the-head processes a reader uses to make sense of what is being read. Because these internal processes are not easily observable and can be hard to gauge based solely on having readers retell a story or answer comprehension questions, we frequently must guess whether our students are using strategies. Listening to students work through texts by reading aloud gives us a "window on the reading process" (Goodman, 1982).

Within the last four decades, a strong body of research has been developed to describe what good readers do when they read printed texts, all of which can be applied toward Web texts (see Pressley & Afflerbach, 1995; Block & Pressley, 2002, for a review). Teachers recognize the need for quality, explicit instruction of strategies as a way to provide students with tools for their mental reading toolbox (Figure 3.4). Even more

 Strategy instruction is only useful insofar as it leads our kids to better understand the text, the world, and themselves so they can gain insight, anticipate hurdles, solve complex problems, and make progress toward a goal.
—Harvey and Goudvis (2013, p. 433)

effective comprehension occurs when a reader knows when, why, and how to use a strategy (Paris, Lipson, & Wixson, 1983). Strategy instruction is not an end in itself but a means to help our students to better understand texts, themselves, and the world

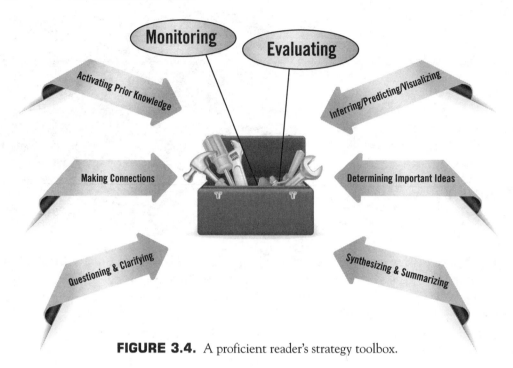

FIGURE 3.4. A proficient reader's strategy toolbox.

(Harvey & Goudvis, 2013). Reading comprehension strategies are sometimes categorized as cognitive strategies (mental processes that assist with making meaning) and metacognitive strategies (thinking about one's own strategy use).

Cognitive Strategies

The path from novice to expert reader includes the development of cognitive strategies that lead to understanding texts. Within the last decade, we have begun to understand how these strategies are applied online. "In essence, readers' strategies for identifying and learning text content bear remarkable resemblance to one another in both traditional and Internet reading, although the places in hyperspace in which readers find the texts and how they arrive at a particular text (or chance upon it) vary" (Afflerbach & Cho, 2010, p. 210). Because online texts are multimodal and nonlinear, today's readers are gaining information from a wide variety of sources in a variety of ways. Although an overlap exists between the strategies used by print and Web readers, there are some notable differences:

 TEACHER: How do you know when you find good information for your inquiry project?

STUDENT: When you can turn what you found into something bigger.

- Online reading is more complex and therefore requires higher level thinking (Coiro, 2011a).
- Online reading requires locating texts and navigating within and across websites (Coiro & Dobler, 2007; Leu, Kinzer, et al., 2013).
- Online reading places a heavier load on the metacognitive strategies of monitoring and evaluating (Afflerbach & Cho, 2015).

Activating Prior Knowledge and Making Connections

Strategic readers use prior knowledge to check whether their construction of meaning matches what they know about the topic and structure of the text (Duke & Pearson, 2002) by developing connections between the text and themselves, the text and other texts, and the text and the world. These connections help link together new information with what is already known. Readers with greater prior knowledge can remember more, determine the important information in the text, and draw conclusions from what they read.

Web readers must also rely on their prior knowledge to form connections and make meaning. In addition, they draw from their experiences with locating and navigating content (Dwyer & Harrison, 2008; Henry, 2006). Experienced online readers rely on their prior knowledge of the Web to determine the most appropriate reading paths within a shifting problem space. These readers expend less cognitive energy navigating, leaving more attention available for comprehension (McEneaney, Li, Allen, & Guzniczak, 2015). All of these additional demands on prior knowledge add another layer to the complexity of the Web reading process, so that skilled print readers sometimes find themselves frustrated and disoriented on the Web.

Questioning and Clarifying

Questioning is among the first comprehension strategies typically taught because it is so natural to young learners. Unfortunately, schools tend to focus on having students *answer* questions, to the point that kids' questions nearly disappear by about fifth grade (Harvey & Goudvis, 2007). Asking questions is a powerful way for readers to check comprehension and clarify unfamiliar or confusing ideas (Palincsar & Brown, 1984; Raphael & Pearson, 1985). Students learn more effectively and retain more information if they continuously ask questions while reading (Rothstein & Santana, 2011). Explicitly teaching the strategy of asking questions of text lets students know that actively seeking answers while reading and asking new questions that emerge along the way is an effective comprehension tool (Fisher et al., 2012). A clarification is a special type of question that leads to a deeper understanding, especially for concepts that are new, unfamiliar, or difficult to understand.

When reading on the Web, it is especially important to ask questions and clarify misconceptions, not just about texts and tools but about the entire information space. Questions may range from simple ("Where is the 'About Us' link?") to complex ("Which sites are not being shown by this search engine?"). Clarification questions play a special role in helping the Web reader remain in a constant state of metacognitive awareness; for example, "How does this information connect with what I read earlier?" Because Web reading can be confusing to even the most experienced of readers, it's crucial for readers to be constantly seeking clarification of unfamiliar words, concepts, tools, and so on.

Inferring, Predicting, and Visualizing

When inferring, the reader acts like a detective, drawing conclusions from the text through a process of mentally combining her own knowledge with details found within the text. An inference must be based on text evidence (NGA & CCSSO, 2010), not just on what a reader thinks. A prediction is special kind of inference in which the reader draws from her prior knowledge to make an informed guess about what information will come next based on the details from the text so far. Good readers make predictions before, during, and after reading. Accurate predictions rely on a sensitive balance of prior knowledge of the topic, other experiences with similar types of text, and a sense of wonderment or curiosity (Pressley, 2002). The strategy of predicting involves three steps: making the prediction, gathering information from the text to confirm or disconfirm the prediction, and making a judgment about the accuracy of the prediction. Visualizing is another type of inference that allows readers to create a mental representation to fill in the gaps not fully explained in the text, based on evidence in the text and their own experiences. This internal strategy helps readers understand and remember what they read.

> 📖 **A reader's level of metacognitive awareness about which strategies are best suited to locate, critically evaluate, and synthesize diverse online texts is likely to foster a deeper understanding of the texts they encounter on the Internet.**
> —Coiro (2011b, p. 108)

Readers of Web texts also rely on inferring, predicting, and visualizing. However, not only do Web readers make predictions about what is to come in the text and within other multimedia elements, but they also make predictions about how to move through the text in order to find information. This has been termed *forward inferential reasoning* (Coiro & Dobler, 2007). For example, if a reader clicks on the hyperlink "olley," she is mentally making a prediction that the link will lead her toward learning more about this skateboarding trick. Making and confirming predictions is an essential goal of efficient Web reading. Randomly clicking on links without thoughtful predictions may be interesting when browsing, but this strategy is not only frustrating but also a waste of time when searching for information.

Determining Important Ideas

Strategic readers mentally reduce text into manageable chunks of key ideas by sifting out the important from the unimportant. They determine which important ideas on which to focus their attention during the reading process and which unimportant details deserve little or no attention (Afflerbach & Johnston, 1986). This process of

> 📖 **Given that accomplished readers regularly assess their knowledge, their strategies, and their progress toward goals, we need to specify the means for helping less able readers develop self-assessment mind-sets and strategies.**
> —Afflerbach (2002, p. 99)

determining important ideas differs according to a reader's purpose for reading but is especially crucial when reading informational text. Here, the reader must both decide and remember what is important if she is going to learn something from the text or find the answer to her question(s). Text features often provide clues to the reader about what is important through the use of subtitles, bold print, and captions.

Determining important ideas when reading Web text is similar to the process used for reading print text; however, Web readers face the dual task of deciding what is important (from the author's point of view) and what is relevant (from the reader's point of view). Web texts have the capacity to provide a wider variety of cues than printed texts regarding what is important. In addition to headings and captions, a reader might also draw information from icons, hyperlinks, and interactive graphics. Meanwhile, commercial intrusions are intentionally used to attract the reader's attention (Fabos, 2004). Experienced Web readers learn which visuals are merely distractors and which are likely to provide important and relevant information.

Synthesizing and Summarizing

Synthesizing and summarizing are considered to be the most challenging of the comprehension strategies (Dole, Duffy, Roehler, & Pearson, 1991; Harvey & Goudvis, 2007). Proficient readers learn to stop every so often to summarize what is being read and how this information supports the construction of meaning. Strong readers sort and summarize the most important ideas not only from within single texts but also between texts in order to synthesize ideas to help create an understanding of what is being read.

Synthesis of Web texts provides a chance for readers to formulate new ideas or understandings as information is gathered from one place or by summarizing ideas from several locations. As with printed text, this process is not easy, because a reader must determine what is most important and hold those ideas in her memory (if not on a notepad) as she navigates within and between websites (Guinee & Eagleton, 2006; Henry, 2006). Unlike novices, experienced Web readers *expect* to read in more than one place within a website or to read more than one website to locate the answer to a question (Coiro & Dobler, 2007). They understand that the "answer" will likely not jump out at them but rather will require making inferences while summarizing and bringing together ideas from separate locations. In Chapter 8, we delve more deeply into both summarizing and synthesizing, as they play key roles in making the information we locate on the Web manageable and useful.

Metacognitive Strategies

When cognitive strategies have been practiced to the point of automaticity, readers are able to reflect on their use of each strategy. This is known as *metacognition*, or thinking about one's own thinking. Two reading comprehension strategies, sometimes called "superstrategies," require a high level of metacognitive awareness right from the start: monitoring and evaluating.

Monitoring

Monitoring underpins each of the strategies we have discussed thus far. Strategic readers possess the metacognitive ability to monitor their process of making meaning by pausing and mentally checking to make sure they understand and remember what they are reading. When meaning breaks down, expert readers select an appropriate mental tool or strategy such as rereading, clarifying, or adjusting their reading rate to repair or "fix up" comprehension (Pressley, 2002). All of the reading strategies described thus far can serve as effective fix-up strategies for a skilled reader; in fact, a reader may use two or more of these strategies simultaneously. Shifting the pace of reading requires skillfully maneuvering between skimming, scanning, and slow, careful reading. Proficient readers use skimming by glancing over the text to determine the topic and type of text and decide whether these ideas match their purpose for reading. Scanning is used to quickly read a text, noting headings, bold words, dates, numbers, or other details that stand out for the reader. Careful reading requires moving through the text at a pace slow enough to notice, understand, and remember details (Beers & Probst, 2013).

> Screen reading, unlike book reading, may include video and sound; on the monitor images float past us, words move around, videos pop up, and music joins in; we scan and jump and scroll. Screen reading is likely to be faster and less contemplative than book reading.
> —Beers and Probst (2013, p. 14)

Web readers must also monitor and repair their comprehension throughout the reading process. "Online readers apply fix-up strategies to help them reread, refocus, adjust their speed or direction, or clarify their understanding before they move on" (Coiro, 2011b, p. 109). Online reading increases the need for monitoring because multiple "strategies come into play when Internet readers simultaneously conduct the tasks of managing information and comprehending text(s)" (Afflerbach & Cho, 2010, p. 213). In addition, proficient Web readers know that online information may be hidden below the screen or beneath several layers of links. Monitoring comprehension through these various layers is more complex than merely checking whether the text is making sense to the reader. The reader must also have a sense of where she is within the text(s) and have a fairly good idea of how to find the information she needs. A reader who wants to reread a text must know how to find it again, whether this is done through the use of the back button or the history list. During all of this forward and backward movement, readers may lose sight of their question(s) or forget information they already read unless they are actively monitoring their strategy use and progress toward their goals.

Evaluating

Evaluating relies on a complex weaving of the information gathered through the other comprehension strategies with a reader's metacognitive ability to determine what is important, what is useful, and what is truthful. Although printed materials have been vetted before reaching the library or classroom bookshelves, readers still bear the responsibility for evaluating whether the information is useful for answering their question or solving their problem. They must also determine whether the information is up to date and represents multiple sides of an issue. Critical evaluation is an important skill, whether students are reading books, thumbing through magazines, or watching TV. The cognitive strategy of determining important ideas is elevated to the level of a metacognitive strategy when readers are simultaneously tasked with deciding what is important while also evaluating what is useful and truthful. Readers must be aware of what they want to remember and what they plan to discard.

Online reading makes even greater demands on critical evaluation than does print reading. From the first moment, Web readers must spring into an evaluative stance as they begin with a search tool, decide what keywords to enter, and move to predicting which websites might be worthy of viewing. While wading through massive amounts of unfiltered content, readers must simultaneously identify reliable information that meets their needs and make sense of the information, whether it is presented as words, images, or video. This balancing act is not easy, and to do it quickly and with great frequency requires metacognitive awareness and higher level thinking. Evaluating websites for truthfulness and usefulness will be explored in greater depth in Chapter 7.

> Clicking through hyperlinks and scrolling through text can be much like turning the page, or they may be more akin to opening Pandora's Box.
> —Afflerbach and Cho (2010, p. 220)

Foundational Reading Skills

In addition to orchestrating cueing systems, alternating stances, and flexibly applying comprehension strategies, being a skilled reader involves proficiency with foundational skills. When foundational skills become automatic or unconscious, cognitive energy is available for comprehension. Skills that must be in place for readers to achieve automaticity include decoding, fluency, and vocabulary knowledge. Spelling is also important when reading on the Web if the activity involves using keywords to search for information. Although important for reading print text, automaticity is especially crucial for reading Web text, because the reader can encounter massive amounts of information and must make reading decisions quickly so as to effectively understand and use the information encountered. If a student is weak in one or more of these areas, she will need appropriate scaffolding in order to comprehend effectively.

Decoding

The ability to decode, or sound out, unfamiliar words is an important complementary, or foundational, skill for comprehension. Students must be able to read texts with a reasonable degree of accuracy before they can make much sense of them. If readers cannot recognize a substantial number of sight words and easily decode unfamiliar words, they will not be able to extract meaning from the text. Decoding is a gatekeeper skill for independent reading in print and on the Web because today's search results lists and Web texts still contain heavy amounts of print (Leu et al., 2011; Castek et al., 2011). In some cases, the cognitive load of decoding can be greatly aided by interactive graphics, multimedia, hyperlinks to definitions, virtual assistants, and text-to-speech tools (Dalton & Proctor, 2008), but these supports are not always available.

Fluency

Fluency is another foundational skill for effective reading comprehension. If readers are laboriously slogging through texts, either silently or orally, the cognitive load of remembering what was read will overcome their ability to make sense of the text. Clearly, fluency relies on decoding ability, but being able to decode accurately is insufficient. Readers must be able to decode quickly and with ease in order to be considered fluent (Pikulski & Chard, 2005; RAND Reading Study Group, 2004), and they must have adequate syntactic awareness to attend to punctuation cues. The key is automaticity—being able to effortlessly use the skills of phrasing, tone, and pacing to read in a way that enhances understanding.

Fluency on the Web is important to the comprehension process because readers often face large volumes of text and must make continual decisions about relevancy. Dysfluent Web readers can easily get discouraged if the effort to move smoothly through text is too high to sustain their interest and stamina.

Vocabulary Knowledge

Also essential to reading are vocabulary skills (Blachowicz & Fisher, 2003). Like those with decoding and fluency deficits, readers with weak vocabulary skills will most likely struggle with comprehension (Beck, McKeown, & Kucan, 2013; Overturf, Montgomery, & Smith, 2013). Perhaps you have known readers who can decode just about any word they encounter and can even read fluently but cannot truly understand what they read. Unless there is a significant language or learning disability, vocabulary is usually the culprit. Second-language learners often have difficulty in this area, as do any of us when reading in unfamiliar genres with unusual terminology, such as medical texts or legal contracts.

> If reading is about mind journeys, teaching reading is about outfitting the travelers, modeling how to use the map, demonstrating the key and the legend, supporting the travelers as they lose their way and taking circuitous routes, until, ultimately, it's the child and the map together and they are off on their own.
> —Keene and Zimmerman (1997, p. 28)

Vocabulary on the Web represents additional layers of complexity in the reading process. As with print text, a reader encountering search engines and Web text must have a good working knowledge of key vocabulary and concepts related to the topic at hand (Dwyer & Harrison, 2008). An additional challenge in the area of vocabulary development lies in the need for the reader to also be proficient with the vocabulary of the Web itself. An understanding of terms such as *search engine, back button, scroll, drop-down menu, hyperlink,* and *icon* supports the reader as she locates and understands information.

Another complexity arises when the reader is crafting the wording for an inquiry question and determining keywords (Guinee, Eagleton, & Hall, 2003). The selection of an accurate keyword or combination of keywords hinges on the reader's ability to identify vocabulary to match her topic and purpose. Overly broad keywords yield an overwhelming number of search results. Unduly narrow keyword combinations can yield few or no search results. Selecting just the right keyword or phrase allows search tools to provide adequate results so that the reader has choices about where to locate information without feeling overwhelmed. We return to the topic of keyword strategies in Chapter 6.

Spelling and Keyboarding

Being able to spell correctly and type accurately are not usually issues that arise when reading printed text; however, when students search for information online, spelling can rise to the foreground as a gatekeeper skill (Dwyer & Harrison, 2008). Even though most search tools have spellcheckers, if the spelling is too far off, the spellchecker will be useless. The issue of spelling may diminish as we shift toward searching for information in Web 3.0 environments, but for now, it merits attention as one of the challenges of reading on the Web.

Keyboarding is a foundational skill that is required by the CCSS (NGA & CCSSO, 2010). Smooth and accurate keyboarding facilitates clearly expressing your thoughts through searching, writing, and the creation of projects. Keyboarding and touchscreen typing may become obsolete as more and more people use speech recognition technologies, but for now, they are the means by which we communicate our thinking in the digital world.

Informational Text

Throughout history, as texts have changed, we have adapted our literacy goals from reading Bibles to reading textbooks and novels to reading websites. Throughout these modernizations of texts, we have adjusted our view of what it means to be literate. In each case, the way the text is structured, or organized, influences what a person needs to know to be able to read the text. Knowing how to identify a verse is important when reading a Bible, whereas identifying structures such as cause–effect or compare–contrast is important

 Social Studies Standard: **Cite specific textual evidence to support analysis of primary and secondary sources.**

when reading a textbook. Similarly, when reading a narrative, it is important to be able to identify common story elements such as characters, setting, and plot. In other words, our literacy instruction responds to the types of texts we are expected to read in order to be considered productive, successful members of society.

In the United States, the CCSS call for a 50:50 split between informational and narrative texts in the primary grades, gradually increasing to a 70:30 split in high school (NGA & CCSSO, 2010). This expectation, coupled with the fact that informational text is often more difficult to comprehend than is narrative text (Coiro, 2011b; Fisher et al., 2012), necessitates that educators teach strategies for comprehending informational texts.

Informational Text in Print

Skilled readers of informational text develop a mental organization system to help locate, sort, and store important ideas by relying on cues provided by text features (e.g., table of contents, index, glossary), organizational aids (e.g., headings, captions, bold print), graphic aids (diagrams, timelines, maps), and text structures (e.g., sequential, compare–contrast,

In general, research suggests that almost any approach to teaching the structure of informational text improves both comprehension and recall of key text information.
—Duke and Pearson (2002, p. 217)

problem–solution). Readers who can identify, understand, and use these types of cues and structures can recall more textual information than those who are not as knowledgeable and can more easily predict the types of information and potential challenges to be found within the text.

Explicit instruction in informational text structures prepares students to activate their prior knowledge about such structures while they're reading. Students can be taught to recognize signal words such as *first–last, although, same–different, however, if–then,* and *and so on,* which alert the reader to the type of text structure being used. Common informational text structures include the following:

- *Descriptive*—Describes the characteristics of persons, places, things, and events.
- *Sequential*—Arranges information and events in order, often chronologically.
- *Compare–contrast*—Organizes information about two or more topics according to their similarities and differences.
- *Cause–effect*—Provides reasons or explanations for events or concepts.
- *Problem–solution*—Poses a problem and its potential solution(s).

Information within a printed text is sometimes presented using several text structures. For example, a book or magazine article about owls may describe the habitats and behaviors of owls while also providing a sequential description of an owl's growth and a persuasive section about the need to protect owl habitats. Readers must possess high levels of metacognitive awareness and cognitive flexibility in order to maintain comprehension while shifting between various text structures for a variety of purposes.

Informational Text on the Web

As mentioned previously (see Figure 3.2 in this chapter), cues such as text features, organizational aids, and graphic aids are found in digital texts as well as printed texts. Unfortunately, websites are inconsistent in their use of these features. For example, some web pages display links across the top of the screen, whereas others display links on the sides or the bottom. Still others display links as images or icons without words.

 Science Standard: **Analyze relationships across given contexts to predict and explain events in new contexts.**

Each time a reader encounters a new website, she must reorient herself to the location of key elements, adding more complexity to the reading process. Now, more than ever, a reader must be skilled at adapting to changes in the structures and features within and between websites.

When reading informational text offline or online, readers tend to skip around rather than read in a linear fashion. Printed texts such as encyclopedias, textbooks, and magazines typically rely on tables of contents and page numbers to help readers locate information and maintain a sense of where they are in the text. In contrast, online texts use hyperlinks in the form of buttons, tabs, image links, maps, icons, scroll bars, and text links to help the reader navigate within and across websites. These varied navigational cues can serve to either orient or disorient learners in this complex, multidimensional space, depending on their experience and dispositions (Figure 3.5).

FIGURE 3.5. Web readers need to stay focused.

The Reciprocal Nature of Learning

Before we close this chapter on what it means to become Web literate, let's take a moment to consider the reciprocal nature of learning. We have known for a long time that readers benefit from writing and writers benefit from reading. The same holds true for Web literacies. In fact, online reading and writing have become so closely intertwined that it is nearly impossible to separate them (Leu et al., 2011). "We read online as authors and we write online as readers. Online communication involves the use of texting, blogs, wikis, video, shared writing spaces such as Google docs and social networks such as Nings" (Castek et al., 2011, p. 95). We are observing a similar fusion between offline and online practices. This is especially the case with adolescents, many of whom construct their personal identities in virtual and actual spaces, with a blurry distinction between these seemingly disparate worlds (Gardner & Davis, 2013; Turkle, 2011).

 Successful online readers are able to manage texts that often change from one day to the next with patience, persistence, and flexibility.
—**Coiro (2012, p. 645)**

Perhaps the most exciting aspect of the reciprocal nature of learning is the fact that online literacy practices benefit offline literacy practices, and vice versa. Although some weak readers of printed text struggle when reading search results lists and text-heavy online

Library Media Standard: **Use strategies to draw conclusions from information and apply knowledge to curricular areas, real-world situations, and further investigations.**

content (Macedo-Rouet et al., 2013), others who struggle with printed texts perform surprisingly well online. Multimedia supports such as text-to-speech tools, annotation tools, and scaffolds for summarizing, synthesizing, and reflection make it possible for struggling learners to access online content, solve real-world problems, and actively contribute to the classroom community (Dalton & Proctor, 2008). Web reading can even improve students' reading comprehension because many of the cognitive strategies involved in print-based reading (e.g., inferring, visualizing, synthesizing) are enhanced by opportunities for explicit practice with multimedia.

Some educators may be surprised to know that skilled print readers are not necessarily skilled Web readers (Coiro, 2014). The key is whether or not learners have a positive attitude and experience with navigating the Web. Prior knowledge of the architecture of the Web and how to skillfully navigate among its nodes is a stronger predictor of online reading success than is prior knowledge of a topic or print reading ability. "Skilled online readers are often actively engaged in reciprocal acts of reading, writing, and reflecting. This interactive response process typically involves summing up key ideas, making connections, looking deeper, asking questions, and contributing their own ideas in response to the posed challenge" (Coiro, 2011b, p. 109). In sum, Internet inquiry can improve students' online and offline reading skills while building their capacity to learn how to learn (Castek et al., 2011).

SUMMARY •

In this chapter we connected traditional and modern understandings of what it means to be literate, noting that *reading is a very complex cognitive and metacognitive process*. We applied cueing systems and transactional theories to reading on the Web. We also investigated the reading comprehension strategies used by expert readers of both print and Web text, noting that these strategies occur in tandem with each other as readers adapt their thinking to the text elements encountered and to their purposes for reading. Foundational skills were explored, along with the ways these skills are utilized by proficient readers of both print and Web-based texts, noting that digital texts can be more challenging because of their additional complexity. We highlighted the role of informational text in print and on the Web and the reciprocal nature of learning.

Chapter 4 introduces the QUEST model of Internet inquiry and helps educators to determine their own level of preparation, both technically and conceptually. Several formal and informal assessment tools are described and/or provided in order to gauge students' level of readiness. Many of these assessments can be used before, during, and after Internet inquiry so that you and your students are aware of the progress that is being made.

(4) Preparing for the QUEST

KEY IDEAS ●

- The QUEST model of Internet inquiry provides a process for developing Web literacy skills that includes **Q**uestioning, **U**nderstanding, **E**valuating, **S**ynthesizing, and **T**ransforming.

- Before launching a Web inquiry project, it is crucial to be technically prepared. Technical preparation involves networking and file storage, a plan for curating resources, hardware, software, and applications (apps).

- Conceptual preparation includes establishing and reinforcing fundamental knowledge of the Internet and the Web, URLs and domain names, library databases, search engines, and keywords.

- Formal assessments of Internet inquiry strategies are currently in development.

- Various assessment tools can be used to help teachers gauge the level of scaffolding their students will need in order to be successful with Web inquiry. Many of these assessments can be used as pre- and posttests as well as reflective teaching tools.

[Not teaching students to be savvy Internet users] leaves them to navigate the information superhighway without a map, a tank of gas, and a spare in the trunk.
—Kajder (2003, p. 49)

57

In this chapter we introduce the QUEST model of Internet inquiry, which includes Questioning, Understanding, Evaluating, Synthesizing, and Transforming. Chapters 5 through 9 in *Reading the Web* delve into each of these aspects of inquiry individually. The focus for this chapter is on ideas and materials that will help you determine how well prepared you and your students are for Internet inquiry. First, we cover technical preparation by suggesting minimal requirements for school networking and file storage options and by recommending essential hardware, software, and apps. Then we discuss conceptual preparation by providing some basic information and vocabulary related to the Internet and the Web, such as URLs and domain names, library databases, search engines, and keywords. Finally, we offer several types of assessment tools from which to choose so that you can determine your students' level of preparedness to engage in Internet inquiry and their level of progress after instruction in Web reading strategies.

The QUEST Model of Internet Inquiry

Because we believe that children learn best when they practice skills and strategies within the context of authentic learning activities rather than artificial ones, we have designed a model of Internet inquiry—QUEST—that engages and supports students as they tackle the complexities of reading on the Web (Figure 4.1). QUEST also serves as an ideal metaphor for the active *quest* for information that characterizes our daily lives, whether at home, in school, or in the workplace. Our QUEST model should not be confused with the term *WebQuest* (*webquest.sdsu.edu*), a lesson plan format for Web-based learning.

The QUEST model illustrates the cyclical nature of Internet inquiry. The QUEST model visually reminds students that Internet inquiry is a multistep *process*, not a one-time *event*, much like our leaders in writing instruction have shown (Calkins, 1994; Graves, 1983). We like to point out to students that the word *research* is composed of

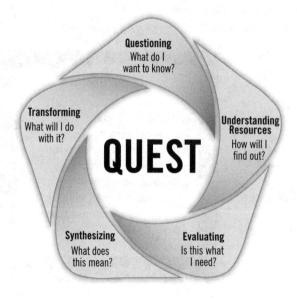

FIGURE 4.1. The QUEST model of Internet inquiry.

the prefix *re-* and the root word *search*, thus emphasizing the notion that the process is recursive. For example, readers may come across information that sparks more questions, thus initiating a new round of Questioning. Similarly, learners cycle through the Evaluating phase repeatedly as they encounter new information and must decide whether it meets their needs.

Note that there are several preparatory steps that must be taken before students actually start reading and Synthesizing information; this is analogous to the prereading and prewriting activities used by proficient readers and writers. These preparatory activities are important because they help activate prior knowledge and set the stage for strategic, reflective learning. In schools where resources are scarce, it is especially prudent to engage students in presearch activities before they actually sit down in front of the computer to begin searching for information (Rouet et al., 2011).

 Writing Standard: **Use technology, including the Internet, to produce and publish writing and to interact and collaborate with others.**

The QUEST model is based on our observations of hundreds of learners and is consistent with existing models of information literacy, most of which do not differ significantly in concept but use diverse terminology. Examples include: Big6 (Eisenberg & Berkowitz, 2001); Guided Inquiry (Kuhlthau et al., 2007); SEARCHing (Henry, 2006); Research Cycle (McKenzie, 1999); and Pathways to Knowledge (Pappas & Tepe, 2002). Having used several of these models in the classroom, we have found that a visual model with a memorable acronym is optimal for students and teachers.

The QUEST model was initially presented in the first edition of this text (Eagleton & Dobler, 2007). Since that time, many teachers have given us anecdotal examples of how useful the model is to their teaching of information literacy skills and in promoting effective Web reading. We love hearing stories of the ways QUEST guides classroom activities and promotes the type of higher level thinking we all value in our students.

The teacher's role during Internet inquiry is to scaffold the process until each learner is able to self-reflect and self-regulate. Scaffolding includes frequent metacognitive reminders, such as "What are you trying to find out?" "Which search engine is the best match for your question?" "Where do you think that link will take you?" "Does this web page have the information you're looking for?" or "How do

" " I think your graphic of the Internet inquiry process is outstanding. It's a graphic that all of us are using on the seventh grade team now. There are different ways of viewing the research process, but I think that the cyclical nature of this one is really great.
—Deborah, special education teacher

you know this information is reliable?" Scaffolding also involves frequent teacher modeling of both the process and, if applicable, a final product. We strongly suggest that teachers conduct authentic inquiry alongside their students so the learners can observe what an expert inquirer thinks and does.

As you read, please keep in mind that internalizing complex strategies and skills takes a long time, so you can't teach the entire QUEST model in one brief lesson. Internet inquiry strategies must be taught recursively throughout the K–12 curriculum (Leu, Kinzer, et al., 2013). Our approach has been to focus on one strategy at a time; for example, we have done 6-week Internet inquiry units focusing on keyword selection strategies and 4-week units emphasizing notemaking techniques. While focusing on one strategy or stage of the process, remember to provide scaffolds (models, templates, etc.) for the other strategies so that students are not overwhelmed with too many challenges at once. Please note that although we have provided numerous suggestions for each phase of the QUEST, reproducibles and lesson plans should be treated as a menu of possibilities rather than a prescription to use them all.

Internet inquiry is an effective way for students to develop and apply traditional literacy skills and Web literacy skills *while practicing generative metacognitive strategies that lead to more self-regulated learning.* The teachers with whom we've worked value Internet inquiry because it fulfills multiple instructional objectives across content areas and meets local, state, and national standards for learning. Throughout Chapters 5 through 9, this text presents the QUEST model, along with learning standards from language arts, library media, history and social studies, science and technical subjects, and math.

> " Inquiry accomplishes about 20 things I feel I need to do as a language arts teacher. It supports writing, nonfiction reading, putting texts into your own words, and documentation.
> —Tracey, eighth-grade language arts teacher

Technical Preparation

So you're thinking about trying out some Web inquiry with your students? That's great! Let's make sure you have all the technical requirements in place and that you and your students know how to use them. After reading the following three sections on networking and file storage, hardware, and software, you can use the Technical Preparation Checklist (Handout P-4.1) to ensure that you are technically prepared to launch a Web project. An acceptable use policy (AUP) is a must for communicating expectations to parents and students. If your school doesn't have one in place, you can find examples by searching for <school AUP>. The AUP is a signed agreement among students, parents, and school district personnel. Among other things, it may state that students will not visit inappropriate websites, use offensive language, plagiarize, or harm the system. In return, the district agrees to keep the network in working order and protect students by using software filters and disallowing personal information exchanges.

An ideal situation for Web inquiry is a school with a stable network, high-speed Internet, up-to-date devices for every student, and friendly technical support personnel on demand. If this dream vision is not descriptive of your school, you're not alone. We have worked with teachers who have cobbled together a collection of devices (a desktop computer or two, a few tablets, a couple of laptops) or are in districts in which students can bring their own devices (BYOD). We have found that students are generally forgiving of unreliable systems or the need to share devices. When difficulties arise, flexible teachers shift to collaborative work or whole-class instruction, perhaps using a projector. Remind your students to save their work often and always have a

> If we want classrooms brimming full of kids who are engaged, enthusiastic, and independent learners, they must have ownership in what they study and investigate.
> —Harvey and Goudvis (2007, p. 231)

backup lesson plan if technology issues arise. It's best to try everything out yourself in advance of teaching a lesson with technology, even if you are an experienced Internet user. Technology changes quickly, including websites and applications. Never assume that everything will work as it should.

Besides being flexible, teachers and students must see themselves as problem solvers. No single person can know all of the answers when it comes to technology—frankly, there is just too much to know! The goal is to work together to solve problems and to learn from each other. As the instructional leader in the classroom, you have the power to create a classroom that promotes this mindset through your own modeling of problem solving or troubleshooting techniques. When you encounter an aspect of technology that doesn't work, do you throw up your hands and put in a work order, complaining about how long it takes for someone else to come and fix things? Or do you resist this helpless stance and start working to find solutions? Two excellent problem-solving strategies are to ask for help from tech-savvy students and to search for online troubleshooting tutorials.

When troubleshooting hardware, check the power switch and the wireless or cable connections, as these are often the culprits and are fairly easy to fix. When troubleshooting software, try closing programs and starting them up again. With a frozen PC, try the "three-fingered-salute," which means pressing the <Ctrl+Alt+Delete> keys all at once to shut down programs and/or restart the machine. On a frozen Mac, you can shut down a program by pressing <Command+Option+Escape> and then restart the device by pressing the Power key or choosing Shut Down from the Special menu. If that doesn't work, press <Command+Option+Shift+Power> to restart the machine. If an app on a tablet is wonky (our favorite technical term!), try closing out of the app, shutting down and restarting the tablet, or deleting the app and reinstalling it.

> **"** My students see their tablet as a personal work station. Although the school owns the devices, the students treat their tablet like gold, because they know it's their connection to the world outside of the classroom.
>
> **—Angela, fourth-grade teacher**

Networking and File Storage

Your school probably has a local area network (LAN). This means that you can access the school network, the Internet, and peripherals such as printers and scanners from any device in your school. If this is the case, you and your students only need to know how to log on to the school network and how to save, move, and access files in their proper location. Many schools assign teachers and students unique user names and passwords, as well as personal storage space to save files and images. Some schools also dedicate open-access file folders where teachers can put assignments and handouts for students to download. If you are inexperienced with your school network, ask your district or school technology specialist to give you a quick tutorial. It's easier than you think.

If your school doesn't yet have a network, then each device must be able to connect to the Internet (via cable or wireless) with sufficient bandwidth to enable multimedia. The main disadvantage of using non-networked machines is that a student must use the same device every time, because that student's work will be stored on that particular device. This creates a hazardous file storage situation, because devices may fail or be unavailable at the time students are trying to retrieve their work. Alternately, students can keep their work on a memory stick (sometimes called a thumb drive or flash drive), which plugs into a USB port.

Student work can also be stored online. Google Drive, Dropbox, and other services provide free online storage with the option of purchasing additional storage if needed. Online storage sites may also enable users to work collaboratively on documents. The purpose of all forms of electronic document storage is to save one's work, but in today's world of anytime, anywhere learning, the goal is also to give students access to their work beyond the walls of the classroom.

Curation

In education, collecting and sorting content has traditionally fallen into the realm of the library media specialist, and this professional remains the curation expert in many schools. However, with the massive amount of content at our online fingertips, all users must become curators of their own information. This role is new for many students and teachers, so it's helpful to have a plan to avoid "infowhelm," or becoming overwhelmed amidst massive amounts of information (Crockett, Jukes, & Churches, 2011). When you come across a useful website, do you have a systematic, reliable way to find it again later? Digital curation focuses on the use of online tools to collect, organize, and share web resources about a topic.

Online curation tools give students access to their collection from any computer with Internet access. Some of our favorite online curation tools include Zotero (*zotero. org*), Pinterest (*pinterest.com*), Symbaloo (*symbaloo.com*), and Diigo (*diigo.com*). Others can be located by searching for <digital curation>. Once you choose a curation tool and create an account, you can begin adding favorite websites that can be annotated and tagged with key words for sorting and retrieval. Your collection can be made public and shared with others who have similar interests or kept private for your own use.

> Much like a museum curator is constantly improving the museum collections and putting them on display, a digital curator is using curation tools in order to strategically identify new content and organize it in a way that makes sense for personal use as well as the use of others.
>
> —Summey (2013, p. 146)

Device Requirements

While working on inquiry projects, you will need enough Web-enabled devices (computers, laptops, tablets, cell phones, etc.) for individual students or small groups. Blocks of 45–60 minutes are a good target for grades 3–5, and 60–90 minutes is preferred for grades 6–8. If this amount of time is not possible in your situation, don't let that stop you from initiating inquiry projects. Teachers are highly skilled at squeezing every minute out of the instructional day, so for a short time you may have to "borrow" time from other subjects or other teachers.

If your school is using laptop or tablet carts, make sure the devices are fully charged and that you have power boosters turned on. Convenient access to a reliable printer is ideal, but make sure your students don't abuse printing privileges or you will find yourself replacing ink cartridges and paper at an alarming rate. We don't allow students to print out web pages—only their own work may be printed for review or submission. If you have students with special needs in your classroom, be sure to inquire about any assistive technologies they may need, such as height-adjustable computer tables, touchscreens, or augmentative communication devices. It is helpful to have a document camera, projector, and/or digital whiteboard for modeling, instruction, and presentation of student work.

Microphones, scanners, webcams, and digital cameras are useful for Internet inquiry if you don't have devices with those functions built in. Note that digital cameras often capture pictures at a very high resolution, such as 600 or 1,200 dpi (dots per inch), so they'll look sharp in print. When the images are transferred to a device such as a computer, your students may need to reduce the file sizes of these pictures using image editing software (discussed next) so they don't appear too large on screen or take up too much space; 150 dpi is usually sufficient for printing, and 72 dpi is fine for online viewing.

> While media and technology formats continue to change, the comprehensive nature of information literacy prepares individuals to adapt to shifting information environments.
> —Mackey and Jacobson (2011, p. 70)

Software, Apps, and Web Tools

One type of tool that is absolutely essential for Internet inquiry is a Web browser such as Google Chrome (*google.com/intl/en_us/chrome/browser*), Firefox (*mozilla.org/en-US/firefox/new*), or Safari (*apple.com/safari*). If not already installed on your devices, these can be freely downloaded. If you have administrator privileges on your school devices, be sure to faithfully update your Web browser when prompted so that website features will function properly when searching for information. Also, note that some websites have browser preferences, so if a website is not playing media or responding to your actions, you may need to try a different browser.

Another essential utility for young children, struggling readers, and students with visual impairments is a text-to-speech (TTS) or screen reader application (app). These tools read digital texts aloud, providing access to content by alleviating the burden of decoding. Some offer accessibility features such as highlighting words as they are read aloud, whereas others only perform the function of reading. Some use synthetic speech and others use natural voices. Newer systems and browsers come with TTS, but if you need to obtain your own or if any of your students require more sophisticated accessibility features, you can search for <free TTS download>.

For multimedia design, many schools use the Microsoft suite of tools, including Microsoft Word and PowerPoint. Mac users can also utilize Keynote and Pages. These programs and apps are useful for creating written documents,

> " I have a terrible time reading. So you know, the Internet's not really the best place for me to go because it's like reading a giant book.
> —Kevin, middle school student

fliers, brochures, scrapbooks, and multimedia slide shows. A web-based alternative to PowerPoint is Prezi (*prezi.com*), which allows students to present information in an interactive 3D concept map. Prezi employs a zooming user interface (ZUI) that permits users to place multimedia and text on a virtual canvas and navigate between links and nodes by panning and zooming.

Free image editing software includes Windows Live Photo Gallery and iPhoto, a free application for Apple devices. Audacity (*audacity.sourceforge.net*) is a free audio editing program for Mac and PC, and GarageBand (*apple.com/mac/garageband*) can be used with Apple devices. Lots of tools are available for projects incorporating voice and/or images—too many to list—but a few of our favorites include Voice Thread (*voicethread.com*), Tellagami (*tellagami.com/*), PicCollage (*pic-collage.com*), and Glogster (*edu.glogster.com*). Microsoft MovieMaker and Apple's iMovie enable students to create dynamic multimedia projects.

If you would like to teach your students to make web pages so they can present their work to a broader audience, you can search for free Web design software using keywords <free website builder>. Several free website building and hosting sites are available so that students can create their own websites with little training or special software. Two of our favorites are Weebly (*weebly.com*) and WiX (*wix.com*). Web authoring tools have become as easy to use as word processors, and all have helpful online tutorials. Many teachers publish student work or links to projects on the school website so families can easily access them. If your web authoring tool requires you to publish, ask your technology specialist for details—typically, you'll need the FTP (file transfer protocol) address and domain name, the directory (a master file folder), a user name, and a password.

Conceptual Preparation

In addition to being technically prepared, make sure you and your students are conceptually prepared for online inquiry. Some of the fundamental teaching points that you will want to reinforce are listed below and are explained in more detail in Chapter 6.

The Internet and the Web

The Internet is a massive network that includes email, instant messaging, newsgroups, and the Web. It connects millions of devices together, forming a global network in which any device can communicate with any other device so long as they are both connected to the Internet. Devices are connected to the Internet through phone lines, cables, or wireless connections that transmit digital information. Information that travels over the Internet does so via a variety of languages known as protocols. Email uses SMTP, and the Web uses HTTP to connect web pages via hyperlinks. The Internet and the Web are not synonymous terms, but most people use them interchangeably.

> When students articulate the goal of an Internet inquiry, they are developing habits of mind by developing a thoughtful and inquiry-based stance.
> —Harrison, Dwyer, and Castek (2014, p. 99)

URLs and Domain Names

Every website needs a unique identifier so that your device will know where to find it on the web. It's like an email address or a postal address that enables people to send mail to you and only you. A URL (Uniform Resource Locator) is the address or location of a website or other Internet service; for example, *http://www.pbs.org*. When you visit a website, it is important to notice the host, or domain, of the website (e.g., pbs) so you have an idea where the information originated. Each website has a domain suffix that indicates the type of organization that published the information (e.g., .org). The domain suffix is the small group of letters that comes after the host name. For example:

.edu = educational (*arizona.edu*)
.org = nonprofit or not-for-profit (*pbs.org*)
.com = commercial or individual (*readinga-z.com*)
.net = alternate to .com (*www.starfall.net*)
.gov = government (*whitehouse.gov*)
.mil = military (*army.mil*)
.uk = country (*ico.org.uk*)

Online Library Databases

A library database lets users search for information in a closed system bounded by the access provided by the library. A school district may subscribe to a single database, such as Destiny, which gives online access to search the materials available within the district. A district may also give students and teachers access to

Library Media Standard:
Demonstrate mastery of technology tools for accessing information and pursuing inquiry.

other databases and resources, perhaps providing access to print and online materials through interlibrary loan arrangements. The process of searching a closed information system is similar to searching the Web, albeit with fewer search results and fewer concerns about quality since the materials have been preselected.

Customized Search Tools and Directories

Between the closed system of a database and the open access of the Internet lie custom search tools and directories. One way to create a custom search tool is by collecting websites using Google's customized search engine. When students conduct a search, their results will be limited to the preselected websites. Another way to post preselected sites is by creating a hyperlinked list in a word processing document or by building a website with a main page serving as a portal. A portal is a jumping-off point for finding websites listed by topic or in alphabetical order. The expertise of the portal creator helps to give credibility to the quality of the preselected links. KidsClick (*kidsclick.org*) is an annotated directory of websites for kids that is created and maintained by librarians. The directory can be searched by keyword, by category, by Dewey decimal number, or alphabetically.

Search Engines

Search engines such as Google, Bing, and Yahoo! are software programs that let us search the Web by browsing through categories or entering keywords. Search engines don't actually go out and search the Web when search queries are entered; rather, they have already located and indexed the sites before you search—that's why your search results come back so fast. Search engines are becoming increasingly flexible, allowing users to enter natural-language phrases and questions instead of keywords. Commercial search engines are money-making enterprises, so businesses pay to advertise their products and websites within the search results. We provide more information about Understanding search engines in Chapter 6 and about Evaluating websites in Chapter 7.

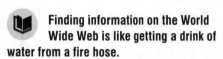

Finding information on the World Wide Web is like getting a drink of water from a fire hose.
—Grisham (2001, n.p.)

Keywords

One of the biggest secrets to searching the Internet is knowing which words to use in your search. These are called *keywords, key terms,* or *key phrases.* Keywords are useful for obtaining specific results. For example, if you want to find out about the history of skateboarding, it's more efficient to use the keywords <skateboard history> than the broad term <skateboard>. Using a combination of terms increases the likelihood that you will home in on the information you seek. Sometimes keywords consist of phrases rather than single words; for instance, you may need to search for <tree frogs> instead of <frogs>, or <Chicago jazz musicians> instead of <musicians>. Keyword strategies are discussed further in Chapter 6.

Assessing Internet Inquiry Strategies

Educators are beginning to take notice of the important role that Web literacies play in our students' success in school, out of school, and in their future lives in the workplace. Many people are asking "What do our students know?" "What can they do?" and "How well can they do it?" when it comes to finding, understanding, and using information. Authentic Internet inquiry gives teachers an opportunity to make observations and examine student work. Ongoing formative assessment of students' performance is used to plan programs, develop curricula, and determine individual student progress. When the emphasis is placed on assessing *for* learning, Internet inquiry assessments can promote quality instruction in an area that has traditionally received little attention. By assessing these skills, a clear message is given to educators, students, and caregivers: knowing how to be an efficient and effective Internet reader and writer is critical. Formative assessment tools are provided later in this chapter.

Science Standard: Observe patterns to guide organization and classification.

Formal Assessments

Several forces are driving the formal assessment of Web literacy skills, including economic competition, technology growth, and learning standards. National and state standards are increasingly focused on preparing students to find, understand, and use information from a variety of sources. Formal assessments for higher education include iSkills, created by Educational Testing Services (2014; *ets.org/iskills*), and the Standardized Assessment of Information Literacy Skills (SAILS) created by Kent State University (*projectsails.org*; Project SAILS, 2014).

For K–12 educators and students, the CCSS (NGA & CCSSO, 2010) emphasize the need for students to be college- and career-ready, including knowing how to gather information from multiple resources, both print and digital, and how to create information for the technology of today and tomorrow. However, no U.S. states currently assess students' ability to locate information on the Web, understand search results, or evaluate website information (Leu, Forzani, et al., 2013). A challenge faced by assessment developers is the need to design assessments that keep pace with the changing nature of the Internet. New and flexible types of pre- and postassessments are needed to capture the critical-thinking and problem-solving skills of the strategic online reader, as described below.

One assessment showing promise is the Online Research Comprehension Assessment (ORCA), a performance-based online reading assessment that determines how well students use the Internet to locate, critically evaluate, synthesize, and communicate information (see Coiro & Kennedy, 2011; see also Leu, Kulikowich, Sedransk, & Coiro, n.d.).

The Tool for Real-time Assessment of Information Literacy Skills (TRAILS) focuses on information literacy skills for both print and online research (Kent State University Libraries, 2014; *trails-9.org*). TRAILS is aligned with the CCSS (NGA & CCSSO, 2010) and the 21st Century Learner Standards (American Association of School Librarians [AASL], 2007). This multiple-choice assessment is designed for grades 3, 6, 9, and 12 but can be utilized by other grade levels. Teachers can receive class and individual student report summaries with benchmark data.

> Effective instruction cannot take place without effective assessment to inform that instruction, but this can only happen when assessment is used appropriately.
>
> —Leu et al. (2013, p. 231)

Informal Assessments

Before launching a Web inquiry project, you will want to have a sense of your students' spelling skills, decoding ability, reading comprehension strategies, reading fluency, vocabulary, and writing ability (see Chapter 3). You'll also want to have a sense of students' information literacy skills, their understanding of the research process, and their ability to stay organized and focused. If your students have weaknesses in any of these areas, they will need extra scaffolding in order to be successful with Web inquiry. It's especially important to observe your students' keyboarding (and/or touchscreen typing) skills because keyboarding is required by the CCSS (NGA & CCSSO, 2010). There are many inexpensive games and apps that students can use at school and/or at home to improve their keyboarding speed and accuracy.

We strongly recommend that you conduct some preassessments to determine what your students already know about the research process and the Web. Many students have gaps in their understanding about what the process of inquiry entails (offline or online), and most have misconceptions about search engines, keywords, and/or the Web. Next we offer several types of assessment tools from which to choose, depending on your class size and access to technology. Some of these assessments can then be used for group discussion and reflection, thus serving as highly effective teaching tools. Note that we would not expect a teacher to use *all* of the assessments we provide with all students. Think of them as a menu of possibilities, from which you can select the assessments that best meet the needs of your students and your instruction.

The first two assessments are individually administered, so they require more time than the subsequent whole-class measures. If possible, it is optimal to use one or the other of the individual assessments in conjunction with some of the whole-class instruments. With any of the whole-group assessments, allow young learners and older students with writing difficulties to dictate their responses so that you can get a more accurate measure of their Web experience and knowledge. Similarly, you may want to read aloud the questions, ensuring that your weaker readers are not stymied by decoding.

> Just because our students are able to cruise through the Internet with speed and what looks like skill doesn't mean they know what they are doing.
> —Kajder (2003, p. 49)

Web Search Strategies

The most accurate assessment tool is the 10-minute Online Web Strategies Assessment—Individual (Handout P-4.2), in which the teacher sits right next to each individual student and asks him or her to *show* how he or she typically goes about finding information on the Web. You can record the session for later analysis and/or take notes using the Online Web Strategies Scoring Guide—Individual (Handout P-4.3) while you watch each student carry out the task. In addition to noting each student's keyboarding or touchscreen typing skills, you will want to observe and record students' strategies for (1) turning on the device; (2) logging on to the school network; (3) launching browser software (such as Mozilla Firefox or Safari); (4) going to a search engine (such as Google or Bing); (5) entering keywords (such as <lory care>); (6) choosing a website; (7) scanning for information (such as dietary or housing needs for a lory); and (8) finding relevant information. If no relevant information is found on the first site, observe and record students' recovery strategies for (1) choosing a new website; (2) choosing a new search engine; or (3) choosing new keywords.

Once each student feels that she or he has found relevant information, ask how the student knows whether it is "good" information, what he or she would do with this information, and what he or she would do next if this were a real research project. Stop after 10 minutes, regardless of whether the student has been successful. This tool can be used as a posttest as well.

1. go to a search site.
2. type in what you are looking for.
3. press search.
4. and read the answer.

FIGURE 4.2. Web Strategies Assessment—weak.

If you have too many students or lack easy access to a Web-enabled device, you can glean some of the same information by doing the 5-minute Oral Web Strategies Assessment—Individual (Handout P-4.4). With this tool, you ask a student to *tell* you how her or she would go about finding specific information on the Web, while you record his or her responses on a notepad and/or tape recorder.

If you cannot afford the time it takes to administer individual assessments, the most time-saving tool to measure your students' Web strategies is the group-administered Written Web Strategies Assessment—Group (Handout P-4.5). You can score responses to the both the oral and written tools using the Web Strategies Scoring Guide—Oral or Written (Handout P-4.6). For the written assessment, we recommend that you have students trade papers for scoring. This serves as an excellent teaching and group discussion tool. Figures 4.2 and 4.3 show two contrasting Web Strategies Assessments written by eighth graders.

Technology Experience

Another quick assessment is the Technology (Tech) Survey (Handout P-4.7), which helps you gauge which students are likely to be proficient and which are likely to struggle. It is also a great way to find out who your "tech-savvy" students are so that they

1. Double Click Browser
2. Put in search engine web site in the adress and hit go
3. Type in search order make sure correct spelling
4. Search the hits of web sites and pick a good one
5. Browes the site and try to pick up info. (print)
6. if the web site is not good try to rephrase search
7. repeat step 4-6 until everything is done
8.
9.

FIGURE 4.3. Web Strategies Assessment—strong.

can be recruited to serve as in-house technical support for you and the rest of your class(es).

A very interesting assessment tool we like to use is the Internet Drawing (Handout P-4.8), which simply asks students to draw a picture of the Internet and use captions, if desired. This is a quick method for evaluating the degree of sophistication of students' mental models of the Internet as a place to find information. For example, do they accu-

Library Media Standard: **Use technology and other information tools to analyze and organize information.**

rately depict it as a global network of networked devices (Figure 4.4), or do they draw a picture of the Google search engine (Figure 4.5)? Do they have only a vague mental image of the Internet (Figure 4.6), or do they have misconceptions

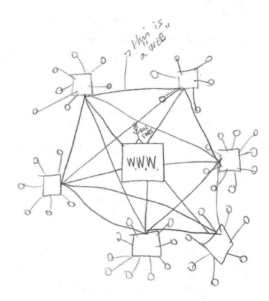

FIGURE 4.4. The Internet as a global network.

FIGURE 4.5. The Internet as Google.

FIGURE 4.6. A vague image of the Internet.

about the Internet, such as thinking that there are robots behind the walls finding web pages (Figure 4.7)? Because the Web is the most frequently used resource for student research, let's make sure our kids really understand what it is—and isn't. We usually describe the Internet as a huge network of networks (devices that are all hooked together so they can share data) and the Web as a bunch of interconnected websites containing information (some of it valuable and some of it not), rather like a large, disorganized virtual library. Search engines are tools for finding the information you want in this immense network of websites.

Finally, we offer a tool for assessing students' Internet Vocabulary (Handout P-4.9), which you can measure with the Internet Vocabulary Scoring Guide (Handout P-4.10). This quick assessment will not only inform you of your students' fluency with technology terms and help identify your tech-savvy students but will also serve as a guide for you as you're teaching with the Internet. The vocabulary words on this tool are the terms with which your students should be conversant in order to be considered Web literate.

Once you have administered some of the preceding assessments, show students the QUEST Inquiry Model (Handout P-4.11) and have a discussion about what each phase of Internet inquiry involves. It's always advisable to begin with scavenger hunts and mini-inquiries before diving into major inquiry projects.

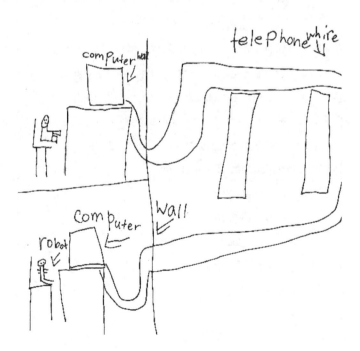

FIGURE 4.7. A misconception of the Internet.

SUMMARY •

Just as you must gather equipment and knowledge for a hike in the woods, you need to be technically and conceptually prepared for Internet inquiry. Technical preparation includes making sure you have appropriate networking and file storage, hardware, and software. Conceptual preparation includes knowing some basics about the Internet, URLs and domain names, search engines, and keywords. You also need to determine your students' level of readiness for a QUEST so that you know what needs to be taught and scaffolded; therefore, we provide several assessment tools from which to choose. Many of these assessments can be used before, during, and after a QUEST so that you and your students are aware of the progress that is being made.

In Chapter 5, on Questioning, we offer research-based suggestions for helping young inquirers figure out what they want to know and develop a plan for finding the information they seek. This first step in the QUEST Internet inquiry cycle often includes research themes, topics, focus areas, and questions while considering the audience, purpose, and final formats for demonstrating what has been learned.

Handouts

The following chart lists the handouts discussed in this chapter on preparing for the QUEST. Individual assessments provide the most data, but they can be time-consuming to administer, so we also offer group assessments to help identify tech-savvy students and compare pre- and posttest data. Choose or adapt the tool or tools that best serve your needs.

Number	Name of handout	Purpose
P-4.1	Technical Preparation Checklist	Ensure you are prepared
P-4.2	Online Web Strategies Assessment—Individual	Assess Web strategies
P-4.3	Online Web Strategies Scoring—Individual	Score Web strategies
P-4.4	Oral Web Strategies Assessment—Individual	Assess Web strategies
P-4.5	Written Web Strategies Assessment—Group	Assess Web strategies
P-4.6	Web Strategies Scoring—Oral or Written	Score Web strategies
P-4.7	Technology (Tech) Survey	Assess technology experience
P-4.8	Internet Drawing	Assess Internet knowledge
P-4.9	Internet Vocabulary	Assess technical vocabulary
P-4.10	Internet Vocabulary Scoring	Score technical vocabulary
P-4.11	QUEST Inquiry Model	Model of the process

HANDOUT P-4.1. Technical Preparation Checklist

NETWORKING and FILE STORAGE

☐ Internet access (circle all that apply)   classroom   cart   library   lab   BYOD

☐ User names and passwords for all students

☐ Signed AUPs from all families/students

☐ File storage: online/cloud   school   network   flash drive(s)   other: _____

HARDWARE

☐ Web-enabled devices: computers _____   laptops _____   tablets _____   other: _____

☐ Ratio of devices to students _____

☐ Time on computers: 30 min   45 min   60 min   90 min   other: _____

☐ Headsets or individual student earbuds: How many? _____

☐ Printer: Closest location _____   Backup printer location _____

☐ Projector, screen, and speakers for modeling and demonstration _____

☐ Assistive technologies (if needed for specific students) _____

☐ Document camera (optional)

☐ Microphone, webcam (optional)

☐ Scanner, digital camera (optional)

SOFTWARE

☐ Web browser: Google Chrome   Safari   Firefox   Other: _____

☐ Text-to-speech tool or screen reader app

☐ Speech-to-text tool or voice recognition app (optional)

☐ Multimedia editor: Word   PowerPoint   Keynote   Pages   Other: _____

☐ Image editor: Windows Live Photo Gallery   iPhoto   Other: _____

Name(s) and contact info for tech support _____

_____

_____

_____

Names of tech-savvy students _____

_____

_____

_____

HANDOUT P-4.2. Online Web Strategies Assessment—Individual

Name _____ Class _____ Date _____

☐ Pretest   ☐ Posttest

1. Explain to student that you want to see how people find information on the Web. Say that this activity will take **10 minutes**.

2. Say to student: **"Let's say you were doing Internet research on the lory, which is a type of parrot people keep as pets. Show me how you would find information about how to feed and take care of a lory. Please talk through every step as you go so I can understand what you're thinking."** [Spell "lory" for student.]

3. Record or write down everything the student does. If students forget to talk out loud, prompt them frequently; for example, "What are you doing now?" "Why did you choose that link?" "What is going through your head right now?"

4. End the test at 10 minutes. Ask what the student would do next if there were more time.

Search Engine Prompt:

If necessary, prompt, "What else could you try?" If that doesn't work, say, "Have you ever used Google or Bing?" If the student doesn't know how to get to a search engine, provide the URL (*google.com*; *bing.com*). Stop the test if the student has no other ideas about search engines.

Keywords Prompt:

If student has tried only the "main topic" approach (typing "lory" by itself into a search engine), prompt, "What else could you try?" If that doesn't work: "Are there any other words you could use that would help you find the information you need?" Stop the test if the student has no other keyword ideas.

POSTTEST PROMPT: Instead of the lory, use the anole (UH-NO-LEE), which is a type of lizard people keep as pets.

HANDOUT P-4.3. Online Web Strategies Scoring—Individual

Name _____ Class _____ Date _____

☐ Pretest   ☐ Posttest

	1	2	3	Score	Comments
Keyboarding or Touchscreen Typing	Hunt and peck	Slow, looking at letters	Fast, not looking at letters		
Logging On	Novice	Intermediate	Expert		
Managing the System	Novice	Intermediate	Expert		
Launching Web Browser	Novice	Intermediate	Expert		
Using Databases	Novice	Intermediate	Expert		
Using Search Engines	Novice	Intermediate	Expert		
Selecting Keywords	No idea what to do	Too big or too small	Just right		
Spelling Ability	Weak	Average	Strong		
Reading—Decoding	Weak	Average	Strong		
Reading—Comprehension	Weak	Average	Strong		
Choosing a Website from Search Results	No idea what to do	Random, numerical choices	Judicious choices		
Identifying Relevant Info	Novice	Intermediate	Expert		
Evaluating Info	Novice	Intermediate	Expert		
Navigating Websites	Novice	Intermediate	Expert		
Overall Speed	Slow	Medium	Fast		
Overall Effectiveness	Novice	Intermediate	Expert		
			TOTAL SCORE		

HANDOUT P-4.4. Oral Web Strategies Assessment—Individual

Name _____ Class _____ Date _____

☐ Pretest ☐ Posttest

1. Explain to student that you want to know how he or she usually finds information on the Web. Say that this activity will take **5 minutes**.

2. Say to student: **"Let's say you were doing Internet research on the history of soccer. Tell me exactly how you would gather information on the Web, explaining every step so I can picture what you would actually do. Start by imagining yourself preparing to get online."**

3. Record or write down everything the student says. Prompt if needed: "What would you do next?"

4. End the test at 5 minutes. Ask what the student would do next if there were more time.

Search Engine Prompt:

If the student doesn't mention using a search engine, prompt, "Have you ever used a search engine such as Google or Bing?" (If so) "Explain how you would use it to find information on the history of soccer."

Keywords Prompt:

If student has mentioned only the "soccer.com" or "main topic" approach (putting "soccer" by itself into a search engine), prompt, "What other keywords would you try?" If that doesn't work, "Are there any other words you could use that would help you find the information you need?"

Notemaking Prompt:

If student doesn't mention making notes, prompt, "What would you do with the info once you find it?"

POSTTEST PROMPT: Instead of the history of soccer, prompt for the history of baseball or any other popular sport in your region.

HANDOUT P-4.5. Written Web Strategies Assessment—Group

Name _____ Class _____ Date _____

□ Pretest   □ Posttest

List every step a person needs to do when searching for information on the Web. Please use the back of this paper if you have more than 10 steps.

1. _____

2. _____

3. _____

4. _____

5. _____

6. _____

7. _____

8. _____

9. _____

10. _____

HANDOUT P-4.6. Web Strategies Scoring—Oral or Written

Name _____ Class _____ Date _____

☐ Pretest   ☐ Posttest

	If student says or writes:	Points	Wording/Comments
Get Ready	Find a computer/turn on computer	0	
	Get online/open browser	1	
	Sign on/log on/username/password	1	
Have a Plan	Think about your topic/have a focus	3	
	Have a research question in mind	4	
Find a Site	Type in URL field/go to a website	1	
	Click on search icon	2	
	Go to a search engine	4	
Search	Look for/click on/type in search box	1	
	Check your spelling	2	
	Click enter/go/search	1	
Use Keywords	Type in main topic	1	
	Ask the computer a question	1	
	Search for specific keywords	4	
	Narrow search/reduce keywords	3	
	Use advanced search features	4	
Search Results	Look at the search results	1	
	Pick any site	1	
	Look at/read site descriptions	2	
	Pick a promising site	2	
Plan "B"	Get help	1	
	Try a new website/do the cycle over	2	
	Try a new search engine	3	
	Rephrase keywords	4	
Find Info	Get info/find info on page	1	
	Find the information you need	3	
	Read through/skim site	2	
	Evaluate site for usefulness/quality	4	
Gather Info	Print/save	1	
	Copy/paste	1	
	Bookmark for future use	2	
	Make notes in your own words	4	
All Done	Sign off/log off/close window	1	
	Review information	2	
TOTAL POINTS OUT OF 75			

HANDOUT P-4.7. Technology (Tech) Survey

Name _____ Class _____ Date _____

☐ Pretest   ☐ Posttest

		1	2	3	4	Number
1.	Do you like using technology (tech)?	I hate it.	It's OK.	I like it.	I love it.	
2.	Do you have tech at home (computer, laptop, tablet, smartphone, etc.)?	No.	Yes, but I don't use tech very much.	Yes, I use tech pretty often.	I have my own device.	
3.	Do you get online at home?	No.	Yes, but I rarely get online.	I get online a few times per week.	I get online nearly every day.	
4.	Are you good at using tech?	No.	I'm OK.	I'm pretty good.	I'm really good.	
5.	Do you use tech to find info online?	No.	Sometimes.	Pretty often.	Really often.	
6.	Are you good at finding online info?	No.	I'm OK.	I'm pretty good.	I'm really good.	
7.	Are you fast when finding online info?	No.	I'm OK.	I'm pretty good.	I'm really good.	
8.	Are you fast when texting or sending email?	No.	I'm OK.	I'm pretty good.	I'm really good.	
9.	Are you good at posting things you create?	No.	I'm OK.	I'm pretty good.	I'm really good.	
10.	Are you good at fixing tech problems?	No.	I'm OK.	I'm pretty good.	I'm really good.	
					TOTAL OUT OF 40	

Please list your favorite online tech activities (for example: Pinterest, Instagram, Snapchat): _____

_____

_____

_____

_____

HANDOUT P-4.8. Internet Drawing

Name _____ Class _____ Date _____

☐ Pretest   ☐ Posttest

Directions: Draw a picture to show what the Internet looks like.

HANDOUT P-4.9. Internet Vocabulary

Name _____ Class _____ Date _____

☐ Pretest   ☐ Posttest

Score:
/ 10
%

Directions: Put a letter in front of each vocabulary word to match its definition.

VOCABULARY	DEFINITION
Bookmark/Favorites	a. A worldwide network of networks
Boolean operator	b. A method of remembering a good website
Domain extension	c. A way to find specific info using a search tool
Host	d. Words or icons that connect to other webpages
Internet	e. A group of connected web pages
Keyword	f. The type of website (.com, .edu, .org)
Link or hyperlink	g. Tool used to find information on the Web
Search engine	h. A punctuation mark used to filter searches
URL	i. The organization that posted the website
Website	j. The address of a website

HANDOUT P-4.10. Internet Vocabulary Scoring

Give 1 point for each correct answer for a total of 10 possible points.

	VOCABULARY	DEFINITION
b	Bookmark/Favorites	a. A worldwide network of networks
h	Boolean operator	b. A method of remembering a good website
f	Domain extension	c. A way to find specific info using a search tool
i	Host	d. Words or icons that connect to other webpages
a	Internet	e. A group of connected web pages
c	Keyword	f. The type of website (.com, .edu, .org)
d	Link or hyperlink	g. Tool used to find information on the Web
g	Search engine	h. A punctuation mark used to filter searches
j	URL	i. The organization that posted the website
e	Website	j. The address of a website

Questioning
What do I
want to know?

**Understanding
Resources**
How will I
find out?

Transforming
What will I do
with it?

QUEST

Synthesizing
What does
this mean?

Evaluating
Is this what
I need?

(5) Questioning

Questioning
What do I
want to know?

Transforming
What will I do
with it?

Understanding
Resources
How will I
find out?

QUEST

Synthesizing
What does
this mean?

Evaluating
Is this what
I need?

KEY IDEAS ●

- Children and young adolescents often initiate research without explicit research questions or a plan of action.

- Key questions that guide the Q phase of the inquiry process are "What do I want to know?" and "What is my plan for finding out?"

- We ask questions before, during, and after reading and inquiry.

- Student choice is crucial for successful inquiry.

- Research questions must be of an appropriate scope and must be researchable.

- The Q phase includes theme selection, topic selection, focus areas, research questions, audience, purpose, final format, and project planning.

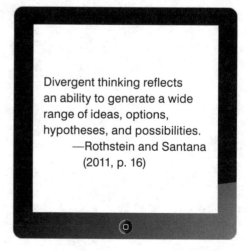

Divergent thinking reflects an ability to generate a wide range of ideas, options, hypotheses, and possibilities.
—Rothstein and Santana (2011, p. 16)

This chapter covers the first phase of Internet inquiry, the Questioning phase. Using an easy-to-follow Why, When, What, and How format, we present background information, teaching ideas, and numerous tools for teaching an instructional unit focused on Questioning. Questioning strategies are useful across disciplines and in life, so the time you spend guiding your students through this process will be time well spent.

Why Is Questioning Important?

Humans are natural questioners. Anyone who has been around a 4-year-old for more than 5 minutes can attest to the innate human need to know (Figure 5.1). Unfortunately, this passion for asking questions seems to diminish as students reach the upper grades, most likely because schools have traditionally prioritized answers over questions. In Chapter 3 we discussed the cognitive strategy of asking questions when reading to activate prior knowledge, check comprehension, clarify unclear ideas, and focus attention on the task. In this chapter we expand our definition of questioning to include its role as the first step in the inquiry process and a key element of information literacy.

Cultivating a sense of wonder is crucial for humans in order to advance our understanding of the world. We might still be traveling by land and water if the Wright brothers and others hadn't wondered what it would be like to fly. Curiosity leads to questions and questions lead to learning. Asking questions is a spiraling process in which each new understanding generates additional questions. This spiral is more easily built when students begin to "think in questions" (Rothstein & Santana, 2011). The key is for learners to ask their own questions, because these are the questions that matter and that will motivate the search for answers. Some would argue that "the most essential skill of the 21st century is knowing how to ask the most interesting questions" (November, 2012, p. 5). Learning how to ask questions also leads to improved learning outcomes, greater student engagement, and more ownership of the learning process (Rothstein & Santana, 2011).

FIGURE 5.1. Young children are natural inquirers.

Key questions that guide the Q phase of the inquiry process are "What do I want to know?" and "What is my plan for finding out?" Numerous researchers have found that children and young adolescents initiate research without clear goals or explicit research questions, which obscures their sense of purpose and their ability to target and recognize the information they seek (e.g., Colwell et al., 2013; Dwyer & Harrison, 2008). Keeping a strong focus on a guiding question while reading on the Web is crucial because of the incredible volume of information that can distract a reader from her original intent (Beers & Probst, 2013; DeStefano & LeFevre, 2007; Figure 5.2). Cognitive surplus refers to the idea that with the Internet we have access to more information than one could ever use (Shirky, 2010); therefore, guiding questions are essential for managing information and avoiding overload.

Just as we must thoughtfully plan and prepare for a hike in the woods or a trip to the beach, learners need to have a plan of action before beginning their QUEST for information on the Web, or they will waste valuable time aimlessly surfing. The goal-setting process is critical for learning and reading, and it is essential for effective (accurate) and efficient (fast) Web searching (Henry, 2006; Kajder, 2003). In addition

---

Unit 4 Inquiry Questions (PowerPoint)

TEAM 1: How did the things that make up our planet form?

- Conjecture: "We think people built some things, and some things grew."

TEAM 2: How are dinosaurs alike and different to animals we have today?

- Conjecture: "We think they all drink water, they all eat food, and they all have teeth."

TEAM 3: How was the Earth formed?

- Conjecture: "We think people were made by God and Earth by a meteor."

TEAM 4: How are volcanoes on land the same or different than volcanoes underwater, or in outer space?

- Conjecture: "We think it's hotter on land."

TEAM 5: What was the life of a young dinosaur like?

- Conjecture: "We think young dinosaurs were small and were hatched from eggs very slowly."

TEAM 6: How does a volcano erupt?

- Conjecture: "We think it comes out of the ground and out of the volcano."

FIGURE 5.2. Guiding questions from a third-grade inquiry unit.

to asking questions, planning for inquiry includes defining research topics and focus areas, identifying audience and purpose, and (when appropriate) deciding on a final format (e.g., report, poster, website) to demonstrate what has been learned (Guinee & Eagleton, 2006; Kuhlthau, Maniotes, & Caspari, 2007).

When Do We Ask Questions?

We ask questions all the time in our daily lives, so it seems natural that skilled question asking would spill over into the classroom, but this isn't always the case. Students have extensive experience with *answering* questions, especially simple questions with literal answers, but not as much in-school experience with asking questions that require deep thinking and critical analysis. In fact, many students see it as the teacher's role to ask the questions, and these questions likely reflect the curriculum. So in a sense our students are operating in two spaces: their experiences from life outside of school and the curriculum content of the classroom. Developing effective questions for Internet inquiry relies on building a bridge between these two spaces, or the creation of a "third space" in which a teacher provides opportunities for students to "use their cultural knowledge and experiences from everyday life to help them understand the curriculum content" (Kuhlthau et al., 2007, p. 31). This third space represents an overlap of real life and school, in which learners use their own knowledge in tandem with what they learn in school to create new ways to develop questions that guide their learning.

We ask questions before, during, and after reading and inquiry. Questions that come before inquiry are used to guide the process, but learners must also ask numerous decision-making questions during and after online reading, such as "Where do I want to go next?" "Is this the information I need?" "Do I have enough information?" and "What am I going to do with this information?" As students become more engrossed in an inquiry topic, they naturally generate more questions based on new information. This is an excellent outcome; however, students and teachers need to find a balance between adherence to an original question or set of questions and capricious topic-hopping based on haphazard findings, reactive decision making, or fears that the original question will require too much work.

> Rather than asking for simple responses, inquiry addresses deeper issues. Taken literally, inquiry means not just questioning, but questioning into something. This type of questioning is rich because of the depth of exploration it encourages, and because each good question typically leads to more questions.
> —Thornburg (2004, p. 2)

What Characterizes "Good" Questions?

Good questions for Internet inquiry are open-ended and promote deep, divergent thinking. They:

- Do not always have one right answer.
- May have many answers.
- Cause us to ponder and wonder.

- Dispel or clarify confusion.
- Challenge us to rethink our opinions.
- Lead us to seek out further information.
- Are subject to discussion, debate, and conversation.
- May require further research (Harvey & Goudvis, 2007).

Research questions are characterized as thin versus thick, skinny versus fat, surface versus deep, or closed- versus open-ended. Each of these constructs shares a commonality: A research question is off target if it is either too small or too large in scope. This has been dubbed the "Goldilocks principle" (Harrison et al., 2014). Questions that are too small can be answered in a few words or sentences after minimal research; for example, "Which country hosted the 1988 World Exposition?" In contrast, questions that are too large cannot be answered in one inquiry project (if at all), such as, "Why is there war?"

In addition to having an appropriate scope, an inquiry question must be "researchable." By this we mean that the answer to the question can be found using available resources. One third grader explained it in this way: "Make sure you can get information on what you are searching." Examples of questions that are difficult to research include evaluative questions that rely solely on opinion, vague questions that have no real answers, and personal questions that can't be answered using public resources such as interviews, primary documents, print materials, or the Web.

Another type of question to avoid is one about which the student has either too much or too little prior knowledge. We have seen students select topics about which they already know everything there is to know, particularly popular culture topics such as sports and celebrities. In this case, there are no authentic questions to be asked, because the student already knows all the answers. In contrast, when a student has such a low level of prior knowledge about a topic that she can't even generate a reasonable question (one of our personal favorites is "Where did Harriet Tubman get her education?"), then it is advisable to allow her to explore the topic a little bit before committing to it and formulating definitive research questions.

Learners who ask their own questions are more motivated to seek answers because their questions stem, at least partially, from their personal fund of knowledge. Our family, friends, community, and culture play a role in development of knowledge (Moje et al., 2004), and when our questions can connect to these areas, we pursue the things that matter to us. As one third grader put it, "You should choose something you want to learn more about because it's never fun doing something you don't enjoy learning about." We agree. Developing the skills needed to ask effective questions hinges on giving students opportunities to ask their own questions throughout the inquiry process. Four essential rules for brainstorming questions include:

> **TEACHER: How do you choose a good question for inquiry?**
>
> **STUDENT: You just brainstorm through what you want to learn about.**

1. Ask as many questions as you can.
2. Do not stop to discuss, judge, or answer the questions.

3. Write down every question exactly as it is stated.

4. Change statements into questions (Rothstein & Santana, 2011, p. 19).

Many students need guidance in asking appropriately scoped research questions based on their age, ability, and the constraints of the task. Educators play an important role in leading students through the process of question generation, possibly by providing question prompts or helping rephrase underdeveloped questions. This support is important because "the construction and phrasing of a question shapes the kind of information you can expect to receive" (Rothstein & Santana, 2011, p. 57). Sometimes young children and older students with learning difficulties need support in choosing questions within broad themes and carrying these through the inquiry process. Beth visited a third-grade class in which the teacher introduced students to an inquiry unit theme based on the reading curriculum and assisted students with generating their own inquiry questions. Early in the school year, the teacher and the students worked through the inquiry process together, but as time went on, students worked more independently, although the teacher still reserved the right to approve each inquiry group's question. Throughout the year, he taught students that the question served as a guidepost or reminder of their purpose. Each group's question was kept in a prominent place during the inquiry block, and when the teacher conferenced with individual groups, he always asked group members to reiterate their inquiry question. If their project seemed to veer off course, he reminded students of their question as a way to steer them back to center.

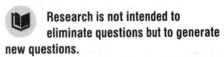

Research is not intended to eliminate questions but to generate new questions.
—Short and Burke (1991, p. 59)

In sum, a good inquiry question is one for which:

- We do not already know the answer.
- The answers are defensible.
- The door is opened for in-depth research and projects.
- Anything from a class project to a doctoral thesis can be created.
- The focus is on causes (understanding), not surface knowledge.
- Other questions emerge (Thornburg, 2004).

How Do We Teach Questioning Strategies?

If you haven't administered any of the preassessments presented in Chapter 4, we recommend that you do so first. Before engaging in large-scale inquiry projects, you may want to assign "mini-inquiries," which are short investigations focused on a single strategy that can be concluded within one or two class periods. We also strongly suggest that you conduct your own inquiry project alongside your students so that you can frequently model the process. Using teacher think-alouds is a powerful method for helping make explicit the in-the-head processes used by expert inquirers.

Assessing Questioning Strategies

Before beginning an inquiry unit focused on Questioning strategies, we recommend that you assess your students' understanding of what makes a "good" research question for an inquiry project by using or adapting the Research Questions Assessment (Handout Q-5.1). One option is to have students trade papers for scoring while you guide them through Research Questions Scoring (Handout Q-5.2). We have found that this is an excellent tool to springboard a lively conversation about questioning.

After being assessed, students are ready to move forward with selecting themes, topics, focus areas, and research questions. If this is more than just a mini-inquiry, students should also consider audience, purpose, and final format(s). Remind the students frequently that the focus of the unit is on the Q part of the QUEST. Although some students are impatient with this preparatory stage, making a plan is an essential part of the initial phase of inquiry and should not be skipped. Emphasize that initiating an inquiry QUEST is analogous to preparing for a journey, so good planning is crucial.

The next eight sections can be completed in any order that makes sense to you and your students: theme selection, topic selection, focus areas, research questions, audience, purpose, final format, and project planning. Allow as much student choice as possible *so long as the choices match your instructional objectives*. Be sure that your objectives don't confuse the methods with the content; for example, if your objective is for students to learn how to develop persuasive arguments, that doesn't mean that every student must write a five-paragraph essay. There are lots of ways for students to demonstrate their understanding of an effective argument without writing an essay. On the other hand, if your instructional objective is for students to learn how to write a five-paragraph essay, then you can provide choices with the topic while keeping the format fixed (Novak, 2014; Lapinski, Gravel, & Rose, 2012).

> **We need to explicitly teach the skills of goal formation and asking meaningful questions, choosing appropriate search engines for the task focus, generating and revising search terms, and investigating search results with a critical eye.** —Harrison, Dwyer, and Castek (2014, p. 116)

Theme Selection

Think of the theme as a starting point, providing students with a stimulus for generating questions. A theme can also serve as a beacon, as if on a lighthouse, guiding students back on track if they become lost in the fog of the inquiry process. If you teach in the content areas or work with a themed basal reader, you may not be able to offer much student choice regarding inquiry themes. However, if you have some flexibility, have the class vote on a group theme or allow students to select their own. Short et al. (1996) recommend broad concepts (e.g., cycles, change, conflict, adaptation, culture, community, mysteries, perspectives, systems, sense of place, interdependence, discovery), because they provide "many possible points of connection that naturally weave across the day and year and do not limit the topics and questions that students can pursue" (p. 19).

TABLE 5.1. Interesting Inquiry Topics

People	Places	Animals
Heroes	Outer space	Endangered
Royalty, celebrities	Craters	Weird, rare, extinct
Humanitarians	National monuments	Deadly, gigantic, tiny
Issues	Events	Science
Controversial	Natural disasters	Inventions
Current	Rebellions, coups	Exploration
Future	Elections	Technology
Popular Culture	Phenomena	Wonders of the world
Music	Weird	Ancient
Movies	Mysterious	Natural
Sports	Religious	Modern

Table 5.1 lists a wide range of themes that will hook even the most reluctant inquirers. Themes can be presented as statements, phrases, or words; for example, "heroes inspire us," "rocks: clues to the past," or "conservation."

Topic Selection

Once a theme has been established, students should select topics of personal interest within that theme. Themes and topics are often chosen before questions are generated; however, some students find it easier to start with questions. Allow each student to proceed in whatever order feels natural to her. Some teachers have students keep an ongoing list of inquiry topics in their journals or writing folders so that there is always a bank of ideas from which to select. Teacher modeling is always beneficial. For example, when reading a piece of literature or a portion of a textbook, the teacher might wonder aloud, "That's really interesting. I don't know much about that topic; I might want to research it at some point."

Although some students have an endless list of inquiry topics, others don't seem to be interested in anything. These unenthusiastic inquirers should be prompted until they come up with a topic about which they are passionate. Here are some prompts that are sufficiently broad to allow student ownership of the endeavor (adapted from Armstrong, 2000):

"What animals do you find interesting or weird?"
"Who are some people you admire [or don't admire]?"
"Where would you like to go [or not go] on vacation?"
"What are your favorite hobbies or sports?"
"What issues do you care about?"
"What would you like to be an expert on?"

"What are you curious to know more about?"

"What do you think is the best invention [or what needs to be invented]?"

As with all aspects of inquiry and learning, student choice with topic selection is crucial. Maya once overheard an eighth-grade teacher ask a student to switch topics because the teacher did not think the Olsen twins were sufficiently "heroic." The young adolescent's affect took an immediate nosedive. Angrily flipping through a book on presidents, she randomly selected one, retorting, "I am not psyched about anything in school anyway, so who cares?" Later, when Maya suggested to the student that she construct an argument to defend her choice of the Olsen twins, the teacher permitted her to keep the topic. Asking students to spend the time required for quality Internet inquiry on a topic of no interest does not make any sense.

At times, young students and struggling learners come up with topics that are too big, too small, too vague, or unresearchable, as discussed previously in relation to research questions. In this case, the teacher or a more capable peer can help the student adjust the topic to an appropriate scope for whatever length of time has been allotted for the project. Previous student topics and projects can also serve as inspiration. Once a topic has been chosen, we ask students to use the Topic Knowledge Assessment (Handout Q-5.4) as a pretest so that we have a sense of their prior knowledge about the topic. This tool flags students who know either too little or too much about a topic so that the teacher can intervene.

This pretest also alerts the teacher to students who do not know how to depict categories and subcategories of topics; for example, a student who chooses to research Walt Disney might create a concept map with his name in the center bubble, then place details about his life into subcategories such as "creations," "appearance," and "family life" (Figure 5.3). In contrast, students who produce what we term "spoke-shaped," or nonhierarchical, concept maps list all their knowledge of a topic at the same level of importance, as shown in Figure 5.4. Spoke-shaped concept maps are often an early indicator that these students will have trouble searching the Internet because they don't understand that information is arranged hierarchically on the Web.

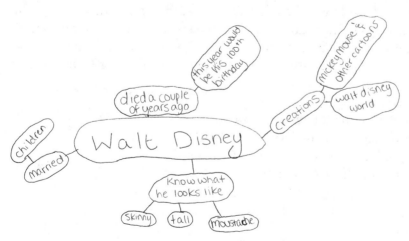

FIGURE 5.3.
Topic knowledge, hierarchical.

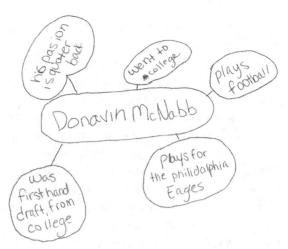

FIGURE 5.4. Topic knowledge, nonhierarchical.

Focus Areas

Once a theme and topic have been selected, many students think they are ready to begin researching. However, we strongly suggest that students develop one or two focus areas within their topic that are of particular interest rather than trying to cover the entire topic in one inquiry project. For example, in a famous-person project, a student might zero in on the person's childhood. Similarly, in a sports project, the history of the sport might serve as an interesting focus area. This not only helps direct student inquiry and results in more interesting projects but also leads to the development of specific keywords, as discussed in the next chapter.

 Language Arts Standard: **Conduct short as well as more sustained research projects based on focused questions, demonstrating understanding of the subject under investigation.**

If students are having difficulty with choosing focus areas, it might be a good idea to generate research questions first, then come back to focus areas. Focus areas can be derived by having students brainstorm as many questions as they can about their topics, then grouping similar types of questions together. Most students find that obvious categories of questions emerge. At this point, it is useful to come up with a label for each category and then choose one or two categories that are most interesting, saving the rest of the questions for another project. Handout Q-5.5, Choosing Focus Areas, guides students through this process.

Research Questions

As mentioned earlier, sometimes the generation of research questions precedes topic and focus area selection. It depends on the student. The most important consideration is the scope of a topic or research question, as discussed earlier. Is the subject something that can be researched in a few weeks, or would it take a year? Is it something that can be answered with a simple yes–no, or is it something that requires synthesis and transformation? A useful method for evaluating the quality of a research question is to use the Inquiry Question Rubric (Handout Q-5.3).

One of the most effective inquiry planning tools that we've used is the Category Flowchart (Handouts Q-5.6, Q-5.7, and Q-5.8). The flowcharts shown in these handouts can serve as guided and/or independent practice in identifying themes, topics, focus areas, and questions. The goal is to teach students that the most effective Web research questions contain a topic and a focus area. For example, the question "What is the history of hockey?" has "hockey" as its topic and "history" as the focus area, and "Where do polar bears live?" contains the topic "polar bear" and the focus area "habitat." Handout Q-5.5 helps students generate topics and focus areas from words that are directly stated in the question. Handouts Q-5.6 and Q-5.7 require students to fill in the topic and focus areas by substituting words or phrases from the questions. Finally, Handout Q-5.8 is left blank for teachers and students to generate their own flowcharts. In Chapter 6, we discuss how topic and focus area words can conveniently be used as keywords for searching the Web.

A classic questioning tool is the K-W-L Chart. The *K* stands for "what I already **Know**," the *W* stands for "what I **Want** to know," and the *L* is used to record "what I **Learned**" during and after reading and/or inquiry. Zwiers (2004) offers a variety of adaptations of the K-W-L, including K-W-H-L-S, which stands for "what we think we **Know**," "what we **Want** to learn," "**How** we will learn it," "what we **Learned**," and "how we will **Show** what we learned" (Figure 5.5).

Another classic method of helping students generate questions is the 5WH technique, which helps students brainstorm questions using *Who, What, Where, When, Why,* and *How* as sentence starters. You can also get creative by turning a lesson on questioning into a whole-class or small-group game in which one team asks questions and another team has to categorize the questions as too big, too small, or just right for a typical inquiry project. Have fun with it, and keep at it until you feel confident that your students really understand what constitutes a reasonable research question.

 Science Standard: **Ask questions about relationships between forms and events and the factors that influence them.**

K	W	H	L	S
What we think we KNOW	What we WANT to learn	HOW we will learn it	What we LEARNED	How we will SHOW what we learned

FIGURE 5.5. K-W-H-L-S chart.

If students are having difficulty generating questions about their chosen topic, an activity that we always find helpful is to have students ask each other genuine questions about the topics. This often stimulates new ideas that students had not even considered and helps to remind them that there is a real audience for their inquiries. Be sure to have someone record all the questions that are asked so nothing is forgotten.

Table 5.2 shows some themes, topics, focus areas, and questions that our students have successfully researched on the Web. While some of the questions are a bit clunky, the topics and focus areas are interesting and easily converted into keywords for searching.

Audience

Part of the initial phase of inquiry involves knowing one's audience. Whenever possible, we like to provide the broadest, most authentic audience for student inquiry. An audience of one (namely, the teacher) is not really a true audience. At the very minimum, students should present the results of their inquiries to each other, but you will find that the students' level of effort and the quality of the inquiry will rise dramatically if they are asked to present to another class or set of classes, to their grade-level peers, to the whole school, to parents, to teachers, to the community, or even to a global audience via the Web. If students are asking important questions that have real answers, they will

TABLE 5.2. Themes, Topics, Focus Areas, and Questions

THEMES	Topics	Focus areas	Questions
ANIMALS	Siberian tigers	Extinction	Why are Siberian tigers becoming extinct?
	Platypuses	Classification	What makes the platypus a mammal instead of a bird?
	Grizzly bears	Size	How big are grizzly bears compared to other bears?
SPORTS	Snowboarding	Equipment	How do they change snowboarding equipment for sandboarding?
	Stanley Cup (hockey)	History	What is the history of the Stanley Cup?
	Williams sisters (tennis)	Biography	What was the Williams sisters' childhood like?
HEROES	Martin Luther King, Jr.	Personality	What was Martin Luther King, Jr. like?
	Nelson Mandela	Peace Prize	Why did Nelson Mandela win the Nobel Peace Prize?
	Shirley Temple Black	Career	What did Shirley Temple Black do in her career?

take pride in demonstrating their findings to an authentic audience. Handout Q-5.9, Knowing Your Audience, helps students determine their audience before launching an inquiry project.

Purpose

Often students don't have a sense of purpose during the inquiry process. This is similar to not knowing the purpose of a writing assignment. Is it to inform? To entertain? To persuade? To express oneself? The purpose, whether assigned by the teacher or chosen by students, will have a significant impact on the types of questions that are pursued, the types of information located, and the types of formats that are used to represent what has been learned (discussed in the next section). Therefore, it is important that students identify the purpose of their inquiries in advance. Handout Q-5.10, Understanding Purposes, helps to highlight how the entire focus of a writing or inquiry project can change depending on the purpose that is selected.

> **Reading initiated by a question differs in important ways from reading that is not.**
> —Leu, Kinzer, Coiro, Castek, and Henry (2013, p. 1165)

Final Format

A simple search for a small fact or piece of information does not require a final product, but full-scale inquiry projects usually result in some sort of final product to demonstrate what has been learned. Whenever possible, we like to give students choices as to how they will represent their findings (e.g., poems, posters, podcasts, wikis, websites). Unfortunately, students often choose final formats according to (1) teacher requirements; (2) familiarity and comfort; (3) convenience; or (4) a perception of what seems "fun," such as glitter-spangled posters or colorful slide shows that lack substantive content (Eagleton, Guinee, & Langlais, 2003). Therefore, we always require that students gain approval of their intended final format very early in the inquiry process. Having a strong vision of a final format in advance really helps students stay on target while searching for information. Table 5.3 shows some common formats.

Final formats must be appropriately matched to research questions, purposes, and audiences; should be of a reasonable size and scope; and must demonstrate the content learning that has taken place. This last point is harder to achieve than it sounds. Many students do not know how to express knowledge; therefore, we must teach this skill through modeling and scaffolding and by providing plenty of practice and feedback (see Chapter 2). One of our

> *Library Media Standard:* **Display initiative and engagement by posing questions and investigating the answers beyond the collection of superficial facts.**

favorite examples of a final format that did not demonstrate content knowledge was an eighth-grade student's ceramic bust of Jerry Garcia (Figure 5.6). Although this project showed wonderful creativity, it did not reflect 4 weeks of inquiry into the life and music of Jerry Garcia. In fact, it did not communicate any information at all other than his facial appearance. In contrast, another student's digital time line of Walt Disney's career represented a lot of information about her topic and focus area (Figure 5.7).

TABLE 5.3. Final Formats

Written formats

Autobiography	Biography	Booklet
Book report	Diary	Essay
Glossary	Journal	Letter
List	Magazine article	Newspaper article
Poem	Questionnaire	Report
Review	Script	Survey

Visual formats

Advertisement	Brochure	Cartoon
Comic strip	Commercial	Diorama
Drawing	Flier	Game
Mural	Photo essay	Poster
Sign	Storyboard	Timeline

Presentation formats

Dance	Drama	Interview
Mock debate	Music	Oral report
Puppet show	Role play	Speech

Digital formats

Blog/Vlog	Podcast/Vodcast	Wiki
Slide show	Ebook	Webpage
Word cloud	Interactive concept map	Digital poster
Game	Animation	Mixup/Mashup

FIGURE 5.6. Final format—insufficient content.

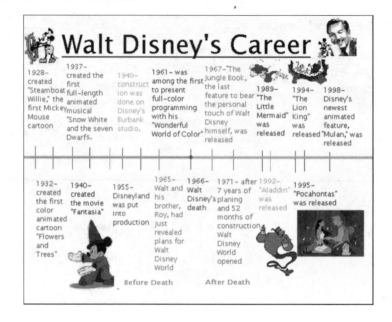

FIGURE 5.7. Final format-sufficient content.

When creating a final product using technology, many students get caught up in the bells and whistles of the technology tool rather than focusing on content. One example that demonstrates this point is a sixth grader who spent so much time creating a digital version of his robot drawing that he had little remaining time to research the ways a robot can help a person with a disability (Figure 5.8). In contrast, his classmate created a well-researched movie trailer presenting information about an artificial eye and the ways it can be useful (Figure 5.9).

FIGURE 5.8. The creation process must not detract from the content to be learned.

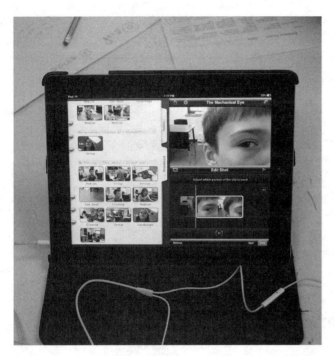

FIGURE 5.9. A final project should reflect the learning of content and skills.

At the beginning of an inquiry project, we always ask students to brainstorm a list of the various ways that information can be presented and show them examples of past student projects as models. We return to the topic of final formats in Chapter 9, when we discuss the Transforming phase of inquiry.

Project Planning

Before embarking on a major inquiry project, we ask students to collaborate in designing project criteria, due dates for major milestones (Figure 5.10), and grading rubrics for how their efforts will be assessed. These are printed out as metacognitive reminders and stored in students' Reflection Log journals (discussed in Chapter 10), in which they write during the last 5 minutes of every class period. The Sample Grading Rubric (Handout Q-5.11) is a useful way of assessing student productivity. For inquiry projects lasting more than 2 weeks, we have students complete several grading rubrics to encourage ongoing self-reflection and so they can receive frequent feedback on how they are progressing.

Because many students initiate research without a clear plan, we also ask that some students fill out a Project Planning Flowchart (Handout Q-5.12) and that all develop a Project Plan (Handout Q-5.13) to cement the intended theme, topic, focus area(s), question(s), audience, purpose, and final format(s). This document serves as a road map for the QUEST, helping students and teachers stay on course toward the targeted objective of the activity. The project plan must be previewed by one or more peers and approved by the teacher or librarian in an individual conference (Figure 5.11). Handouts Q-5.14 and Q-5.15, the Project Planning Lessons for Elementary and Middle Levels, provide guidelines for walking your students through the planning process.

Note: All assignments are due at the BEGINNING of the period!				
ITEM	ASSIGNMENT	DUE DATE	Student initials and date	Teacher initials and date
1	Project Plan			
2	Website Evaluation Chart			
3	Notes—first draft			
4	Notes—second draft			
5	Focus Area #1—3 paragraphs			
6	Focus Area #2—3 paragraphs			
7	Project—first draft			
8	Project—final			
9	Works Cited			
10	Project Presentation			

FIGURE 5.10. Due dates checklist.

FIGURE 5.11. Teacher-student planning conference.

SUMMARY ●

The Q phase of the QUEST includes theme selection, topic selection, focus areas, research questions, audience, purpose, final format, and project planning. Children and young adolescents frequently initiate research without explicit research questions or a plan of action; therefore, we need to help them develop strategies for this important first step in the inquiry process. As teachers, we can reinforce these strategies by conducting our own inquiry process alongside our students while providing appropriate modeling, scaffolding, practice, and feedback. Whenever possible, we allow student choice so that young inquirers will sustain interest in their QUEST over the long haul.

In Chapter 6, on Understanding Resources, we share research and practical suggestions for helping students develop strategies for identifying resources, managing computers, utilizing the Internet, choosing search tools, and selecting keywords. Although we always like to see students using as many resources as possible to answer their research questions—people, books, mass media, and technology tools—there is no doubt that today's students need strategies for using the Internet as a resource for inquiry and learning.

Handouts

The following chart lists the assessment tools, activities, and handouts discussed in this chapter on Questioning. Remember that it is not advisable to have students use everything we've provided in one project. Choose several that appeal to you and save the rest for another time. Feel free to modify any of these tools to suit your specific needs.

Number	Name of handout	Purpose
Q-5.1	Research Questions Assessment	Assess research question knowledge
Q-5.2	Research Questions Scoring	Score research question assessment
Q-5.3	Inquiry Question Rubric	Assess quality of research questions
Q-5.4	Topic Knowledge Assessment	Assess topic knowledge
Q-5.5	Choosing Focus Areas	Help choose focus areas
Q-5.6	Category Flowchart—Literal	Find focus areas in question
Q-5.7	Category Flowchart—Substitution	Substitute words in question
Q-5.8	Category Flowchart—Blank	Create your own flowchart
Q-5.9	Knowing Your Audience	Help identify your audience
Q-5.10	Understanding Purposes	Transform purposes
Q-5.11	Sample Grading Rubric	Method of assessing progress
Q-5.12	Project Planning Flowchart	Guide inquiry project
Q-5.13	Project Planning Template	Scaffold inquiry project
Q-5.14	Project Planning Lesson—Elementary Level	Teach project planning strategies
Q-5.15	Project Planning Lesson—Middle Level	Teach project planning strategies

HANDOUT Q-5.1. Research Questions Assessment

Name _____ Class _____ Date _____

☐ Pretest   ☐ Posttest

Directions: *Decide whether these questions would be effective for a Web research project by circling "strong" or "weak." If you circle "weak," choose one of the four reasons.*

			Reason	
1. What is the life cycle of a zebra?	strong	weak	Too small	Too big
			Opinion	Not a question
2. What is the zebra's habitat?	strong	weak	Too small	Too big
			Opinion	Not a question
3. What are zebras?	strong	weak	Too small	Too big
			Opinion	Not a question
4. Are zebras endangered?	strong	weak	Too small	Too big
			Opinion	Not a question
5. All about zebras.	strong	weak	Too small	Too big
			Opinion	Not a question
6. How big are zebras?	strong	weak	Too small	Too big
			Opinion	Not a question
7. Why do zebras have stripes?	strong	weak	Too small	Too big
			Opinion	Not a question
8. Are zebras better than horses?	strong	weak	Too small	Too big
			Opinion	Not a question
9. What are stripes?	strong	weak	Too small	Too big
			Opinion	Not a question
10. How many zebras live in the San Diego zoo?	strong	weak	Too small	Too big
			Opinion	Not a question

HANDOUT Q-5.2. Research Questions Scoring

Directions: *Give 1 point for each correct answer.*

#	Question	strong/weak	Too small	Too big	Opinion	Not a question
1.	What is the life cycle of a zebra?	(strong) weak	Too small	Too big	Opinion	Not a question
2.	What is the zebra's habitat?	(strong) weak	Too small	Too big	Opinion	Not a question
3.	What are zebras?	strong (weak)	Too small	(Too big)	Opinion	Not a question
4.	Are zebras endangered?	(strong) weak	Too small	Too big	Opinion	Not a question
5.	All about zebras.	strong (weak)	Too small	(Too big)	Opinion	(Not a question)
6.	How big are zebras?	strong (weak)	(Too small)	Too big	Opinion	Not a question
7.	Why do zebras have stripes?	(strong) weak	Too small	Too big	Opinion	Not a question
8.	Are zebras better than horses?	strong (weak)	Too small	Too big	(Opinion)	Not a question
9.	What are stripes?	strong (weak)	Too small	(Too big)	Opinion	Not a question
10.	How many zebras live in the San Diego zoo?	strong (weak)	(Too small)	Too big	Opinion	Not a question

HANDOUT Q-5.3. Inquiry Question Rubric

Name _____ Class _____ Date _____

Directions: *Use this rubric to evaluate whether your inquiry question is of high quality.*

Inquiry Question _____

Quality	4 points	3 points	2 points	1 point	Student Score	Teacher Score
Answer is unknown	Neither teacher nor student knows an answer in advance	Teacher may have a general answer for the question	Teacher knows the answer in depth	Student knows the answer in depth		
Answer is defensible	Highly likely to find solid evidence for an answer	Some good sources are likely to be found	Very little reliable information exists	Results are likely to be nearly impossible to verify or defend		
Leads to deep research	Topic has excellent potential for deep exploration	Topic has good potential for deep exploration	Topic has limited potential for deep exploration	Topic has almost no potential for deep exploration		
Can apply at any grade level	Topic is worthy of research at all levels, K-12	Topic limited to grades 3-8	Topic limited to student's grade level	Topic worthy of research at grade level below that of student		
Leads to other questions	Topic triggers numerous other interesting questions	New questions are limited to variations of the original question	Very few questions are triggered by the topic	No new questions are likely to emerge while exploring the topic		
				Student Score		
				Teacher Score		

HANDOUT Q-5.4. Topic Knowledge Assessment

Name _____

Class _____ Date _____

☐ Pretest   ☐ Posttest

Directions: *Draw a bubble map that shows everything you know about your topic.*

HANDOUT Q-5.5. Choosing Focus Areas

Name _____ Class _____ Date _____

Directions: *Follow these steps to choose some focus areas and research questions for your topic.*

Step 1: Brainstorm at least 10 questions about your topic on 3x5 note cards—one question per card. If you run out of ideas, invite other people to ask some questions about your topic.

Step 2: Sort the note cards into categories; in other words, group similar questions together.

Step 3: Figure out a word to describe each category. For example, if you are researching an animal, you might have words such as *life cycle, appearance, diet,* and *habitat.*

Write the category words here: _____

_____

_____

_____

_____

_____

_____

_____

Step 4: Choose at least two of the categories and turn them into research questions with a topic and a focus. For example, if you are researching a sport and you are interested in the history of the sport, one of your research questions might be, "What is the history of soccer?"

Write your research questions here: _____

_____

_____

_____

_____

_____

_____

_____

HANDOUT Q-5.6. Category Flowchart—Literal

Name _____ Class _____ Date _____

Directions: *Fill in the missing information in the flowchart. The first one has been done for you.*

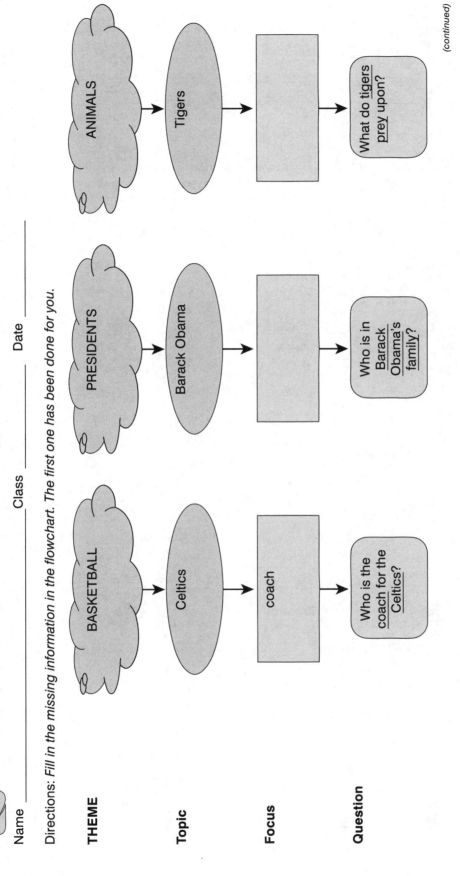

THEME

BASKETBALL   PRESIDENTS   ANIMALS

Topic

Celtics   Barack Obama   Tigers

Focus

coach

Question

Who is the coach for the <u>Celtics</u>?   Who is in <u>Barack Obama's family</u>?   What do tigers <u>prey upon</u>?

(continued)

Category Flowchart—Literal *(page 2 of 2)*

Make up your own flowchart:

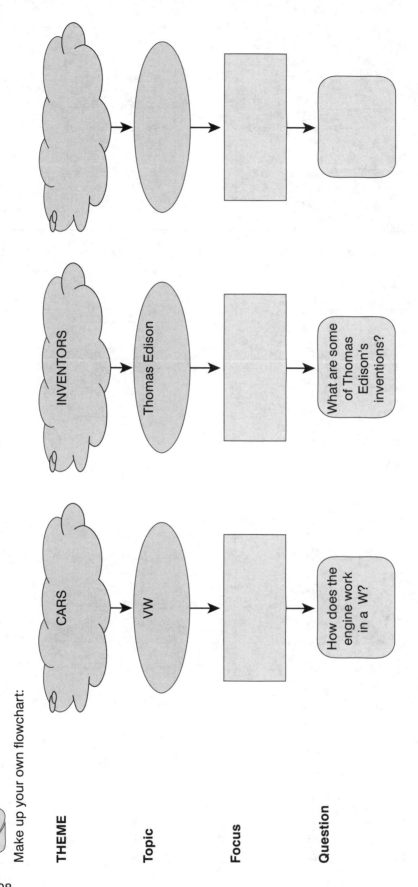

THEME

CARS | INVENTORS

Topic

VW | Thomas Edison

Focus

Question

How does the engine work in a VW? | What are some of Thomas Edison's inventions?

HANDOUT Q-5.7. Category Flowchart—Substitution

Name _____ Class _____ Date _____

Directions: Fill in the missing information in the flowchart. The first one has been done for you.

THEME

ANIMALS → AUTHORS → FOOTBALL

Topic

Tigers → J. K. Rowling → Jets

Focus

Habitat or range → [ ] → [ ]

Question

Where do tigers live? → What has J. K. Rowling written? → Where is the Jets' hometown?

(continued)

From *Reading the Web, Second Edition*, by Elizabeth Dobler and Maya B. Eagleton. Copyright 2015 by The Guilford Press. Permission to photocopy this handout is granted to purchasers of this book for personal use only (see copyright page for details). Purchasers can also download and print this handout at *www.guilford.com/dobler-forms*.

Category Flowchart—Substitution *(page 2 of 2)*

Make up your own flowchart:

THEME

ANIMALS

PAST PRESIDENTS

Topic

Pandas

Bill Clinton

Focus

Question

Where do pandas come from?

What does Bill Clinton do for a living now?

HANDOUT Q-5.8. Category Flowchart—Blank

Name _____ Class _____ Date _____

Directions: *Fill in the missing information in the flowchart using three different themes.*

THEME

Topic

Focus

Question

HANDOUT Q-5.9. Knowing Your Audience

Name _____ Class _____ Date _____

Directions: *Write down what you know and can predict about your audience.*

	Enter your answers in this column:
1. The audience for my project includes these kinds of people:	
2. My audience is similar to me in these ways:	
3. My audience is different from me in these ways:	
4. My audience probably knows the following about my topic:	
5. My audience probably feels this way about my topic:	
6. These are questions my audience might ask me about my topic:	

HANDOUT Q-5.10. Understanding Purposes

Name _____ Class _____ Date _____

Almost any topic can be used for a variety of purposes. There are four basic purposes for any writing or inquiry project: to inform, to entertain, to persuade, and to express.

Directions: *Read the chart and fill in the missing blanks. Create your own topics and purposes in the blank rows.*

TOPICS	PURPOSES			
	to inform	**to entertain**	**to persuade**	**to express yourself**
kangaroos	kangaroo life cycle	the crazy story of the dueling kangaroos	TV ad for saving the Australian outback	my kangaroo poem
skiing	history of skiing	skiing comics	letter asking for money to build a ski resort	how skiing changed my life
Einstein	Einstein's childhood	weird creatures that live in Einstein's hair	why Einstein should win the Nobel prize	
whales	different types of whales	all the things you can do with blubber		collection of haunting whale sounds
rap music	famous rap musicians		why kids should be able to play rap in school	my rap song
Hawaii		surfing bloopers	poster to convince tourists to visit Hawaii	video clip of my hula dancing

HANDOUT Q-5.11. Sample Grading Rubric

Name _____ Class _____ Date _____

PROCESS	4	3	2	1	0	STUDENT SCORE	TEACHER SCORE
Effort	I put forth a *ton* of effort	I put forth *a lot* of effort	I put forth *some* effort	I put forth a *little* effort	I didn't put forth any effort		
Citizenship	I *always* respected my peers	I *usually* respected my peers	I *sometimes* respected my peers	I *rarely* respected my peers	I never respected my peers		
					TOTAL PROCESS		

PROGRESS	4	3	2	1	0	STUDENT SCORE	TEACHER SCORE
Making Notes	I *totally* had enough notes for my project	I *mostly* had enough notes for my project	I *somewhat* had enough notes for my project	I *sort of* had enough notes for my project	I didn't have any notes		
Finding Information	I found my info *super fast*	I found my info *pretty fast*	I found my info *but it took a little while*	I found my info *but it took a long time*	I couldn't find any information		
					TOTAL PROCESS		

PROGRESS	4	3	2	1	0	STUDENT SCORE	TEACHER SCORE
Citing Sources	I gathered info from *four or more* sources	I gathered info from *three* sources	I gathered info from *two* sources	I gathered info from *one* source	I didn't gather any info		
Research Topic	I learned *nearly everything* about my topic	I learned *a lot* about my topic	I learned *some* stuff about my topic	I learned a *little* about my topic	I didn't learn anything new		
Final Project	My project *totally* showed what I learned	My project *mostly* showed what I learned	My project *somewhat* showed what I learned	My project *sort of* showed what I learned	My project didn't show what I learned		
					TOTAL PROCESS		

	TOTALS	
TOTAL POSSIBLE FOR THIS CATEGORY: 8 PROCESS		
TOTAL POSSIBLE FOR THIS CATEGORY: 8 PROGRESS		
TOTAL POSSIBLE FOR THIS CATEGORY: 12 PRODUCT		
TOTAL out of 28 points		
PERCENT		

HANDOUT Q-5.12. Project Planning Flowchart

Name _____ Class _____ Date _____

Directions: *Enter your theme, topic, two focus areas, and two questions into the flowchart.*

THEME

Topic

Focus

Questions

HANDOUT Q-5.13. Project Planning Template

Name _____ Class _____ Date _____

Directions: *Enter a plan for your project in the chart.*

	Enter your answers in this column:
1. My theme is:	
2. My topic is:	
3. I chose this topic because:	
4. My first research question is:	
5. My second research question is:	
6. The audience for my project is:	
7. The purpose of my research is (to inform, persuade, entertain, or express):	
8. I will show what I've learned by making a (report, brochure, digital poster, webpage, etc.):	

HANDOUT Q-5.14. Project Planning Lesson—Elementary Level

Objective

Students will demonstrate the ability to plan an inquiry project by brainstorming and categorizing research questions.

Time

One or two class periods

Materials

1. QUEST Inquiry Model (Handout P-4.11)
2. Choosing Focus Areas (Handout Q-5.5)
3. Project Planning Flowchart (Handout Q-5.12)
4. 3x5 notecards (10 or more per student)
5. Rubber bands or paper clips (5 or more per student)
6. Pencils

Assessment Options

1. Web Strategies Assessment (Handout P-4.2, P-4.4, or P-4.5)
2. Web Strategies Scoring Guide (Handout P-4.3 or P-4.6)

Introduction

1. Make sure you have covered themes, topics, audience, purpose, and formats before doing this Project Planning Lesson.
2. Tell students you will be teaching them a strategy for planning an inquiry project that many other students have found useful. Contextualize the lesson using the QUEST Inquiry Model (Handout P-4.11) by pointing out that they are in the **Q** phase of the QUEST, which includes creating a plan.
3. Have students brainstorm why planning is useful in this class, in other classes, and outside of school. This can be done in pairs, in small groups, or as a whole class.
4. Generate excitement and get student buy-in on the purpose of the lesson before proceeding. Tell students that strong project plans and appropriately scoped focus areas and research questions will improve their ability to find information on the Internet.

Modeling

1. Follow the process in Handout Q-5.5 to model brainstorming questions, sorting them into categories, and creating a name to describe each category.
2. Pass out materials.

Practice

1. Students brainstorm what they want to know about their topics by putting one question on each index card.
2. Students sort the cards into categories with similar questions.
3. Students create a name for each category and enter the names in Step 3 of Handout Q-5.5.

(continued)

4. Students choose two categories (focus areas) and corresponding questions to put in Step 4 of Handout Q-5.5 and then in the flowchart on Handout Q-5.12.
5. Toward the end of the class period, have each student place a rubber band or paper clip around all the index cards and put his or her name in a prominent location on the top card.
6. Collect all materials.

Scaffolding

1. An excellent activity for helping students generate questions is to have them ask each other questions about their topics. This works well in small groups so long as someone who writes quickly and legibly can accurately record the questions.
2. If anyone is struggling to generate questions, you may want to have that student use the 5WH technique (Who, What, Where, When, Why, How).
3. If students are struggling to categorize their questions, name their categories, or convert categories into research questions, pair them up or help them individually.
4. If anyone is struggling with writing, have a more capable student serve as a scribe.
5. For students who are overwhelmed with two focus areas, have them just do one.
6. If anyone is having serious difficulty with the whole procedure, have him or her go through the process again from the start with you or a more capable peer. Have the student talk aloud as you go through each step together. Choose another topic if necessary.

Feedback

Have individual conferences to ensure that students have appropriately scoped focus areas, "good" research questions, and well-matched purposes and formats before proceeding to the next QUEST phase: **U**nderstanding Resources.

Ticket Out the Door

Have each student tell you his or her topic and focus area(s) before leaving class.

HANDOUT Q-5.15. Project Planning Lesson—Middle Level

Objective

Students will demonstrate the ability to plan an inquiry project by brainstorming and categorizing research questions.

Time

One or two class periods

Materials

1. QUEST Inquiry Model (Handout P-4.11)
2. Choosing Focus Areas (Handout Q-5.5)
3. Project Planning Flowchart (Handout Q-5.12)
4. 3x5 notecards (10 or more per student)
5. Rubber bands or paper clips (5 or more per student)
6. Pencils

Assessment Options

1. Web Strategies Assessment (Handout P-4.2, P-4.4, or P-4.5)
2. Web Strategies Scoring Guide (Handout P-4.3 or P-4.6)

Introduction

1. Make sure you have covered themes, topics, audience, purpose, and formats before doing this Project Planning Lesson.
2. Tell students you will be teaching them a strategy for planning an inquiry project that many other students have found useful. Contextualize the lesson using the QUEST Inquiry Model (Handout P-4.11) by pointing out that they are in the **Q** phase of the QUEST, which includes creating a plan.
3. Have students brainstorm why planning is useful in this class, in other classes, and outside of school. This can be done in pairs, in small groups, or as a whole class.
4. Generate excitement and get student buy-in on the purpose of the lesson before proceeding. Tell students that strong project plans and appropriately scoped focus areas and research questions will improve their ability to find information on the Internet.

Modeling

1. Follow the process in Handout Q-5.5 to model brainstorming questions, sorting them into categories and creating a name to describe each category.
2. Pass out materials

Practice

1. Students brainstorm what they want to know about their topics by putting one question on each index card.
2. Students sort the cards into categories with similar questions.
3. Students create a name for each category and enter the names in Step 3 of Handout Q-5.5.

(continued)

4. Students choose two categories (focus areas) and corresponding questions to put in Step 4 of Handout Q-5.5 and then in the flowchart on Handout Q-5.12.
5. Toward the end of the class period, have each student place a rubber band or paper clip around all the index cards and put his or her name in a prominent location on the top card.
6. Collect all materials.

Scaffolding

1. An excellent activity for helping students generate questions is to have them ask each other questions about their topics. This works well in small groups so long as someone who writes quickly and legibly can accurately record the questions.
2. If anyone is struggling to generate questions, you may want to have that student use the 5WH technique (Who, What, Where, When, Why, How).
3. If students are struggling to categorize their questions, name their categories, or convert categories into research questions, pair them up or help them individually.
4. If anyone is struggling with writing, have a more capable student serve as a scribe.
5. For students who are overwhelmed with two focus areas, have them just do one.
6. If anyone is having serious difficulty with the whole procedure, have him or her go through the process again from the start with you or a more capable peer. Have the student talk aloud as you go through each step together. Choose another topic if necessary.

Feedback

Have individual conferences to ensure that students have appropriately scoped focus areas, "good" research questions, and well-matched purposes and formats before proceeding to the next QUEST phase: Understanding Resources.

Ticket Out the Door

Have each student tell you his or her topic and focus area(s) before leaving class.

6 Understanding Resources

Questioning
What do I want to know?

Transforming
What will I do with it?

QUEST

Understanding Resources
How will I find out?

Synthesizing
What does this mean?

Evaluating
Is this what I need?

KEY IDEAS ●

- The key question that guides the U phase of the inquiry process is "How will I find the answers to my questions?"

- Identifying appropriate resources for inquiry requires the ability to match resources with research questions, whether these resources are people, books, media, or the Internet.

- Choosing search tools means knowing the difference between typing a search topic straight into the URL field and using a search engine.

- Because search tools differ in their algorithms and features, it is important to understand how several popular ones work and to know when to use them.

- The linchpin to selecting keywords for searching is to avoid being too broad or too wordy. A reliable method is the <topic focus> keyword strategy.

- Experienced Internet users utilize power search strategies to increase efficiency.

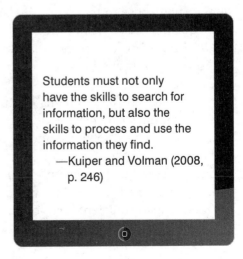

Students must not only have the skills to search for information, but also the skills to process and use the information they find.
—Kuiper and Volman (2008, p. 246)

In this chapter on Understanding Resources, we share research-based practical suggestions for helping students develop strategies for identifying resources, managing devices, utilizing the Internet, choosing search tools, and selecting keywords. Whereas many of the strategies presented in the preceding chapter on Questioning are similar for print-based and Web-based learning, the Understanding Resources phase requires unique strategies that have no print corollary. For example, because search engines are currently the primary mediators of information on the Internet, understanding how to use them effectively is critical. To move forward in an online search, a learner must condense a question into a meaningful query, so it is essential that students have strategies for selecting keywords. We conclude this chapter with numerous handouts to help your students become more strategic with technological resources.

Why Is It Important to Understand Resources?

There is so much information available to us today that it is important to have knowledge of available resources and to have flexible strategies for finding answers and solving problems. There is no doubt that the Internet has far exceeded every previous information technology in breadth, depth, and recency. The Internet has become an integral tool for gaining information in schools, at home, and in the workplace; however, as mentioned throughout this text, researchers have found that people of all ages are surprisingly inefficient at finding information using this uniquely flexible resource. If we want to prepare today's students to be successful in school and to compete in tomorrow's workplace, we had better start teaching them to be Web literate.

When Do We Need to Use Resources?

It is a high compliment to describe someone as "resourceful." A resourceful person may not know all the answers, but he is strategic and tenacious at finding them; for example, he may know the right person to call, know the right reference book to peruse, or know how to find the information online. When stumped, a resourceful person does not give up but, rather, tries to think of another resource to consult. These are exactly the kinds of transferable strategies that we need to be teaching our students, and providing instruction in the types of resources that are available via the Internet is especially crucial today.

Strategies for Understanding Resources come into play throughout the inquiry process but are especially helpful after the Questioning phase, when topics and research questions have been solidified and it's time to figure out the most expedient means for gathering the target information. Certain types of research questions lend themselves to primary data collection methods, such as interviewing people or conducting surveys. Others require a trip to the library or the local museum. Still others may require a combination of many different kinds of resources, including the Web. The trick is knowing which types of resources to consult at which times.

What Characterizes Effective Use of Resources?

There are five fundamental aspects of Understanding Resources with which students must be strategic in order to be successful with Web-based inquiry projects, as follows: (1) identifying resources; (2) managing devices; (3) utilizing the Internet; (4) choosing search tools; and (5) selecting keywords. If you have used some of the assessment tools provided in Chapter 4, you will know which of your students need assistance in each area.

TEACHER: What have you learned about inquiry?

STUDENT: It takes time. You don't have to get it all done in one day.

Identifying Resources

The first step in Understanding Resources is identifying the most promising and easily accessible resources for answering research questions. Although the chief focus of this text is Web-based resources, we like to give students experience with all the different types of sources that real researchers use: primary source materials, people (adults, peers, experts), print (books, magazines, encyclopedias), media (TV, film, radio), and the Internet (email, websites, social media). Notice how these forms of representation map onto the semiotic sign systems

Library Media Standard:
Demonstrate confidence and self-direction by making independent choices in the selection of resources and information.

discussed earlier in the text. Humans use a wide variety of representational forms to communicate information, and being literate involves interpreting and making use of a variety of culturally valued forms.

Managing Devices

If a student decides that a technological resource is indeed a good match for his research questions, then we need to ensure that he knows how to manage devices that access the Internet, such as computers, tablets, and other devices. Keyboarding is essential because most schools use computers, laptops, or tablets for Internet access. Furthermore, because the CCSS (NGA & CCSSO, 2010) specifically state that students must be proficient with keyboarding. Just as a young learner needs to know how to hold a pencil and form letters in order to write, he needs to be able to use a keyboard and a touchscreen, track-pad, or mouse to work with computers. Using the laborious keyboard technique known as "hunting and pecking" is a barrier to learning on the Web (Figure 6.1).

As discussed throughout this text, navigation is also fundamental to Web reading. Unlike books, which typically proceed in a linear fashion, Web reading necessitates nonlinear navigational strategies, or the linking of ideas in various sequences, in order to move through the system with ease. Web navigation requires an understanding of the system and the ability to make rapid, informed decisions about where to go next . . . and next . . . and next.

FIGURE 6.1. Hunting and pecking at the keyboard.

Finally, learners need some basic troubleshooting strategies in order to manage technology effectively. Although we don't advocate having youngsters dismantle computer hardware at school, it is helpful if your students know a few tricks to escape from frozen programs and error messages. A good rule of thumb to preserve your sanity as a teacher is to train students to solicit help from three knowledgeable classmates before coming to you with questions or problems (aka, "ask three before me").

Utilizing the Internet

After assessing your students using some of the tools presented in Chapter 4, you will have a sense of their level of Internet knowledge, abilities, and attitudes. The following are some additional questions you will want to ask about your students:

- Do they know how to get on the Internet?
- Do they know how to navigate the Web efficiently?
- Do they know about the "refresh" and "history" features on Web browsers?
- Do they know what to do when commercial ads appear?
- Do they know how and where to save images, multimedia, and text?

In order for students to develop these skills, we strongly suggest starting with closed information searches (i.e., library portals, customized searches, or teacher-created websites with links to preselected sites) in the lower grades before moving to open-ended searching on the Web. A social bookmarking site, such as Diigo (*diigo.com*) or Delicious (*delicious.com*), is a handy way to collect and organize websites. One fifth-grade teacher developed a collection of websites with information about the Civil War within Diigo. During this unit of study, students received an invitation to access the group and could view the collection. Another fifth-grade teacher on this same grade-level team created a website using the tool Weebly (*weebly.com*) to display the Civil War websites she wanted her students to access. A third teacher on this team created Quick Response (QR) codes for each website. These are two-dimensional barcodes that look like a box with a unique series of black-and-white square dots arranged on a grid. With a QR code reader app on a tablet or smartphone, a person can scan this image and be taken directly to the website through a browser. This teacher printed the QR codes on paper and displayed each one around the room as a part of a social studies learning station.

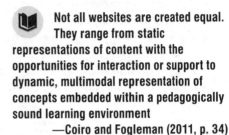

Not all websites are created equal. They range from static representations of content with the opportunities for interaction or support to dynamic, multimodal representation of concepts embedded within a pedagogically sound learning environment
—Coiro and Fogleman (2011, p. 34)

Choosing Search Tools

At this time in history, in order for anyone to find anything in the multidimensional system that is the Internet, a person must be able to understand and use tools such as databases, directories, and search engines. Although some students know of the existence of several search engines, they tend to use one search engine—usually Google—regularly. Web readers are often unaware of the advanced features offered by search engines, even on

Math Standard: Use appropriate tools strategically.

Google, and those who are aware of them use them infrequently. One problem is that most students do not understand how search engines work. In our research with students in grades 3–8, we have found it very enlightening to pose the question, "When you ask a computer to do an Internet search, what does the computer do with your request?" Table 6.1 shows typical responses to this query, sorted into degrees of sophistication.

Another problem is that search engines, and the ways users interact with them, are always changing. Commercial search engines compete for business in the form of users. As a result, faster and easier search algorithms are continually being developed. As Web 3.0 tools become more sophisticated, online searching has begun to more closely mimic the way people actually ask a question and seek an answer in real life. One of the main reasons Google enjoys such popularity is that it is smart about interpreting natural language searches. As Beth's daughter (23 years old) remarked, "I can talk to Google." Similarly, Beth's son (20 years old) commented, "Google is intuitive and knows me." Competing search engines, directories, and databases aim to be more "Google-like" because this is the search experience most users know and understand.

Although the evolution toward Google-style searching may seem convenient, using natural language sometimes hinders a search. The more precise our search terms, the closer a search engine can get to pinpointing information that matches our needs.

TABLE 6.1. Children's Beliefs about Search Engines

How does a search engine work?

Novice

- I don't know. It gets it really fast.
- It goes to this other computer with a person on it and it types in where you want to go and it somehow connects you.
- Takes it to a computer that someone's on and they actually search and find information and send it back to your computer.
- It goes in a small cycle through a telephone wire, back through the wall, into your computer. I think it's a robot that does it.
- It has the information I type onto it and it brings it to the computer's main frame. It brings the energy pulses, the signals.

Intermediate

- It will scan a bunch of websites and it will show all the websites related to what you typed in.
- It sends what you type to this site. It analyzes all that information and sends you the links that match your description.
- Goes through every site that has the word on it, or talks about it.
- It goes through miles and miles of documents.

Advanced

- Sends it to the server and it processes it in a script and looks through the database and returns what results you have.
- It browses the registered webpages for the information that you search for and finds the closest matches.
- I think it searches the information it has on its sites for words that you've used.

For a query seeking a fairly straightforward answer, using a broad search engine such as Google and simply typing your question directly into the search box may be adequate. However, for a query requiring the synthesis of information from various sources, or one requiring highly accurate and reliable information, a more specialized search tool and more specific search terms may be a better choice.

As you can imagine, these rapid changes mean that the information in this text regarding search engines will quickly become outdated. Our best advice is to become familiar with several search tools. Visit each search tool's home page, find the About link, and read the site's description. Check to see whether this description matches what you know about online searching or whether your own processes need a bit of updating before you pass this information on to students.

To choose the best search tool, we begin by asking ourselves the questions, "What does each search tool offer?" and "What are the differences between search engines developed for children and those developed for adults?" Some Internet readers, including adults, figure out how to use a search engine with little or no instruction. Maybe you are like us and began Internet searching by muddling your way through the use of a search engine. Though you may eventually find some information, are you being efficient and effectively finding the most useful information? A system relying on luck and guessing may work very well, especially if you are not pressed for time when searching for information. Students, on the other hand, are often pressed for time. When searching at school or the public library, students may have a limited amount of time for using the computer. When working at home, time may also be a consideration for students who are busy with other assignments, after-school activities, and pressures from other family members who are sharing Web devices.

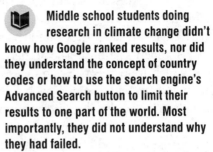 Middle school students doing research in climate change didn't know how Google ranked results, nor did they understand the concept of country codes or how to use the search engine's Advanced Search button to limit their results to one part of the world. Most importantly, they did not understand why they had failed.

—November (2012, p. 50)

In school settings, we have observed students using three approaches to locating information on the Web: (1) the dot-com formula; (2) the shopping mall; and (3) search engines (described in detail in Guinee et al., 2003). We briefly discuss the first two strategies before moving into an in-depth discussion of search engines.

The Dot-com Formula

Many students attempt to find information by substituting their research topic into what Guinee et al. (2003) have dubbed the "dot-com formula" (e.g., *www.mytopic.com*), which is based on the convention for naming corporate websites. With this method, the reader creates a web address using her topic or keyword rather than beginning a search using a search tool. A novice Web user explains this phenomenon: "First of all, you go onto the Internet, and then you write alaska.com or alaskatrip.com or whatever and get onto that, and then you can go through the web pages and finally find what you need."

Commercialization of the Web has led to an abundance of corporate dot-coms, making the dot-com approach fairly effective when trying to find companies. For example, the Nike website (*nike.com*) provides information and opportunities for purchase of Nike products. The proliferation of dot-coms gives many students the impression that the dot-com approach is a good preliminary catch-all search method. This feeling was articulated by one student, who said, "I think also . . . if you want something broad, you can just do like www and like whatever-dot-com nowadays, because there's so many different dot-coms." However, using this approach to find a relevant website for a research project can present problems because companies and their websites generally are not designed to be student reference sources. For instance, a sixth-grade student began his search by typing "www.piranna.com." Spelling error aside, this company's site wasn't related to piranhas or any other fish.

The Shopping Mall

Rather than relying on the dot-com formula, some Internet users treat the Web like a shopping mall, a place with categories of information compartmentalized like stores in a mall—electronics in one store, clothes in another (Guinee et al., 2003). These students go straight to sites they think might contain their desired information. For example, one experienced Internet user said, "I'd go to *expedia.com* and go to the tour guide info and type in 'Alaska' and find out what's there." Another said, "First I'd look to see if there was a brochure of the cruise ship, I'd go to that website . . . and then go to the Coast Guard to see if they rated the safety."

As students gain Internet experience, they become more familiar with various websites, which increases their chances that applying the shopping-mall approach will be effective. However, the approach fails when the student is unsure of where to look or the selected website does not contain the target information. This situation is well demonstrated by the following navigation sequence by an eighth grader who searched for information on the lory bird during the individual Web Strategies Assessment (see Chapter 4). This is the order in which he proceeded: National Geographic.com → Discovery.com → Petco.com → asked researcher, "Is this an extinct bird?" → finally went to a search engine.

Search Tools

There are many search tools on the Web competing for your students' inquiries. As in any product market, different tools work in slightly different ways to try to provide a better product than the competition. Most people use commercial search engines, but there are other tools available, such as librarian-selected databases and educator-created portals. The following discussion of eight search tools provides background information for selecting one that best meets students' needs in various age ranges. If some of the tools are outdated by the time you read this text, try a Web search for <kid friendly search tool>.

KidRex

KidRex (*kidrex.org*) is a *customized search engine* with a dinosaur theme that appeals to younger children ages 6–10. KidRex is useful for filtering out age-inappropriate content and commercial ads (Figure 6.2). Search results are displayed in a clutter-free list with Google-style descriptions of each kid-friendly website. When a reader chooses a site to visit, the website appears in the same browser window, making it easier to navigate back to the search results.

KidsClick

KidsClick (*kidsclick.org*) is a *librarian-selected directory*, so it is useful when a teacher wants to protect children from visiting inappropriate sites, low-quality sites, or web pages with difficult text. According to the KidsClick website, this search tool "is intended to guide users to good sites; not block them from 'bad' sites." As a directory, it is not a completely closed system, because students can leave the preselected sites once they click on a link that goes out to a different website. Students can search using keywords, categories, the Dewey decimal system, or alphabetically. A search for global warming

FIGURE 6.2. KidRex search engine.

reveals two annotated results with an approximate reading level and quantity of illustrations (Figure 6.3). To filter by readability level, the user must use the Advanced Search feature. A disadvantage to this tool is that some topics (e.g., global warming) are not well represented in the directory. Recommended age range is 8–12 years.

ipl2 for Kids

ipl2 for Kids (*ipl.org/div/kidspace*) is a *librarian-selected database* organized by subject. It is useful when a teacher wants to protect children from visiting age-inappropriate or low-quality sites. The reader cannot filter by readability level, but because all the sites are preselected, the reader is unlikely to include highly difficult text (Figure 6.4). ipl2 for Kids is a subsection of the Internet Public Library, which is maintained by professors and students in library and information science programs. When a reader selects a site to visit, a new browser window opens, so the reader needs to know how to toggle back

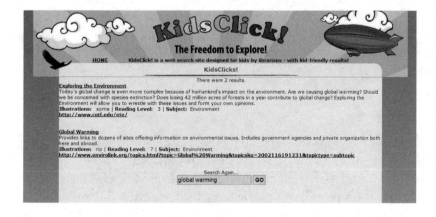

FIGURE 6.3. KidsClick search directory.

FIGURE 6.4. ipl2 for Kids search database.

to the ipl2 site to visit additional sites on the results list. ipl2 for Kids is best for ages 8–12. Older learners can use ipl2 for Teens, which is organized the same way. In addition to using keywords or searching by subject, Web readers can submit a question to a volunteer librarian and receive a well-researched answer within about a week.

instaGrok

instaGrok (*instagrok.com*) is a *visual research tool* that that allows students to organize projects, search concepts, and build multimodal maps around them. instaGrok is suitable for children grades 3 and up (ages 8+). It is useful for readers who don't have a lot of background knowledge about a topic, because they can instantly investigate related terms. instaGrok displays results in an interactive semantic map accompanied by key facts, annotated websites, videos, images, and even more concepts (Figure 6.5). There is a "difficulty" slider that adjusts the complexity of the results. The free version of insta-Grok, both online and as an app, allows users to search, curate, build their own concept maps, share notes and research journals, and take quizzes to check for understanding and practice key vocabulary. The subscription version offers additional capabilities; for example, it allows teachers to monitor student activities (searching, pinning, journaling, quizzes).

Blekko

Blekko (*blekko.com*) is a *search engine* that groups results by *category*. This tool is useful for eliminating sponsored ads. Blekko is best for children in middle school and older (ages 10+). As with all search engines that are designed for adults, students should be taught to include the word <kids> in their keyword search in order to filter out difficult content and, in many cases, ads. A search for <global warming kids> returns lists of sites grouped into three categories: top results, climate, and environment (Figure 6.6).

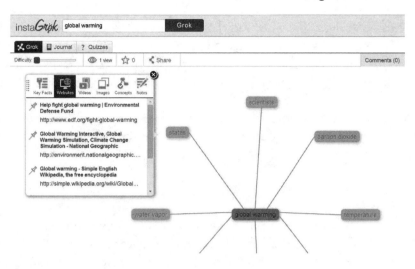

FIGURE 6.5. instaGrok search tool.

Experienced users can make use of Blekko's "slashtags" feature; for example, a search for global warming/edu-games returns sites with educational games related to global warming.

DuckDuckGo

DuckDuckGo (*duckduckgo.com*) is a *hybrid search engine* that is designed to maximize privacy and avoid the "filter bubble" of personalized search results (see Chapter 1). DuckDuckGo distinguishes itself from other search engines by not profiling its users and by showing all users the same search results for a given search term. It is useful for

FIGURE 6.6. Blekko search engine.

teachers of students ages 10+ who want high-quality results in a clutter-free interface. DuckDuckGo always lists one sponsored ad at the top of each search results list, which is far fewer than most search engines (Figure 6.7). As with Blekko, students should include the keyword <kids> to reduce sponsored ads and limit results to kid-friendly sites. If the reader wants to limit the results to a certain domain suffix, for instance, .org, he can add the qualifier <site:org>. DuckDuckGo does not return millions of hits, since it generates results from crowdsourced sites such as Wikipedia and from partnerships with other search engines such as Yahoo! and Bing.

Google

Google (*google.com*) is a *standard search engine*, so it is useful when readers already have strong background knowledge of the information they want to find. If the SafeSearch feature is activated and the word <kids> is added to the search query, Google is appropriate for students ages 10+. Students can conduct separate searches for web, news, video, image, shopping, maps, flights, books, and apps. Like DuckDuckGo, students can add the <site: qualifier> to limit results to certain domain suffixes such as .gov or .edu. Google uses popularity ranking to prioritize sites that are frequently linked and that other people have chosen to visit. A general search for global warming in Google yields almost 64 million websites with sponsored links listed at the top. A search for <global warming kids site:org> removes the ads, limits the search to .orgs, and reduces the number of hits to 900,000 (Figure 6.8). Google provides easy-to-digest videos and infographics entitled "How Search Works" to explain the complexities of online searching.

Bing

Bing (*bing.com*), an acronym for "Because It's Not Google," is a *standard search engine*. It is the default search tool on many Microsoft-driven devices. Like Google, this search

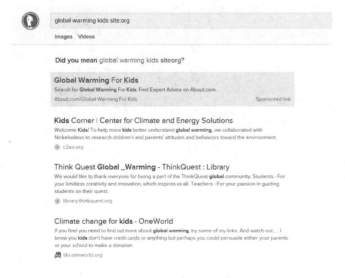

FIGURE 6.7. DuckDuckGo search engine.

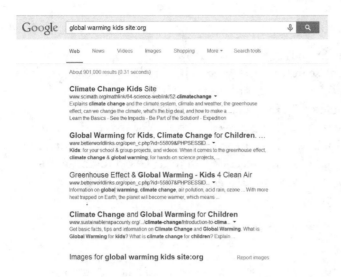

FIGURE 6.8. Google search engine.

engine is appropriate for students ages 10+. A general search for global warming in Bing yields about 17 million websites, including related searches. A search for <global warming kids site:edu> removes the ads, limits the search to .edu sites, and reduces the number of hits to about 200,000 (Figure 6.9). This is still an enormous number of results in comparison to a closed database such as KidsClick, which returned two sites using the broad query <global warming>. Such a large number of search results may have one of two effects on learners. Some feel totally overwhelmed and incapable of making the navigational decisions needed to narrow this huge amount of information. Other students consider a high number of results an affirmation of their search prowess because they can find so many websites. Either way, searchers on the open Web need keyword strategies for narrowing their search to make information retrieval more manageable (discussed next).

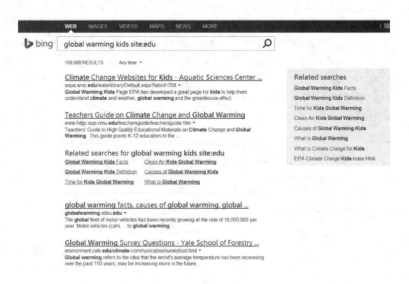

FIGURE 6.9. Bing search engine.

Selecting Keywords

As noted throughout this text, research has repeatedly shown that people of all ages are often inefficient and ineffective at searching the Web. The challenge of using today's search tools centers on keyword selection. According to extensive research conducted by Eagleton and Guinee (e.g., Eagleton & Guinee, 2002; Eagleton et al., 2003; Guinee, 2007; Guinee et al., 2003), children and young adolescents employ five basic strategies for constructing keywords: (1) single words; (2) topic + focus; (3) multiple words; (4) phrases; and (5) questions. For simplicity, we present them in three overarching categories: too broad, just right, and too wordy, similar to gauging the appropriate scope for a topic or a research question (Chapter 5).

Too Broad

The most prevalent keyword strategy we've observed in classrooms is the submission of a single word, usually a research topic, to a search engine. When asked about searching procedures, numerous students report that all you have to do is "type in the topic word that you're searching for." Typical examples of the main-topic approach are volcano, penguins, and Arnold Schwarzenegger. Worse, some children approach keywords from the theme level, using highly inefficient keywords such as animals and states. Still worse, some students use such broad search terms that there is no possibility of success—for example, stuff, free, and info. Although typing in a single keyword can be an effective approach when a student has weak prior knowledge about his topic and needs to learn more before continuing, it is not efficient when searching for something specific.

Just Right

There is research to support the topic focus or topic + focus strategy (Figure 6.10) for choosing keywords (Guinee et al., 2003; Harrison et al., 2014). Students who use this approach are able to locate target information more quickly because they've identified a specific focus area within a research topic. Examples of keywords using this method are bottled water controversy and Mia Hamm childhood. We strongly recommend that you use some of the Category Flowcharts from Chapter 5 to teach this keyword method (Handouts Q-5.5 to Q-5.7).

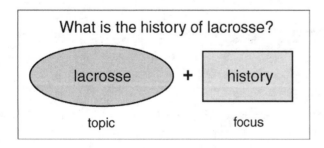

FIGURE 6.10. Topic + focus keyword strategy.

An extension of the topic focus method is to use more than two discrete terms when searching, which we call "multiple keywords." There are times when two keywords are insufficient to narrow the number of search results from a search engine. When searching for something very specific, such as "Who were the first African Americans to win the Nobel Prize for literature?" students must enter at least three sets of keywords "African American" "Nobel Prize" literature to find the answers. Students who neglect to include the keyword literature will incorrectly identify Nobel Peace Prize winner Ralph Bunche rather than writer Toni Morrison. One of our favorite examples of a multiple keyword search is president stuck bathtub, which takes the user straight to amusing websites that recount how a portly U.S. president got stuck in his bathtub on his inauguration day. We share instructional materials for teaching the topic focus and multiple keyword strategies later in this chapter.

Too Wordy

Many Web readers use natural language phrases and complete sentences for keyword searching. Search engines are continually improving their algorithms to predict which words to keep or eliminate in a search query, but computers cannot (yet!) read our minds. The natural language keyword strategy is not always effective because potentially useful websites will not show up if those exact words in that exact order did not appear on any websites. Examples of phrases we've seen students use are pros and cons of being an artist and types of wrestling moves.

An effective approach is to teach students when the use of natural language phrases is more likely to provide useful results. Natural language phrasing is a fine choice for finding specific information; for example, artist Monet's birthdate, because it's a narrow question with a single answer. When making a query that compares and contrasts information or pulls together various ideas, search engines cannot do this efficiently on their own. In other words, a search engine cannot think for us. It can't make value judgments or summarize seemingly unrelated information. For higher level questions, which is where we want our students to be thinking much of the time, search engine results are only as good as the input provided by the user.

> Some students had difficulties in formulating effective queries and some in selecting relevant Web pages from their search results. The inability to predict the relevance of Web pages has an effect on the number of Web pages first selected and then rejected as irrelevant.
> —Kiili, Laurinen, and Marttunen (2008, p. 84)

Another common keyword strategy is to submit an entire question to a search engine; for example, Why do platypuses have beaks and do they lay eggs?. Although such a broad question will certainly yield results in a search engine such as Google, sorting through the massive number of results and pulling out information to answer this two-part question can be a daunting task. Students who habitually use the question keyword strategy are in need of instruction and guidance, because they do not understand how standard search engines function, and they are wasting time typing unnecessary keywords. Until the semantic Web realizes its full potential, it is best to teach students to get in the habit of using the topic focus strategy.

Power Searching

Some search engines and databases have links for Advanced Search or Help, which provide a variety of methods for refining a search (e.g., reading level, language, year, images, videos). If there isn't an Advanced Search feature, savvy online searchers try Boolean operators. Boolean operators are punctuation marks that are used by some search tools to refine a search. The most common operator is the plus sign (+), which means (AND). Google automatically assumes the plus sign, so if you enter African killer bee into Google, it locates web pages that have the words African AND killer AND bee. In this example, the three words would not necessarily be adjacent to each other on all of the websites returned by Google. If you want a search engine to use your exact words (not synonyms or related words) and to keep your keywords together, you must surround your keywords with quotation marks; for example, "Africanized killer bee" or "State of the Union address".

Sometimes it is helpful to include the minus sign, –, or the word NOT in your keyword string. This tells the search engine to omit web pages that contain an undesirable word. For example, a fifth-grade student who was doing research on Hawaii's climate kept getting advertisements for resorts. She used the keyword combination Hawaii + climate –resort to eliminate all the resort sites from the search results list. If she had wanted to filter out all .coms from the results, she could have used Hawaii + climate –.com. Like search engines, library databases are becoming more flexible with natural language queries, but many still rely on Boolean operators. Some online library databases offer a drop-down menu for selecting Boolean operators, providing a scaffold for the search process.

Another power search strategy is to use a colon (:) to narrow results. Maya's daughter (11 years old) was searching for online information on global warming. She became frustrated because her teacher had told the class to avoid .com sites and only use .orgs and .nets. In less than 10 seconds, Maya taught her daughter to add site:org to her search terms: <global warming debate site:org>. In this way the entire list of search results would be limited to .orgs that address the debate about global warming. Recently, Maya used <filetype:pdf> in her own web searching in order to limit results to print-ready research articles in .pdf format.

> With such an abundance of information, however, it is not only difficult to find what you are looking for, but it is also of paramount importance that you know precisely what you are looking for.
> —Kuiper and Volman (2008, p. 246)

All of these examples illustrate that many students (and teachers!) benefit from instruction in Web search strategies. The upcoming activities will help your students gain a better understanding of how to make effective use of online resources.

How Do We Teach Strategies for Understanding Resources?

If you haven't administered any of the assessments presented in Chapter 4, we recommend that you do so first. Then start with one of the preassessments discussed later before moving into an instructional unit. Do not attempt to teach strategies for everything at once; rather, choose one and scaffold the rest. Frequently remind the students that the emphasis of instruction is the U part of the QUEST and that the strategies they learn during these inquiries are highly transferable to other school subjects and to life in general. Our aim is to teach students to be as resourceful as possible, and these days that necessitates a strong working knowledge of search tools and keywords.

Search Tools

To expose your students to various search tools, you may wish to use the Search Tool Comparison—Elementary Level (Handout U-6.1) or the Search Tool Comparison— Middle Level (Handout U-6.2) individually, in pairs, in small groups, or as a class. Afterward, they should be ready to conduct some mini-inquiries on topics of their choosing. Have them keep track of the search tools they use so that they become more metacognitive about their own searching habits. Throughout the inquiry project, have the students keep Reflection Logs and regularly share their search engine strategies with each other.

Keywords

Keyword selection is a linchpin to successful reading and learning on the open Web. If you can't *find* any relevant information, you certainly can't *read* it. After having carried out numerous keyword units with students in grades 3 and up, we feel strongly that this is an area that deserves attention in school every year across content areas. We have done 6-week units focused just on keywords alone. During keyword units, we heavily scaffold all the other aspects of the QUEST process so that students can concentrate on keywords. As an added bonus, focusing on keywords will also stimulate and reinforce students' spelling and vocabulary skills.

One way to quickly assess your students' keyword knowledge is to use the Keywords Assessment (Handout U-6.3) and the accompanying Keywords Scoring Guide (Handout U-6.4). For additional practice, you can use the Keywords Practice 1 (Handout U-6.5) with the Keyword Practice 1 Answers (Handout U-6.6) and the Keywords Practice 2 (Handout U-6.7) with the Keyword Practice 2 Answers (Handout U-6.8). These are not only excellent diagnostic assessment instruments for you but also fabulous teaching tools when used for class discussion and reflection afterward.

A quick method for assessing Web search strategies is Internet scavenger hunts. We have used the Scavenger Hunt Assessments (Handouts U-6.9 and U-6.10) as individual pre- and posttests, as well as a competition between pairs. It's fun for the kids and provides great information for your instruction. While racing to find the answers, students must record their keyword combinations and the URL at which they found the answer. This is analogous to "showing your work" on a math question, because we're more interested in the process than in the answer. Be aware that search engines sometimes display the answer on the results list, so students might find the

> **Young people have a poor understanding of their information needs and thus find it difficult to develop effective search strategies.**
> —Rowlands and Nichols (2008, p. 12)

answer without even visiting a website. We always insist that they visit a website instead of trusting the first thing they see in a search engine results list. As always, save time for a group strategy discussion and/or Reflection Log entry at the end of the activity.

If you find that some of your students need guidance in focused keyword selection, you can assign additional scavenger hunts to be used with individuals or pairs, such as the Literal Scavenger Hunt (Handout U-6.11), the Substitution Scavenger Hunt (Handout U-6.12), and the Double Focus Area Scavenger Hunt (Handout U-6.13). Answers to all the Scavenger Hunts are found in Handout U-6.14, Scavenger Hunt Answers. Note that the layout of these Scavenger Hunts may seem visually unfamiliar if you haven't introduced the Category Flowcharts (Handouts Q-5.6 to Q-5.8) from Chapter 5.

Please note that we are not suggesting that topic focus is the only effective keyword strategy. It's just that we want to ensure that every student has at least *one* reliable keyword method in his inquiry strategy toolbox. After instruction and practice in keyword selection, most students will notice a dramatic change in their speed and accuracy and will be very pleased with themselves. We have fond memories of students who have rushed home to share the topic focus strategy with their family members, thus assuming the "mantle of the expert" that is so desirable in constructivist education. In fact, most of the teachers with whom we've worked have bemoaned that it has taken this long for someone to help *them* learn how to search effectively.

After keyword assessment and instruction, students are eager to try their own inquiry projects. Be sure to reiterate the *important point* that a scavenger hunt is qualitatively different from an inquiry project. The former is a quick search for a specific piece of information, whereas the latter is much more involved, requiring the synthesis of ideas and information from a variety of resources. We recommend that you use some of the project planning materials in Chapter 5 to scaffold students' inquiries, especially Handout Q-5.13, the Project Planning Template. Have them keep track of the search engines and keywords they use so that they become metacognitive about their search habits. Throughout the inquiry project, have the students keep daily Reflection Logs and take time to share everyone's strategies regularly.

 Library Media Standard: **Evaluate own ability to select resources that are engaging and appropriate for personal interests and needs.**

At the end of each of the QUEST chapters in this text, we supply a lesson plan that you can adapt for use in your classroom. In this chapter, we offer the Search Engine Lesson Plan—Elementary Level (Handout U-6.15) and the Search Engine Lesson Plan—Middle Level (Handout U-6.16).

SUMMARY ●

This chapter on Understanding Resources focused on strategies for identifying resources, managing devices, utilizing the Internet, choosing search tools, selecting keywords, and power searching. Researchers have repeatedly found that many people, even adults, have difficulty searching for information on the Web; therefore, these skills must be taught, practiced, and reinforced. Because computer teachers and media specialists do not have sustained time with students, classroom teachers need to help students develop strategies for Understanding Resources.

In Chapter 7, Evaluating, we present strategies for determining the "usefulness" and "truthfulness" of information found on the Web. Not only do students need to be able to determine whether a website is worth visiting when viewing the search engine results, but also, once they are there, they must decide whether the website actually contains the desired information. Further, they must determine whether the information is reliable.

Handouts

The following chart lists the assessment tools, activities, and handouts that were discussed in this chapter on Understanding Resources. Feel free to modify any of these tools, especially if some have become outdated. As with the handouts in all other chapters, do not attempt to use all of them in one lesson or unit. Decide which seem most useful for your students, and save the rest for another time.

Number	Name of handout	Purpose
U-6.1	Search Tool Comparison—Elementary Level	Compare search tools
U-6.2	Search Tool Comparison—Middle Level	Compare search tools
U-6.3	Keywords Assessment	Assess keyword knowledge
U-6.4	Keywords Scoring Guide	Score keyword knowledge
U-6.5	Keywords Practice 1	Assess keyword knowledge
U-6.6	Keywords Practice 1 Answers	Score keyword knowledge
U-6.7	Keywords Practice 2	Assess keyword knowledge
U-6.8	Keywords Practice 2 Answers	Score keyword knowledge
U-6.9	Scavenger Hunt Assessment—Pretest	Assess keyword strategies
U-6.10	Scavenger Hunt Assessment—Posttest	Assess keyword strategies
U-6.11	Literal Scavenger Hunt	Practice keyword strategies
U-6.12	Substitution Scavenger Hunt	Practice keyword strategies
U-6.13	Double Focus Area Scavenger Hunt	Practice keyword strategies
U-6.14	Scavenger Hunt Answers	Score keyword strategies
U-6.15	Search Tool Lesson Plan—Elementary Level	Model search strategies
U-6.16	Search Tool Lesson Plan—Middle Level	Model search strategies

HANDOUT U-6.1. Search Tool Comparison—Elementary Level

Name _____ Class _____ Date _____

Directions: *You are using the Web to find out the most popular cat breed in the world. See what happens in each of these search tools **before** you go to a website for the answer.*

Go to KidRex @ *kidrex.org*

1. Try a broad search for the word **cat.** How many results did you get? _____

2. Try the keywords: **popular cat breed.** How many results did you get? _____

Go to KidsClick @ *kidsclick.org*

3. Go to the letter "C" in the alphabet and choose **cats** (pets). How many results did you get? _____
   _____

4. Go back and try a broad search for the word **cat.** How many results did you get? _____

5. Try the keywords: **popular cat breed.** How many results did you get? _____

Go to instaGrok @ *instaGrok.com*

6. Try the keywords: **popular cat breed.** Find the word **breed** and choose it. What words appear? ___
   _____

7. Move the difficulty slider down and then up. What do you notice? _____
   _____

8. Find the pop-up box that shows Key Facts and Websites. What else does it show? _____
   _____

AND NOW FOR THE ANSWER!

9. What is the most popular cat breed in the world? _____
   _____

10. What search tool did you use to find this info? _____
    _____

11. What keywords did you use to find this info? _____
    _____

12. Which website had the info?   *http://* _____
    _____

HANDOUT U-6.2. Search Tool Comparison—Middle Level

Name _____ Class _____ Date _____

Directions: *You are using the Web to find the most popular cat breed in the world. See what happens in each of these search tools **before** you go to a website for the answer.*

Go to Google @ *google.com*
1. Try a broad search for the word **cat.** How many results did you get? _____
2. Try the keywords: **popular cat breed.** What do you notice? _____

_____

Go to Blekko @ blekko.com
3. Try a broad search for the word **cat.** What categories appear? _____

_____

4. Try the keywords: **popular cat breed.** What do you notice? _____

_____

Go to instaGrok @ *instaGrok.com*
5. Try the keywords: **popular cat breed.** Find the word **breed** and choose it. What words appear?

_____

6. Move the difficulty slider down and then up. What do you notice? _____
7. Find the pop-up box that shows Key Facts and Websites. What else does it show? _____

_____

Go to DuckDuckGo @ *duckduckgo.com*
8. Try a broad search for the word **cat.** What do you notice? _____

_____

9. Try the keywords: **popular cat breed.** What changed? _____

Go to Bing @ *bing.com*
10. Try a broad search for the word **cat.** How many results did you get? _____
11. Try the keywords: **popular cat breed.** What do you notice? _____

_____

AND NOW FOR THE ANSWER!
12. What is the most popular cat breed in the world? _____
13. What search tool did you use to find this info? _____
14. What keywords did you use to find this info? _____
15. Which website had the info? *http://* _____

HANDOUT U-6.3. Keywords Assessment

Name _____ Class _____ Date _____

Score:
/16
%

Directions: *Decide whether these keywords would be effective in a search engine like Google.*
Circle your answer and explain why, using the reasons below. The first two are done for you.

- **Strong** keywords have a topic and a focus.
- **Weak** keywords have no topic, no focus, no topic or focus, or extra words

soccer + history	**strong**	topic and focus
sports	**weak**	No topic or focus
1. What is the history of soccer?	strong weak	
2. soccer + equipment	strong weak	
3. world history of soccer	strong weak	
4. "soccer tournaments"	strong weak	
5. soccer	strong weak	
6. soccer history	strong weak	
7. soccer + sports	strong weak	
8. soccer balls and nets	strong weak	

HANDOUT U-6.4. Keywords Scoring

Give 1 point for the correct answer and 1 point for the reason. Total possible is 16 points.

soccer + history	**strong**	topic and focus
sports	**weak**	no topic or focus
1. What is the history of soccer?	strong (weak)	extra words
2. soccer + equipment	(strong) weak	topic + focus
3. world history of soccer	strong (weak)	extra words
4. "soccer tournaments"	(strong) weak	"topic focus"
5. soccer	strong (weak)	no focus
6. soccer history	(strong) weak	topic focus
7. soccer + sports	strong (weak)	no focus
8. soccer balls and nets	strong (weak)	extra words

HANDOUT U-6.5. Keywords Practice 1

Name _____ Class _____ Date _____

Directions: *Decide whether these keywords would be effective in a search engine like Google. Circle your answer and explain why, using the reasons below.*

- **Strong** keywords have a topic and a focus.
- **Weak** keywords have no topic, no focus, no topic or focus, or extra words

1. tigers	strong weak	
2. tiger + habitat	strong weak	
3. What is the tiger's habitat?	strong weak	
4. tiger + animal	strong weak	
5. tigers around the world	strong weak	
6. "tiger habitat"	strong weak	
7. animals	strong weak	
8. tiger prey and diet	strong weak	
9. tiger + prey	strong weak	
10. tiger diet	strong weak	

HANDOUT U-6.6. Keywords Practice 1 Answers

- **Strong** keywords have a topic and a focus.
- **Weak** keywords have no topic, no focus, no topic or focus, or extra words

1. tigers	strong	(weak)	No focus
2. tiger + habitat	(strong)	weak	Topic and focus
3. What is the tiger's habitat?	strong	(weak)	Extra words
4. tiger + animal	(strong)	weak	Topic and focus
5. tigers around the world	strong	(weak)	No focus
6. "tiger habitat"	(strong)	weak	Topic and focus
7. animals	strong	(weak)	No topic or focus
8. tiger prey and diet	strong	(weak)	Extra words
9. tiger + prey	(strong)	weak	Topic and focus
10. tiger diet	(strong)	weak	Topic and focus

HANDOUT U-6.7. Keywords Practice 2

Name _____ Class _____ Date _____

Directions: *Decide whether these keywords would be effective in a search engine like Google.*

Circle your answer and explain why, using the reasons below.
- **Strong** keywords have a topic and a focus.
- **Weak** keywords have no topic, no focus, no topic or focus, or extra words.

1. "Ben Franklin"   strong   weak

2. "Ben Franklin" + invention   strong   weak

3. inventors   strong   weak

4. "Ben Franklin" invent   strong   weak

5. Famous inventions of Ben Franklin's   strong   weak

6. "Ben Franklin" + career   strong   weak

7. Ben Franklin's career and inventions   strong   weak

8. inventions + career   strong   weak

9. What did "Ben Franklin" invent   strong   weak

10. "Ben Franklin" + "famous invention"   strong   weak

HANDOUT U-6.8. Keywords Practice 2 Answers

Strong keywords have a topic and a focus.
Weak keywords have no topic, no focus, no topic or focus, or extra words.

1. "Ben Franklin"	strong (weak)	No focus
2. "Ben Franklin" + invention	(strong) weak	Topic and focus
3. inventors	strong (weak)	No topic or focus
4. "Ben Franklin" invent	(strong) weak	Topic and focus
5. Famous inventions of Ben Franklin's	strong (weak)	Extra words
6. "Ben Franklin" + career	(strong) weak	Topic and focus
7. Ben Franklin's career and inventions	strong (weak)	Extra words
8. inventions + career	strong (weak)	No topic
9. What did "Ben Franklin" invent?	strong (weak)	Extra words
10. "Ben Franklin" + "famous invention"	(strong) weak	Topic and focus

HANDOUT U-6.9. Scavenger Hunt Assessment—Pretest

Name _____ Class _____ Date _____

Directions:

1. *Open an Internet browser (such as Safari or Firefox)*
2. *Go to a search tool (such as www.google.com or www.bing.com)*
3. *Find answers to the following three questions, noting how and where you found the information. Even if you find the answer on a search results list, you must visit a website and write down the URL where you found the answer.*
4. *You have 10 minutes to complete each search. Your instructor will tell you when to move on to the next question.*

What is the capital of Spain?

Answer _____

Search Tool(s): _____

Keyword(s): _____

URL: *http://* _____

Where is Mount Rushmore?

Answer _____

Search Tool(s): _____

Keyword(s): _____

URL: *http://* _____

Which American president got stuck in a bathtub?

Answer _____

Search Tool(s): _____

Keyword(s): _____

URL: *http://* _____

HANDOUT U-6.10. Scavenger Hunt Assessment—Posttest

Name _____ Class _____ Date _____

Directions:

1. *Open an Internet browser (such as Safari or Firefox)*
2. *Go to a search tool (such as www.google.com or www.bing.com)*
3. *Find answers to the following three questions, noting how and where you found the information. Even if you find the answer on a search results list, you must visit a website and write down the URL where you found the answer.*
4. *You have 10 minutes to complete each search. Your instructor will tell you when to move on to the next question.*

What is the capital of Denmark?

Answer _____

Search Tool(s): _____

Keyword(s): _____

URL: *http://* _____

Where is the Wright Brothers Monument?

Answer _____

Search Tool(s): _____

Keyword(s): _____

URL: *http://* _____

Who was the shortest American president?

Answer _____

Search Tool(s): _____

Keyword(s): _____

URL: *http://* _____

QUEST

HANDOUT U-6.11. Literal Scavenger Hunt

Name _____ Class _____ Date _____

Directions: *Determine the topic and focus, then use them as keywords for searching.*

Question 1: Who was the inventor of basketball?

topic   +   focus

Answer _____
Search Tool(s): _____
URL: _____

EXTRA: In what year? _____

Question 2: How many directors did *Shrek I* have?

topic   +   focus

Answer _____
Search Tool(s): _____
URL: _____

EXTRA: Name them. _____

Question 3: In which country is Mount Everest?

topic   +   focus

Answer _____
Search Tool(s): _____
URL: _____

EXTRA: How tall is Mount Everest? _____

HANDOUT U-6.12. Substitution Scavenger Hunt

Name _____ Class _____ Date _____

Directions: *Determine the topic and focus, then use them as keywords for searching.*

Question 1: Where do marine iguanas live?

topic ⬭ **+** focus ▭

Answer _____
Search Tool(s): _____
URL: _____

EXTRA: What other animals are unique to this area? _____

Question 2: Who played Chewbacca in the original *Star Wars* movies?

topic ⬭ **+** focus ▭

Answer _____
Search Tool(s): _____
URL: _____

EXTRA: How tall is he? _____

Question 3: When was Kingt Tut's tomb found?

topic ⬭ **+** focus ▭

Answer _____
Search Tool(s): _____
URL: _____

EXTRA: Who found it? _____

HANDOUT U-6.13. Double Focus Area Scavenger Hunt

Name _____ Class _____ Date _____

Directions: *Determine the topic and focus, then use them as keywords for searching.*

Question 1: Where is the Country Music Hall of Fame?

topic + focus + focus

Answer _____

Search Tool(s): _____

URL: _____

EXTRA: What other tourist spots are here? _____

_____

Question 2: When did women gain the right to vote in America?

topic + focus + focus

Answer _____

Search Tool(s): _____

URL: _____

EXTRA: What were these female activists called? ____

_____

Question 3: Who was the first African American to win the Nobel Prize for Literature?

topic + focus + focus

Answer _____

Search Tool(s): _____

URL: _____

EXTRA: Name one book written by this author. _____

HANDOUT U-6.14. Scavenger Hunt Answers

Scavenger Hunt Pretest (Handout U-6.9)

QUESTION	KEYWORDS	ANSWER	TYPE OF QUERY
What is the capital of Spain?	Spain + capital	Madrid	keywords in question
Where is Mount Rushmore?	Mount Rushmore + location	South Dakota	one substitution needed
Which American president got stuck in a bathtub?	president + stuck + bathtub	William Taft	three keywords

Scavenger Hunt Posttest (Handout U-6.10)

QUESTION	KEYWORDS	ANSWER	TYPE OF QUERY
What is the capital of Denmark?	Denmark + capital	Copenhagen	keywords in question
Where is the Wright Brothers Monument?	Wright Brothers Monument + location	North Carolina	one substitution needed
Who was the shortest American president?	American + president + shortest	James Madison	three keywords

Literal Scavenger Hunt (Handout U-6.11)

QUESTION	KEYWORDS	ANSWER	EXTRA
Who was the inventor of basketball?	basketball + inventor	James Naismith	1891
How many directors did *Shrek I* have?	Shrek I + directors	2	Andrew Adamson & Vicky Jenson
In which country is Mount Everest?	Mount Everest + country	Nepal	29,035 ft. (8,850 m)

Substitution Scavenger Hunt (Handout U-6.12)

QUESTION	KEYWORDS	ANSWER	EXTRA
Where do marine iguanas live?	marine iguana + location	Galápagos Islands	Galápagos giant tortoise
Who played Chewbacca in the original *Star Wars* movies?	Chewbacca + actor	Peter Mayhew	7 feet 3 inches
When was King Tut's tomb found?	King Tut's tomb + year	1922	Howard Carter

Double Focus Area Scavenger Hunt (Handout U-6.13)

QUESTION	KEYWORDS	ANSWER	EXTRA
Where is the Country Music Hall of Fame?	Hall of Fame + Country Music + location	Nashville, Tennessee	Opryland Hotel
When did women gain the right to vote in America?	women + vote + year	1920	suffragists
Who was the first African American to win the Nobel Prize for Literature?	Nobel Prize + literature + African American	Toni Morrison	*Beloved*

HANDOUT U-6.15. Search Tool Lesson Plan—Elementary Level

Objective

Students will demonstrate the ability to distinguish between ineffective and effective search strategies and will compare the features of two popular search tools.

Time

One or two class periods

Materials

1. QUEST Inquiry Model (Handout P-4.11)
2. Teaching computer and projector
3. Internet computers for students (OK for students to share)
4. Timer or clock
5. Search Tool Comparison (Handout U-6.1) on paper or on the computers

Assessment Options

1. Technology Survey (Handout P-4.7)
2. Internet Vocabulary (Handout P-4.9)

Introduction

1. Tell students you will be teaching them a strategy for searching the Web that many other students have found useful. Contextualize the lesson, using the QUEST Inquiry Model (Handout P-4.11), by pointing out that they are in the **U** phase of the QUEST, which includes using strong search strategies.
2. Have students brainstorm why Web searching is useful in this class, in other classes, and outside of school. This can be done in pairs, in small groups, or as a whole class.
3. Generate excitement and get student buy-in on the purpose of the lesson before proceeding. Tell them that strong search strategies will help them find information faster on the Web.

Modeling

1. Tell the students to imagine that you're doing a research project on cats.
2. Show students what happens when you use the "dot-com" approach by typing *www.cat.com* straight into the URL field instead of using a search tool.
3. Ask the class, "Did we find the info we wanted?" Remark that the "dot-com" strategy is rarely useful for searching. It is only useful for finding known websites.
4. Solicit student suggestions for websites that might have info on cats (Petco, Discovery, etc.). This is the "shopping mall" approach.
5. Before trying any of these sites, say that what you really want to learn is about the types of *cat breeds*.
6. Use a timer or clock to see how long it takes to find info on cat breeds by going straight to some of these commercial sites. Talk out loud as you and the class try to find the info. Stop after 10 minutes.

(continued)

7. Now do a KidsClick (www.kidsclick.org) search for <cat breed> and note the smaller choices of websites, as compared to the shopping mall and dot-com strategies. Read the descriptions for each result and note the close connection to your search for information about cat breeds. Although there are fewer choices, these results are a closer match to the information you are seeking.

8. Finally, show your students the differences between:
   a. intentionally going to a search tool (such as KidsClick),
   b. clicking on the search button on a browser (which typically brings up a default search engine such as Bing), and
   c. searching within a website that has an embedded search tool (a good example is *pbskids.org/go*, which has its own search tool).

Practice

1. Pass out the Search Tool Comparison (Handout U-6.1) or have students bring it up on their computers.
2. Have students work individually, in pairs, or in small groups at the computer.
3. Circulate to observe and offer support.

Scaffolding

1. For anyone with visual disabilities:
   a. Increase the font size in the Web browser (View > Text Size > Largest), or
   b. Make the print larger on the handout.
2. Provide a scribe for weak writers.
3. Provide a typist for weak keyboarders.
4. Pair up weaker readers with stronger readers for decoding.
5. Allow more time for slower workers.

Feedback

1. Have students gather as a whole class to debrief.
2. Discuss the differences between the search tools.
3. Share answers to the "popular cat breed" question.
4. Share any additional observations, opinions, or questions.

Ticket Out the Door

Have each student name two popular search tools for children (i.e., KidRex, KidsClick).

HANDOUT U-6.16. Search Tool Lesson Plan—Middle Level

Objective

Students will demonstrate the ability to distinguish between ineffective and effective search strategies and will compare the features of four popular search tools.

Time

One or two class periods

Materials

1. QUEST Inquiry Model (Handout P-4.11)
2. Teaching computer and projector
3. Internet computers for students (OK for students to share)
4. Timer or clock
5. Search Tool Comparison (Handout U-6.2) on paper or on the computers

Assessment Options

1. Computer Survey (Handout P-4.7)
2. Internet Vocabulary (Handout P-4.9)

Introduction

1. Tell students you will be teaching them a transferable strategy for searching the Web that many other students have found useful. Contextualize the lesson, using the QUEST Inquiry Model (Handout P-4.11), by pointing out that they are in the **U** phase of the QUEST, which includes using good search strategies.
2. Have students brainstorm why Web searching is useful in this class, in other classes, and outside of school. This can be done in pairs, in small groups, or as a whole class.
3. Generate excitement and get student buy-in on the purpose of the lesson before proceeding. Tell them that strong search strategies will help them find information faster on the Web.

Modeling

1. Tell the students you're doing a mock research project on cats.
2. Show students what happens when you use the "dot-com" approach by typing *www.cat.com* straight into the URL field instead of using a search tool.
3. Ask the class, "Did we find the info we wanted?" Remark that the "dot-com" strategy is rarely useful for searching. It is only useful for finding known websites.
4. Solicit student suggestions for websites that might have info on cats (petco, discovery, etc.). This is the "shopping mall" approach.
5. Before trying any of these sites, say that what you really want to learn is about the types of *cat breeds*.
6. Use a timer or clock to see how long it takes to find info on cat breeds by going straight to some of these commercial sites. Talk out loud as you and the class try to find the info. Stop after 10 minutes.

(continued)

---

7. Now do a Google search for <cat breed>, and have everyone note the improvement in speed, as compared to the shopping mall and dot-com strategies. You will probably find a perfect website on the first hit and find the cat breed information in less than a minute.
8. Finally, show your students the differences between:
   a. Intentionally going to a search tool (such as Google),
   b. Clicking on the search button on a browser (which typically brings up a default search engine such as Bing), and
   c. Searching within a website that has an embedded search tool (a good example is *www.nasa.gov*, which has a prominent search box).

Practice

1. Pass out the Search Tool Comparison (Handout U-6.2), or have students bring it up on their computers.
2. Have students work individually, in pairs, or in small groups at the computer.
3. Circulate to observe and offer support.

Scaffolding

1. If someone is overwhelmed by all the text on the handout, increase the line spacing and print it back to back.
2. For anyone with visual disabilities:
   a. Increase the font size in the Web browser (View > Text Size > Largest), or
   b. Make the print larger on the handout.
3. Provide a scribe for weak writers.
4. Provide a typist for weak keyboarders.
5. Pair up weaker readers with stronger readers for decoding.
6. Allow more time for slower workers.

Feedback

1. Have students gather as a whole class to debrief.
2. Discuss the differences between the search tools.
3. Share answers to the "popular cat breed" question.
4. Share any additional observations, opinions, or questions.

Ticket Out the Door

Have each student name three popular search tools. (i.e., Google, Yahoo, Bing).

(7) Evaluating

KEY IDEAS

- Evaluation of information is important in order for citizens to make informed choices as they participate in democracy.

- The guiding questions for this chapter are, "Is this information useful?" and "Is this information true?"

- Evaluating websites is challenging because anyone is free to publish anything on the Internet.

- Clues about the quality of information can be found in the web address (URL) and on the website once an Internet reader knows what to look for and what is meant only as a distraction.

- Comparing and contrasting information found on various websites is an effective way to validate information and develop critical literacy skills.

The key to harnessing and exploiting the internet now is to spot the fakes: to know how to tell the truth from lies, and how to negotiate the grey areas of comment, opinion and propaganda in between.

—Bartlett and Miller (2011, p. 12)

In this chapter, we focus on the skill of evaluating ideas and information, especially those found on the Web. This third—and ongoing—phase of the iterative QUEST Internet inquiry process involves making decisions about whether information is important, useful, and truthful. Critical evaluation must be taught and practiced because it plays a crucial role in all of the information we receive through reading, listening, and viewing. "Without explicit training, many students become confused and overwhelmed when asked to judge the accuracy, reliability, and bias of information they encounter in online reading environments" (Leu et al., 2013, p. 1165).

Why Is It Important to Evaluate?

Evaluation facilitates the separation of the wheat from the chaff, the important from the unimportant, and the useful from the useless. If, as learners, we gave every bit of information we encountered equal consideration, we would drown in a sea of thoughts and ideas. Evaluation helps us to prioritize our time, energy, and money as we strive to make the most informed decision possible when seeking the value or judging the worth of an object or idea. This skill is critical in a society in which citizens are expected to make informed choices as they participate in decision-making processes. So one of our goals as educators is preparing students to find, evaluate, and use quality information in an efficient manner. We must teach students to think critically about what they see and hear and to ask questions of themselves and others as they seek to validate new ideas.

Such a lofty goal is made even more challenging when students are finding, evaluating, and using information from the Web. The novelty of technology and the captivation of multimedia graphics have created an expectation that an answer to every question can be instantaneously located on the Web. Information on the Web looks authentic through what appear to be official publications of everything from rumors to facts, with the boundaries between the two blurred. Traditional indicators of credibility, such as author and publishing information, are often difficult to ascertain. Determining the importance of ideas can become a complex task when information is gathered from the integration of different media—text, graphics, sound, video, animation—and the learner must determine what is useful and what is meant to distract.

Critical literacy skills entail the analysis of written, spoken, visual, and multimedia texts (Hobbs, 2011). Now, more than ever, learners of all ages must be able to analyze the ways politics, economics, and social beliefs and practices influence information (Fabos, 2008). For students, this means becoming critical consumers of information by comparing and contrasting facts and ideas found on websites, *Math Standard:* **Construct viable arguments and critique the reasoning of others.**

blogs, newsfeeds, videos, and other print and online sources. For teachers, this means an increased responsibility for teaching students how to recognize the degree of bias, how to balance information with other sources, and how information fits in a larger context—in other words, teaching students to consider everything they see, hear, and read on the Internet with a critical eye. This role of questioning information extends beyond the text and multimedia features of a website. Learners should question the Web as an information environment, considering who creates the information and for what purposes. The Web is a commercial and political entity, not an educational one, although the Web can be used in many educational ways. Because all information on the Web represents a person's, group's, business's, or institution's perspective, there is no purely unbiased information on the Web. Thus it becomes crucial for educators to help students recognize the characteristics of bias, to recognize various types and degrees of bias, and to compare and contrast information from multiple websites.

Critical literacy combines with other literacies "to develop a continually inquiring human mind," forcing us to "adopt a manner of continuous learning in order to function well in society" (Langford, 2001, p. 18). Critical literacy goes beyond just reading and viewing the Web to include interpreting meaning and assessing appropriateness, whether that information comes from media, print text, or Internet text. Critical literacy also goes beyond our classrooms to promote critical and creative thinking across content areas. "In a knowledge-based world, these critical skills will also impact positively on [students'] work and leisure lives" (Ladbrook & Probert, 2011, p. 118). Such deep thinking calls upon the skills of analysis, evaluation, and synthesis. Critical literacy is tightly woven throughout the inquiry process by empowering learners to be creative, critical, constructive users of information.

> **The online reader is unwilling to expend much cognitive energy on the task of critical evaluation of online information.**
>
> —Harrison, Dwyer, and Castek (2014, p. 128)

When Do We Evaluate?

Evaluation of information is already a part of our lives and the lives of our students. When we encounter new information, we compare the ideas with what we already know to determine whether there is a place to fit this new information into our current understanding. When we integrate information from most non-Web sources, such as print, television, movies, and video games, we know that the content has been vetted by others. Oftentimes, facts and visuals have been checked for authenticity. The reader is the last stop in the chain of authors, editors, and publishers, all of whom contribute layers of evaluation before the content reaches students' hands.

Critical evaluation was important before the advent of the Internet, but now it is absolutely crucial because much of what we find on the Web has not been vetted by experts. The Web reader is often the first stop in the evaluation chain because the Internet has no formal system of checks and balances for evaluating, labeling, or providing indications of appropriateness. As a result, "strategic readers [must] employ evaluative reading strategies during the entire process of searching for, locating, comprehending, and judging Internet information" (Afflerbach & Cho, 2010, p. 215).

Until recently, Web readers were completely on their own when evaluating information. Now, social participation on the Web has provided some support in the form of crowdsourcing. When people share their opinions by tagging blog entries, adding comments to news article discussions, or "liking" ideas on Facebook, the collaborative group helps the reader filter and evaluate information. Crowdsourcing can help, but it's not foolproof. Ultimately, the responsibility for evaluation of online information falls on the learner, which can be a daunting task for our students. Parents and educators share concerns about students encountering incorrect and/or inappropriate information on the Web, which is why we need to teach strategies for evaluation.

> **Users assess authority and trust for themselves in a matter of seconds by dipping and cross-checking across different sites and by relying on favoured brands (e.g. Google).**
> **—Rowlands and Nichols (2008, p. 10)**

Analyzing URLs

Evaluation happens before students even begin reading content on websites. Skilled Web readers evaluate the URLs, or web addresses, on the results list provided by a search tool. Students who analyze URLs are better able to predict the potential usefulness and truthfulness of websites (Walraven et al., 2009; Zhang, Duke, & Jimenez, 2011). A URL can be broken down into parts, as follows:

http://en.wikipedia.org/wiki/Semantic_web				
en	.wikipedia	.org	/wiki	/Semantic_web
language	host or domain	domain suffix	path or directory	file name or topic

Teaching learners to deconstruct URLs goes a long way toward helping them to get their search off on the right foot. Checking the descriptions in the search results reveals additional clues for determining whether the website will be useful and truthful. Figure 7.1 displays one choice listed in the search results for <solar system kids> using Google. The clues found on a search results list help to determine the relevance of the website, the host of the website, and the potential quality of the website.

1. *Title.* The website title can be useful in determining the content of the website; however, sometimes the title does not clearly reflect the topic of the website. Choosing this link will take the learner directly to the site.
2. *URL.* The web address shows that this website is hosted by National Geographic,

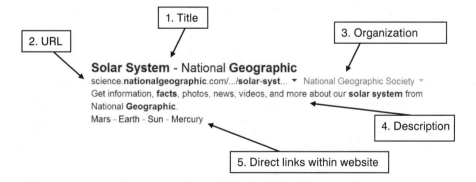

FIGURE 7.1. Clues in the search results list.

a well-known and respected organization. Notice that the domain name suffix in this case is *.com* (not *.edu* or *.gov*), so students must rely on prior knowledge and other clues regarding the reliability of this site.

3. *Organization.* Sometimes the name of the host is listed near the URL. Choosing this link causes a pop-up to appear that validates the reputability of the organization and whether it has received any awards. This is a reasonably strong predictor of reliability.

4. *Description.* A brief description of the types of information found on this website helps the learner to decide whether the website has the information sought. Because the descriptions are brief and often incomplete, important ideas might be left out.

5. *Direct links.* Sometimes there are links that will take the searcher directly to a page within the website that addresses that subtopic. This is helpful if the search was broad (as in this case) and the learner needs to narrow her focus.

Understanding the various parts of a search list entry gives the reader a wealth of knowledge about the type of information likely to be found on each site. For learners to make well-informed choices, they must take time to carefully read each link. Time spent at this early search step may prevent the learner from having to sift through mountains of information in order to answer a question or solve a problem. The search process requires the Internet reader to be an active participant by constantly making decisions about what to read and whether the material she has read meets her informational needs.

What Characterizes Evaluation?

When they are evaluating information, we want learners to be critical consumers by "questioning the validity and accuracy of all information" (American Association of School Librarians, 2007, p. 4) whether that information is found in print or on the Internet. Readers of all types of information must know how to determine the important ideas in what they read and view, discern the quality of the information, and recognize the creators' and their own biases. Within this complex process, Web readers must especially focus on determining the *usefulness* and the *truthfulness* of information (Figure 7.2).

FIGURE 7.2. Evaluating usefulness and truthfulness.

Evaluating Usefulness

In determining the *usefulness* of information, the Internet reader asks herself, "Does this information meet my needs and interests?" This question is the learner's guiding focus as she makes decisions about what to read, when to read, how fast to read, and when to stop reading. Decisions about the usefulness of information on the Internet are often made in a matter of seconds. As we have discussed, elementary and middle school learners often make hasty decisions about what to read on the Web, which causes them to either waste time on irrelevant information or to bypass useful sources of information. Teaching students the self-regulation skills to determine the usefulness of information found on the Web focuses on answering three questions:

> "What do I want to know?"
> "Am I reading carefully with my question in mind?"
> "How does this information connect to what I already know?"

When a teacher models her own responses to these questions during an Internet inquiry lesson, she provides students with effective tools for determining the usefulness of information.

Evaluating Search Results

An Internet reader's evaluation skills come into use from the moment an Internet search begins. Evaluating begins with the selection of a tool such as a search engine, a librarian-selected database, or a teacher-created directory. That said, most people launch their favorite search engine and return to it regularly. In Chapter 6, we described specific search tools and provided information for determining the tool that meets your needs. We also shared several strategies for selecting keywords for searching. Next, we discuss how to evaluate the results produced by a search engine.

After a user selects a search engine and types in a keyword, a list of websites is presented. This search results list is students' first exposure to the information they are seeking and is critical for guiding their progress. Right away a learner uses evaluation skills to select the link that seems to be the most useful by asking herself, "Which website will match my informational needs?" As discussed previously, many students have a hard time identifying useful, high-quality websites from the results list. When a search engine returns a list of potential websites, novices and less skilled searchers sometimes choose the first result on the page and move down the list sequentially, whereas stronger searchers are more selective, using their knowledge of domain names and URLs (see Chapter 6) to determine the likelihood of a good match. Figure 7.3 shows typical middle schoolers' responses to the question, "When you're looking at a results list, how do you decide which websites to visit?"

 TEACHER: How do you know when you find good information for your inquiry project?

STUDENT: I check different books and websites and see what's the same.

TYPE OF STRATEGY	TYPICAL RESPONSE
Random Strategy	"I randomly pick one, and if that doesn't work then I pick the others."
Numerical Strategy	"I just, well, usually I click on the first one, and if that's not the one I want, I go to the second one, and I just go down the list."
Judicious Strategy	"I read the little paragraphs they have underneath and see which one I think is the best for what I want."

FIGURE 7.3. Student website selection strategies.

Regardless of which strategy they employ, it is critical that learners have a research focus firmly in mind by this stage or they will lose valuable time surfing websites that may not contain what they seek. Selecting a useful website activates a learner's prior experiences and skills in critically analyzing the potential quality of a website, based on the limited information on the search results list. A lack of instruction or prior knowledge can cause a learner to struggle with evaluating search results, choosing a site that catches her eye or one that is simply next on the list.

Evaluating Information within a Website

Once a website has been selected, a skilled Web reader quickly evaluates the usability of the website, along with the quality of information. She makes a determination as to whether the website is "user friendly" by determining the ease of navigation and access to information. She also looks for information that is concise and multimedia that support the content. She checks for hyperlinks that are intact and operable. Throughout this usability check, the learner determines whether the content of a site will effectively answer her search question and whether the content is credible. Less skilled Web readers tend to make superficial evaluation checks using the "credibility aesthetic," in which they determine the authenticity of a website based solely on its appearance (Fabos, 2008; Macedo-Rouet et al., 2013; Miller & Bartlett, 2012). Others reject sites outright because there is too much text to read.

 Library Media Standard: **Solicit and respect diverse perspectives while searching for information, collaborating with others, and participating as a member of the community.**

Before the learner can determine whether the information is useful, she must locate the needed information on the web page. Sometimes this is easier said than done. The formats of web pages vary greatly, as discussed previously. With such variation, it's difficult to provide novice Internet readers with consistent tips about where to find information on a website. Teachers can begin by encouraging students to notice the "reader friendliness" of a website, or the direct way a website presents information to make user navigation easy. When reading a website, look for the headings or list of topics that usually runs across the top or down the side of the screen. Also, check for a way to search for a topic within the site by using an internal search engine. Notice an introductory or welcoming message describing the purpose of the site and a sponsor's name or logo to identify the site host. Determine whether the graphics help you understand the information or whether they draw your attention away through the use of bright colors, animation, or sound. All of these features can help or hinder the learner, as the creators of websites know and understand all too well.

After selecting a website with many reader-friendly elements, a reader begins by skimming the web page to gain an overall sense of the type of information found at the website. She may use the Edit > Find strategy to scan for keywords, or she may scan for dates, statistics, people, or topics. When this information appears to be present, the learner takes another pass over the website, this time slowing down for a more careful reading because her initial evaluation has determined the information to be useful. She often makes notes, paraphrasing key ideas (Chapter 9) and citing references.

We have just described a skilled and knowledgeable reader. Wouldn't it be nice if all of our students could read with such confidence and ease? The reality is that not all of our students are skilled at adjusting their reading rate or making reasonable decisions about the usefulness of information. Less skilled Web readers often attempt to read entire websites too thoroughly or, alternately, screen capture and save or print web pages without evaluating them at all. Some rely on the "snatch and grab" (Sutherland-Smith, 2002) method of collecting undigested information rather than paraphrasing key ideas. This method involves looking for a key word, phrase, or image within the body of the website. When this "chunk" is located, it's copied and saved, or the site is bookmarked for later review. More often than not, the text is not thoroughly read and is pasted verbatim into a final project (Guinee & Eagleton, 2006).

> Evaluating is a key aspect of both traditional and Internet reading, but it may be more difficult when text emanates from an unknown source and when text is presented as a snippet, or with little or no attribution related to text source.
> —Afflerbach and Cho (2010, p. 106)

We have also seen cases in which students sit staring at web pages that are not even written in English, at a loss as to why they can't find any information. Conversely, we've watched skilled readers zip right past "perfect" information for their inquiries, completely oblivious that they've overlooked relevant facts. Educators should be careful not to make assumptions about learners' Web reading skills based on their performance with print reading. A slow and careful read may be effective for a textbook but not so effective when sifting through a plethora of websites. For the sake of efficiency and time, students need to be taught specific skills and strategies for identifying and understanding the most useful information available on the Web.

Evaluating Truthfulness

Determining the *truthfulness* of information found on the Internet is challenging for Web readers in general, but especially for students who are still learning the foundations of reading and the process of inquiry. During online reading, each reader must grapple with competing perspectives and conflicting facts that might be explicitly stated or hidden between the lines. The learner must constantly verify information by asking herself, "Is this

> ★ *Language Arts Standard:* Delineate and evaluate the argument and specific claims in a text, including the validity of the reasoning as well as the relevance and sufficiency of the evidence.

information accurate?" This can be a challenge when so much information and so many different types of information are available within and across websites. A learner may encounter accurate information, misinformation, and useless information during just one Internet reading session.

When determining the truthfulness of Internet information, whether text or multimedia, learners can think of themselves as detectives seeking clues in solving a mystery from an array of clues provided by a quality website. Some clues are apparent and some are hidden, but all can provide the puzzle pieces for solving the mystery of the truthfulness of a website. One instructional approach is to teach students to evaluate websites with respect to authority, purpose, objectivity, and timeliness.

Authority

Determining who wrote the information may be one of the most important factors in assessing truthfulness. A credible source can provide students with a good first step toward trusting the information. Typically, the host is identified at the top of the home page or in an opening or welcoming statement. This information may be listed as a personal, company, or organizational name and may include a logo or design to symbolize the host. The author of the site may be the host or someone hired by the host to write the content for the website. Either way, it should be a person who has the background and experience needed to be considered an "expert" on the topic. The most helpful websites provide information about the qualifications and email address of the website author.

> Younger students rarely seek out credibility in relation to authority. Moreover, in the event that elementary school students do evaluate the credibility of the information they read, their decisions are often based on superficial or irrelevant cues.   —Macedo-Rouet, Braasch, Britt, and Rouet (2013, p. 106)

Purpose

The purpose of the website guides the types of information available and the way the information is displayed. Purposes for websites include sharing information, persuading the reader to believe or do something, or entertaining. Determining the purpose helps a learner to recognize the author's view and how this view causes ideas to be written in a certain way. Some websites include an opening paragraph or welcoming statement that provides the reader with the purpose. For example, at the site Wonderopolis (*wonderopolis.org*) learners see the tag line "Where the wonders of learning never cease." For other websites, the reader may need to infer the purpose by considering the reputation of the site host (if known), the graphics, and the text. For example, National Geographic for Kids (*kids.nationalgeographic.com*) does not explicitly state a purpose, but National Geographic is known for providing quality information about topics from around the world.

Objectivity

Although there is no such thing as pure objectivity, it is important to teach students how to spot overt bias and unsubstantiated opinion. This is especially useful when the focus of instruction is on argument or persuasion. Objectivity involves portraying various sides of an issue fairly. Internet readers can tell when a website is biased by identifying propaganda, untrue information, or strong opinions. Unfortunately, when a learner is new to the topic and has little prior knowledge, she may have difficulty detecting bias and opinions versus truth and facts. Website designers may even take advantage of this lack of experience by designing information to contain games, giveaways, or contests as a way to hook the learner. Teach students to watch for overgeneralizations and simplifications expressing opinions not backed up with facts.

Timeliness

One of the major advantages of Internet text over printed text is timeliness, or currency. Websites are able to present information that is up-to-date because it is so easy to post updated material. This consideration is most important with information in which change occurs rapidly, such as weather reports, current events, or statistics. Credible websites usually contain a footer that shows the date on which the site was created or last updated. Failure to find such a date may be a clue to the learner about the lack of timeliness of the information.

Plan B Strategies

What happens when students apply evaluation techniques and determine that the information they have located does not meet their needs? Some students may give up, having decided that the Internet is too confusing, yields too many results, or requires too much thinking. Other students will have the drive and desire to persevere with locating information, especially when

> " When you use search engines, don't give up just because you tried one wording and that didn't work. Because sometimes search engines are picky on how many words you use and what order you put them in, if you use articles or not, and other picky stuff.
> —Marie, sixth-grade student

they are armed with alternative skills and strategies. When students are unsuccessful during their initial attempts to find information on the Web, they need to engage in what we refer to as "Plan B" strategies. Guinee, Eagleton, and Hall (2003) describe four strategies used by students when their initial search queries fail: (1) changing topics; (2) visiting new websites; (3) trying new keywords; and (4) switching search tools.

Changing Topics

We have noted that many students take a reactive stance to searching the Internet, reframing their inquiries around what can be easily found rather than persevering in the face of difficulty. Interestingly, switching research topics midstream can be considered either a dysfunctional or an adaptive technique, depending on the situation. When students select poor keywords for their searches, switching topics will not improve things. This was the case for a youngster who switched topics several times, from the Bahamas to Cuba and back. However,

 Social Studies Standard: Gather relevant information from multiple print and digital sources, using search terms effectively; assess the credibility and accuracy of each source; and quote or paraphrase the data and conclusions of others while avoiding plagiarism.

if a search fails owing to a lack of available information, it's prudent to promptly switch topics, as one fourth-grade student realized during his research project, asking, "Can I change [my topic] 'cause I don't think I can find anything on it?" Alternatively, a student may switch the focus area within a topic. For example, when one eighth grader could not find sufficient information about the Olsen twins' involvement in charitable organizations, she switched her focus to the actresses' current fashion line.

Visiting New Websites

If a website visit proves unhelpful, most students know they should go back to select new websites from the result list (beware: if the keywords weren't good, the result list won't be good either!). A general rule of thumb is that if nothing useful is found on the first page of results, it's time to try new keywords or a new search tool, as discussed next.

Trying New Keywords

One of the most effective Plan B strategies is trying new keywords. This can be done by substituting synonyms or variations of words, narrowing or broadening the focus, checking keyword spelling, or using power search strategies such as Boolean operators (see Chapter 6). As one girl explained, "If the website is not good, try to rephrase your search." This strategy was successful for a student who changed his keywords from <Dodgers + Zack Greinke + Money he makes a year> to <Dodgers + Zack Greinke + Salary>.

Unfortunately, many students make inconsequential changes to their keywords, such as when one student switched from "How many actors played James Bond?" to "How many actors *have* played James Bond?" Keyword selection requires the ability to anticipate what words or phrases will appear on a relevant web page and the knowledge of how search tools work. This is something educators can explicitly teach so as to remove the guesswork.

Switching Search Tools

Another way people can modify unsuccessful search attempts is to switch search tools. As one of our students advised, "If you don't find any results that suit your purpose, try another search engine." Some students apply this technique blindly, using the same broad keywords in multiple search tools. For example, one student searched for <Nashville Tennessee> in Google, visited several sites, and then searched for <Nashville Tennessee> in Yahoo!, still without specifying his focus area. More experienced students make more thoughtful and selective switches. When students understand that search tools use different algorithms and require different types of data entry, they change tools to maximize the fit between these characteristics and their search needs (see Chapter 6).

 TEACHER: What else might you try since you're having trouble finding what you want in your Web search for the lory bird?

STUDENT: How about if I just drive down to Petco? (*exasperated laugh*)

How Do We Teach Evaluation Strategies?

Teaching evaluation strategies involves helping students to develop a discerning eye in order to become Web critics. When searching the Web, we need a set of basic skills to effectively critique and use the information, as follows:

- Choosing appropriate search tools.
- Selecting websites from the search result list.
- Determining the reliability of websites.
- Efficiently sorting through large amounts of information.
- Recognizing the usefulness and truthfulness of information.
- Discarding or ignoring irrelevant information.
- Collecting and organizing large amounts of information.

One way to scaffold the process is to start with whole-class, teacher-led activities before moving to small groups or partners and independent work (Figure 7.4). Whole-class instruction allows the teacher to model and describe the process of selecting and rejecting websites from a search-results list. The game "One-Click" is an example of an offline activity that can promote online skills. The object of the game is to use the least number of clicks to arrive at the desired information. First, the teacher generates a results list for a topic connected to the grade-level curriculum. This list is shared with students, either in paper form or as a shared electronic document. Then students are asked to indicate which sites they would or would not select for various purposes and to explain their reasoning (Leu, Forzani, et al., 2013). The teacher can use student responses to guide a discussion about evaluating search results and making purposeful selections.

Evaluating Search Results

As mentioned earlier, one way to begin the evaluation process is to take a closer look at the clues on the search results list. URL Clues (Handout E-7.1) and Questions about the

FIGURE 7.4. Students move toward independence.

URL (Handout E-7.2) are designed for this purpose. The Results List Evaluation (Handout E-7.3) provides practice in closely analyzing the links available from search engine results. This handout can be used first by students as a whole group and then, after some practice, with partners or individually. Taking a close and careful look at search engine results puts the Internet reading process into slow motion, forcing students to critically analyze the information provided within each link on the list. This is analogous to asking students to slow down when reading printed text so that they can be more metacognitive about their comprehension.

 Library Media Standard: Demonstrate adaptability by changing the inquiry focus, questions, resources, or strategies when necessary to achieve success.

Evaluating Websites

A wealth of resources for evaluating websites is easy to find on the Internet. Among other things, you will find student activities for developing evaluation skills, website evaluation checklists, and hoax (fake) websites to develop students' critical evaluation skills. In this section, we share some activities we have found to be useful, but we also invite you to search for additional ideas using terms such as <lesson plan evaluating websites>.

Evaluation Checklists

Typically, a checklist such as our Reader Friendliness Checklist (Handout E-7.4) is used for evaluating website information. The Quick Website Evaluation (Handout E-7.5) provides students with a list of elements to consider when determining the quality of online information. Before an evaluation lesson, identify and bookmark examples of strong and weak websites. Choose a checklist to complete as a class, pausing to think aloud and discuss various website elements. A variation of this activity is to provide students with a list of preselected websites. Students visit and rank the sites using a checklist, followed by a discussion of these rankings. Agreement is not necessary, but a rich discussion about the rankings will prove interesting and educational.

Questioning the Source

If there is one thing we should teach our students about evaluating, it should be to question the source. This involves questioning whether information is accurate, based on prior knowledge and what we find online. When facts are found in more than one location, the reliability of the information increases dramatically (Figure 7.5). Thinking critically about a web page also requires the learner to question the information, the beliefs of the author, and the purpose of the website. Handout E-7.6, *Bias or Not?*, encourages students to consider and question the various ways a website author may try to persuade the learner to believe or do something.

Another way to encourage the evaluation of website information is the instructional use of hoax websites. This is a fun way for students to practice evaluating truthfulness

FIGURE 7.5. Fact-checking multiple sources.

of information and helps to dispel the "credibility aesthetic" described previously. We have included a list of real and hoax websites for students to analyze in Is It True? (Handout E-7.7), and there are many others that you can access by searching for <hoax website evaluation> or <bogus website evaluation>. If you have the time and technical resources, a highly effective approach is to have students design their own hoax websites. Another approach is to have students compare several websites about a single topic. The website *The Taxonomy of Barney* (*improb.com/airchives/paperair/volume1/ v1i1/barney.htm*) provides seemingly credible information about Barney, the animated dinosaur, that can be compared with the Barney website (*barney.com*) and the *Barney and Friends* website (*pbskids.org/barney*). Comparing and contrasting various sources of information promotes higher order thinking about what is useful and truthful. We also offer Ad vs. Error (Handout E-7.8) to help students distinguish between ads and error messages.

Engaging Plan B Strategies

Even after becoming experts at identifying topics, focus areas, and research questions (Chapter 5); choosing search engines and selecting keywords (Chapter 6); and evaluating results lists and websites (this chapter), students still need to engage in "Plan B" strategies when the first site they visit does not meet their information needs. During an Internet QUEST, it is expected that students will visit more than one website. Therefore, we created the Plan B Checklist (Handout E-7.9), which helps students remember four strategies for deciding what to do next. Finally, we offer Edit > Find Lesson Plans for elementary and middle levels (Handouts E-7.10 and E-7.11), which teach a simple method for determining whether a website has the desired information.

SUMMARY ●

The E phase of the QUEST focuses on evaluating search engine results and websites as learners seek to determine whether the information they find during Internet inquiry is truthful and useful. Because there are no editorial filters in Web publishing, students must become skilled at sifting out the true from the untrue, a daunting task for emergent or struggling readers who are still giving much attention to decoding and fluency. Instruction in these strategies should focus on a gradual release of responsibility from the teacher to the student through modeling and think-aloud procedures, then guided and independent practice. Teachers can help students to become super sleuths throughout the inquiry process by viewing information on the Internet as a collection of clues useful for evaluating.

In Chapter 8, Synthesizing, we explore the "in the head" strategies that Web learners use to integrate ideas within and across websites. Although many of these strategies are similar to those used by readers of print text (Chapter 2), the speed at which many students move through the Internet sometimes makes it difficult for them to take time to ask themselves what the information means.

Handouts

The handouts for Evaluating, listed in the following chart, are meant to give students practice in developing evaluation skills that can be applied as they move into independently seeking answers to their questions using the Internet. Note that because these activities slow down the Internet reading process, they are not meant to be used every time students seek online information.

Number	Name of handout	Purpose
E-7.1	URL Clues	Determine authenticity
E-7.2	Questions about the URL	Determine reliability
E-7.3	Results List Evaluation	Evaluate search engine results
E-7.4	Reader Friendliness Checklist	Evaluate reader friendliness
E-7.5	Quick Website Evaluation	Evaluate website info
E-7.6	Bias or Not?	Determine bias
E-7.7	Is It True?	Determine truthfulness
E-7.8	Ad versus Error	Determine truthfulness
E-7.9	Plan B Checklist	Strategies beyond first site visit
E-7.10	Edit > Find Lesson Plan—Elementary Level	Method for finding specific information and evaluating usefulness of site
E-7.11	Edit > Find Lesson Plan—Middle Level	Method for finding specific information and evaluating usefulness of site

HANDOUT E-7.1. URL Clues

Name _____ Class _____ Date _____

Directions: *Search for a topic of interest, then choose three websites from the results list and break down the URL for each one. Answer the questions below each URL box to predict whether this is a site that can be trusted. The first one is done for you as an example.*

URL EXAMPLE: *kidsdiscover.com/spotlight/endangered-species* _____

host or domain	domain suffix	path/directory	file name/topic
kidsdiscover	*.com*	*spotlight*	*endangered-species*

Do you recognize the domain name? Is it connected to education, government, or a company with a trustworthy reputation?
I know that Kids Discover is a trustworthy magazine because I've seen it in the school library.

Do the path/directory or file name/topic contain words or parts of words that relate to your topic of interest?
The file name/topic says "endangered-species" so I know it will have information on my topic.

URL #1: _____

host or domain	domain suffix	path/directory	file name/topic

Do you recognize the domain name? Is it connected to education, government, or a company with a trustworthy reputation?

Do the path/directory and file name contain words or parts of words that relate to your topic of interest?

(continued)

URL #2: _____

host or domain	domain suffix	path/directory	file name/topic

Do you recognize the domain name? Is it connected to education, government, or a company with a trustworthy reputation?

Do the path/directory and file name contain words or parts of words that relate to your topic of interest?

URL #3: _____

host or domain	domain suffix	path/directory	file name/topic

Do you recognize the domain name? Is it connected to education, government, or a company with a trustworthy reputation?

Do the path/directory and file name contain words or parts of words that relate to your topic of interest?

HANDOUT E-7.2. Questions about the URL

Name _____ Class _____ Date _____

Directions: *Find two websites on a similar topic, then use these charts to see what types of information the websites contain.*

URL #1: _____

Who published the webpage or made it public by putting it on the Web? Look for a host that has a reliable reputation.	

What type of domain does the webpage come from? Domains include:
    .edu (education, college or university)
    .gov (government agency)
    .com or .net (commercial)
    .org (nonprofit and research organizations)
    .k12.ks.us (school district)	

Is this a personal web page hosted by a private individual? Look for the words *users, members,* or *people*. Check for a person's name, the use of a tilde (~), or a percent sign (%).	

URL #2: _____

Who published the webpage or made it public by putting it on the Web? Look for a host that has a reliable reputation.	

What type of domain does the webpage come from? Domains include:
    .edu (education, college or university)
    .gov (government agency)
    .com or .net (commercial)
    .org (nonprofit and research organizations)
    .k12.ks.us (school district)	

Is this a personal web page hosted by a private individual? Look for the words *users, members,* or *people*. Check for a person's name, the use of a tilde (~), or a percent sign (%).	

HANDOUT E-7.3. Results List Evaluation

Name _____ Class _____ Date _____

Directions: *Identify an inquiry question, conduct a search, then choose three URLs from the results list to closely analyze. All of the information you need should be collected from the link on the results list. Don't go to the website.*

URL #1: _____

Website title	Brief description	Links to categories

Does this site match your inquiry question? Why or why not?

URL #2: _____

Website title	Brief description	Links to categories

Does this site match your inquiry question? Why or why not?

URL #3: _____

Website title	Brief description	Links to categories

Does this site match your inquiry question? Why or why not?

HANDOUT E-7.4. Reader Friendliness Checklist

Name _____ Class _____ Date _____

Directions: *Do a search on an appropriate topic and choose a website from the search results list. Go to the website and use this checklist to see whether the site would be helpful for learning about your topic.*

URL:	Yes	No
1. Does the title of the page tell you what it is about?		
2. Is there an introduction or message on the page that tells you what is included?		
3. Are the links easy to distinguish from the rest of the text by color, size, or shape?		
4. Is it easy to find a place to search for information on the website?		
5. If you go to a bunch of other pages within the website, is it easy to get back to the home page without using the back button?		
6. Is each page or section clearly labeled with a heading?		
7. Is the layout uncluttered and easy to use?		
8. Do the visuals help you understand the ideas on the website?		
9. Are there lots of ads?		
10. Would you use this website to help you learn more about the topic? Explain your thinking here:		

_____

_____

_____

_____

_____

_____

_____

HANDOUT E-7.5. Quick Website Evaluation

Name _____ Class _____ Date _____

Directions: *Choose a website and evaluate it using this quick method.*

Name of Website: _____

URL: _____

	LOW SCORE→ → → → → → → → → → → → → →HIGH SCORE				
	1	2	3	4	5
CONTENT How *useful* is the content for your inquiry question?					
ACCURACY Does the information seem reliable and *truthful*?					
CREDIBILITY Is it clear that the author is an expert on this topic?					
APPEARANCE Is the site interesting and inviting?					
NAVIGATION Is it easy to move around the site?					
TOTAL POINTS =					

Would you recommend this site?   Yes   No

Please explain your thinking:

HANDOUT E-7.6. Bias or Not?

Name _____ Class _____ Date _____

Directions: *Follow the steps to decide whether a website is biased.*

1. Write your research question.	2. List possible biases before reading the website.

3. Choose a website and write the URL.

4. Check off bias clues if you see them and give an example.
- ☐ Stereotypes _____
- ☐ Exaggeration _____
- ☐ Appeals to feelings/emotions _____
- ☐ Overgeneralizations _____
- ☐ Opinions stated as facts _____
- ☐ Imbalance in presentation _____
    (were both sides considered?)

5. Based on clues, is this website biased ____ yes ____ no
   If yes, what is the bias?

HANDOUT E-7.7. Is It True?

Name _____ Class _____ Date _____

Directions: *Select three websites to explore from the list below. Some of the sites are real websites with truthful information. Some of the sites are not. Determine whether the information at your site is true by answering the following questions.*

- Dog Island at *thedogisland.com*
- Pacific Northwest Tree Octopus at *zapatopi.net/treeoctopus.html*
- The Venom Cure at *pbs.org/wnet/nature/venomcure*
- Bureau of Sasquatch Affairs at *zapatopi.net/bsa*
- Worm Watch at *naturewatch.ca/english/wormwatch*
- The Jackalope Conspiracy at *sudftw.com/jackcon.htm*

URL #1: _____

1. Does the home page look and work like a typical website? Give specific examples.

2. Does the information seem as though it makes sense? Explain why/why not.

3. Where else can you look to confirm this information? Look somewhere else on the Internet and share what you find.

4. Who created the website? List the author's name and qualifications for being an expert.

5. Is the information on this site true? Why was it created?

(continued)

URL #2: _____

1. Does the home page look and work like a typical website? Give specific examples.

2. Does the information seem as though it makes sense? Explain why/why not.

3. Where else can you look to confirm this information? Look somewhere else on the Internet and share what you find.

4. Who created the website? List the author's name and qualifications for being an expert.

5. Is the information on this site true? Why was it created?

URL #3: _____

1. Does the home page look and work like a typical website? Give specific examples.

2. Does the information seem as though it makes sense? Explain why/why not.

3. Where else can you look to confirm this information? Look somewhere else on the Internet and share what you find.

4. Who created the website? List the author's name and qualifications for being an expert.

5. Is the information on this site true? Why was it created?

HANDOUT E-7.8. Ad versus Error

Name _____ Class _____ Date _____

Directions: *Look for these signs to decide whether a dialog box message is an ad or an error, then draw an example of each.*

Pop-up ad:
 ✓ Blinking graphics (pictures, symbols, words)
 ✓ No easy way to close or minimize the message
 ✓ Music or sounds
 ✓ Message reappears, even after closing it

Error message:
 ✓ Plain background, little color
 ✓ No blinking graphics
 ✓ No music or sound
 ✓ Message does not reappear
 ✓ Message can be closed by clicking on the X in the upper right corner
 ✓ Message can be minimized

DIRECTIONS: Draw an example of a pop-up ad versus an error message.

POP-UP AD	ERROR MESSAGE

HANDOUT E-7.9. Plan B Checklist

Name _____ Class _____ Date _____

Directions: *Use this checklist if you can't find what you want on the Web.*

Step 1: Check your keywords

____ Are your keywords spelled correctly?

____ Did you use topic + focus?

____ Did you put quotation marks around phrases?

____ Other:

Step 2: Check the website

____ Did you use Edit > Find to scan for your keywords?

____ Did you check to see whether there's a search tool on this site?

____ Did you look for links that might lead somewhere useful?

____ Did you find a link that lets you contact the author?

____ Did you notice related keywords that you could try next?

____ Other:

Step 3: Try a new approach

____ Did you try a new website?

____ Did you try different keywords?

____ Did you try a different search tool?

____ Other:

Step 4: Try a new topic or focus

____ Did you try a new focus area?

____ Did you try a new topic that's similar?

____ Other:

HANDOUT E-7.10. Edit > Find Lesson Plan—Elementary Level

Objective

Students will learn a simple method for locating target words and phrases on a website to determine whether it is likely to have the information they seek.

Time

One class period

Materials

1. Internet computer and projector
2. At least two free web browsers, such as Chrome (*https://www.google.com/chrome/browser/*), or Safari (*https://www.apple.com/safari/*)
3. QUEST Inquiry Model (Handout P-4.11)

Assessment Options

1. Web Strategies Assessment (Handout P-4.2, P-4.4, or P-4.5)
2. Web Strategies Scoring Guide (Handout P-4.3 or P-4.6)

Introduction

1. Tell students you will be teaching them an easy way to tell whether a website has the information they need to answer their questions. Display the QUEST Inquiry Model (Handout P-4.11) and remind students of the QUEST phases, specifically the phase of Evaluating, in which we determine whether the website is useful and truthful. Say that today's focus is on deciding whether the information is useful.
2. Discuss the difference between useful information and useless information. Give an example, such as: "If we want to learn about cheetahs, and the website mostly has information about tigers, we would want to choose another website. Even though tigers are interesting, we would not want to keep reading that website because we need to move on and look for information about cheetahs."

Modeling

1. Pose the question, "What do cheetahs eat?" Brainstorm possible foods for cheetahs, then provide the synonym *diet*.
2. Pull up Safari or another browser, go to a search engine, such as Google (*www.google.com*), and search for <cheetah + diet>.
3. Choose a site that looks promising (explain why you think it looks promising).
4. Go to the Edit > Find feature located on the toolbar across the top of the screen in the Edit drop-down menu. Click on Find and search for the word *diet*. If you see it, read the surrounding information to learn more about the diet of the cheetah. Click "Find Next" to see whether *diet* comes up again (on a Mac, go to Edit > Find Again multiple times). If not, quickly leave the site and try other sites until you find something about the diet of cheetahs. Remark that this is a FASTER way to see whether a website has the specific information you want than reading or skimming. Mention that Edit > Find works in all software programs, as well as on search engine results lists.

(continued)

5. Now say that you want to verify the information about the cheetah's diet by fact-checking with another website.
6. Pull up Safari (or another web browser) and go to *www.yahoo.com* to demonstrate that this feature works in any web browser and with any search engine. Search again for <cheetah + diet>.
7. Discuss the way this little trick can help you find information quickly on a website.

Practice

1. Identify a unit of study within the curriculum (e.g., Civil War, inventions). Have students brainstorm possible words related to the topic. Direct students to a predetermined website with information relating to the topic. Have students practice using the Edit > Find feature and keep a running total for the number of times they find the target words.
2. If students are already involved in an inquiry project, have them try the Edit > Find feature on any search engine results list and website related to their topic.

Scaffolding

Pair weaker students with stronger students. However, always be sure that the weaker student has control of the mouse and that the mentor student understands how to support a peer without taking over.

Feedback

1. Circulate around the classroom or computer lab and ask students what they are doing and how it is helpful. If anyone seems unclear about the purpose of this lesson or how to implement it, remediate on the spot.
2. Praise students who are successfully using the Edit > Find feature.

Ticket Out the Door

Have each student tell you a fast method for finding specific words on a results list or website (Edit > Find).

HANDOUT E-7.11. Edit > Find Lesson Plan—Middle Level

Objective

Students will learn a simple method for locating target words and phrases on a website to determine whether it is likely to have the information they seek.

Time

One class period

Materials

1. Internet computer with LCD projector
2. At least two free web browsers, such as Chrome (*https://www.google.com/chrome/broser/*) or Safari (*https://www.apple.com/safari/*)
3. QUEST Inquiry Model (Handout P-4.11)

Assessment Options

1. Web Strategies Assessment (Handout P-4.2, P-4.4, or P-4.5)
2. Web Strategies Scoring Guide (Handout P-4.3 or P-4.6)

Introduction

1. Tell students you will be teaching them a transferable strategy for evaluating the usefulness of a website that many other students have found helpful. Contextualize the lesson using the QUEST Inquiry Model (Handout P-4.11) by pointing out that they are in the **E** phase of the QUEST, which includes deciding whether a website is reliable (truthful) and has the information they want (useful).
2. Have students brainstorm why evaluating is useful in this class, in other classes, and outside of school. This can be done in pairs, in small groups, or as a whole class.
3. Generate excitement and get student buy-in on the purpose of the lesson before proceeding. Tell students that this strategy works in any web browser as well as in most other software programs (Word, PowerPoint, Publisher, etc.). It also works on search engine results lists.

Modeling

1. Tell the class that you already know that modern lacrosse originated with Native American tribes in Canada and the United States but that you want to know what the French had to do with it. Pull up a browser, go to *www.google.com*, and search for <lacrosse + history>.
2. Choose a site that looks promising (explain why you think it looks promising).
3. Check the site for reliability (look at URL and try to find author info).
4. Go to the toolbar at the top of the browser window. Click on Edit and then click on Find. Search for the word *French*. If you see it, read the surrounding info and see whether you find your answer. Click "Find Next" to see whether it's mentioned again (on a Mac, go to Edit > Find Again multiple times). If not, quickly leave the site and try other sites until you find something about the French. Remark that this is a FASTER way to see whether a website has the specific information you want than reading or skimming.
5. Now say that you want to verify the information about the French by fact-checking with another website.

(continued)

6. Pull up a different web browser and use a different search engine to demonstrate that this feature works in any web browser and with any search engine. Search again for <lacrosse + history>.
7. Show that you can use Edit > Find on the search results list, too. Use Edit > Find to search for *origin* on the hit list. Click the "Find" button again to see whether *origin* is listed elsewhere on the hit list.
8. Choose a site that looks promising.
9. Check the site for reliability.
10. Use Edit > Find to search for *French* again. Point out that you can also use the keyboard shortcut "Ctrl + F." Click the "Find" button again to see whether the French are mentioned more than once.
11. See if everyone's satisfied that you've quickly found and verified the information you wanted (the French are credited with inventing the word "lacrosse").

Practice

1. If students are already involved in an inquiry project, have them try the Edit > Find and Ctrl + F feature on any search engine results list and website related to their topic.
2. If this is an isolated mini-lesson, have students quickly think of an interesting topic about which they have fairly strong prior knowledge. Then have them try the Edit > Find and Ctrl + F feature on any search engine results list and website related to this topic.

Scaffolding

Pair weaker students with stronger students. However, always be sure that the weaker student has control of the mouse and that the mentor student understands how to support a peer without taking over.

Feedback

1. Circulate around classroom or computer lab and ask students what they are doing and how it is helpful. If anyone seems unclear about the purpose of this lesson or how to implement it, remediate on the spot.
2. Praise students who are successfully using the Edit > Find feature.

Ticket Out the Door

Have each student tell you a fast method for finding specific words on a results list or website (Edit > Find or Ctrl + F).

(8) Synthesizing

KEY IDEAS •

- Synthesis plays a role in our everyday lives when we make decisions.

- A reader forms a synthesis when mentally linking together kernels of ideas within a text or among texts.

- Synthesis is a complex strategy because it involves a combination of several different reading strategies, including activating prior knowledge, determining important ideas, and making inferences.

- Throughout the inquiry process, synthesis is necessary for readers to understand information gathered from a variety of sources, including text, graphics, and multimedia.

- Readers of varying skill levels benefit from models of synthesis through think-alouds and a gradual release of responsibility.

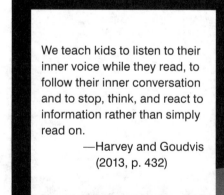

We teach kids to listen to their inner voice while they read, to follow their inner conversation and to stop, think, and react to information rather than simply read on.

—Harvey and Goudvis (2013, p. 432)

In this chapter we look at the process of synthesis, or the connecting of individual ideas to form an understanding. Finding and evaluating information is important, as described in the second and third steps of the QUEST model, but will not be enough unless a deep understanding of the information can be developed through a synthesis of ideas. Therefore, the guiding question for this chapter is, "What does this information mean?"

Why Is It Important to Synthesize?

Synthesis is a thinking tool that affects our daily lives and, more specifically, affects the ways we convert information into knowledge. Synthesis enables us to make both big and small decisions by relying on a combination of our prior experiences and new information gathered from the world around us. For example, while writing this text, we read numerous research articles and books, viewed many websites, and observed hundreds of children during the Internet inquiry process. What you are reading now is a synthesis of what we have read, heard, seen, and done. In everyday life, synthesis is used to help determine which car to purchase, which cell phone plan to choose, or whether one should wear long or short sleeves on an unpredictable spring day.

Even though synthesis is complex, it is a strategy that our students absolutely need in a world in which they encounter massive amounts of information, whether in print or digital form, and must make well-informed decisions about how to interpret and use this information. It is important for readers to learn how to synthesize because it's impossible to store everything we read in our brains (Fisher et al., 2012). Through the inquiry process, readers must not only understand the text but must also be able to "own" the information by developing a line of critical thinking about a concept. The ability to synthesize information is crucial for an informed, democratic society.

Science and Technical Standard: **Compare and contrast the information gained from experiments, simulations, video, or multimedia sources with that gained from reading a text on the same topic.**

When Do We Synthesize?

Synthesis is one of a repertoire of strategies that skilled readers use to make sense of text, images, and multimedia. A synthesis is created when separate and unique ideas are mentally woven together to form a new understanding, much in the way a detective links together clues to solve a mystery. A new understanding is formed as a reader continually shifts back and forth between reading for big-picture ideas to reading for details. When a mental pattern emerges and is refined, a synthesis takes shape. A higher level of understanding is reached when readers personalize the text by integrating words and ideas with their own thoughts and questions, thus creating new insights. Synthesis is not easy. Many students struggle to *find* quality information on the Internet and many more are challenged to figure out what it *means* and what to do with it.

Although teachers sometimes assume that students understand that an inquiry task involves synthesizing information from multiple sources, many students are unaware of this or may struggle to carry it out (Eagleton et al., 2003; Zhang & Duke, 2008). The practice of copying text word for word persists from elementary school through college; in fact, digital resources make it even easier to copy information. One problem is the prevalent "one stop shopping" method, which is an outcome of the erroneous belief that one website should have all the information a student seeks. For example, one student expressed triumph about his Internet inquiry project when he said, "I found that one web page I needed to do my thing!" The "one stop" strategy is ill advised in any type of research, but especially with Web research because websites can, and do, report biased and/or incorrect information (see Chapter 7). To combat this problem, students should be taught to fact-check several sources. This can be enforced by requiring students to visit a minimum number of websites during an inquiry project.

 Language Arts Standard: **Analyze how two or more texts address similar themes or topics in order to build knowledge or to compare the approaches the authors take.**

What Characterizes Synthesis?

As a plant begins from a seed, synthesizing begins from summarizing. Readers must first be able to determine the important ideas and express these in a clear and concise way before they can then make these ideas their own. The terms *synthesize* and *summarize* are often used interchangeably, but they are actually quite different. A summarization is a brief presentation of the main points of a text. A synthesis takes a summary one step further by including the reader's personal response to the text in the form of connections to himself, other texts, and the world (Keene & Zimmermann, 2007). "Our information-rich society requires us to sift through ever-increasing amounts of data to make sense of them and act. We couldn't possibly remember all the information that appears on our radar screen each day. Summarizing and synthesizing allow us to make sense of important information, get the gist, and move on" (Harvey & Goudvis, 2007, p. 19).

Being able to clearly and concisely summarize ideas is crucial to creating a synthesis. Afflerbach and Johnston (1986) use the term *crunching* to describe the way a reader reduces text to more manageable kernels of important information. Skilled readers often begin by scanning a text for relevant words and ideas, then returning to the text for a closer reading. Frequently, these readers pause during reading to mentally crunch new information into a kernel of an idea. These kernels form a summary of the text, and a synthesis is created when the reader uses his insights to link the kernels together. This process of crunching ideas into more manageable units becomes automatic in skilled readers, which makes the process difficult for teachers to observe,

Summarizing is a complex strategy that requires significant amounts of practice. Proficient readers identify main ideas and supporting details and then organize and synthesize this information into smaller units
—Fisher, Frey, and Lapp (2012, p. 115)

explain, and model. Many studies have shown that summarization skills can be improved with explicit instruction, especially when the text is at the appropriate level for the reader (see Duke & Pearson, 2002). Older students respond positively to instruction in summarizing, specifically when the teaching and modeling are part of the total package, such as in the well-researched Reciprocal Teaching method (Palincsar & Brown, 1984; Rosenshine & Meister, 1994).

Synthesis is not an easily observable process, as it occurs in a reader's head as he moves through texts (Figure 8.1). This complex skill is challenging to teach and learn, because learners must understand and apply various comprehension strategies, including activating prior knowledge, determining important ideas, making inferences, and asking questions, while also

Social Studies Standard:
Determine the central ideas or information of a primary or secondary source; provide an accurate summary of the source distinct from prior knowledge or opinions.

developing personal responses or connections to the text (see Chapter 3). In the book *Strategies That Work* (2007), Harvey and Goudvis attribute the complexities of synthesis to the challenge of using critical and creative thinking simultaneously. They describe a synthesis as an idea that evolves slowly over time and occurs only if the reader is focused on making meaning.

Summarizing entails skimming, rereading, mentally listing important elements, and waiting for a new idea, or synthesis, to be constructed (Afflerbach & Johnston, 1986). As this mental process is used more and more, it becomes automatic and even unconscious to the reader. A reader may be quite skilled at creating a synthesis from these key ideas but may have difficulty describing exactly what happens in his mind during this process. Without a clear description, it becomes difficult for a teacher to pass this information on to other students.

Another challenge with synthesizing lies in the fact that the process is iterative. Whether reading, viewing, or listening, throughout the comprehension process, a

FIGURE 8.1. Synthesis is a process that cannot be observed because it occurs in the reader's mind.

synthesis is constantly being constructed and reconstructed as a reader encounters new ideas and weighs these against what is known. "New information is assimilated into the reader's evolving ideas about the text, rendering some earlier decisions obsolete" (Keene, 2008, p. 252). This constant shifting of ideas is disconcerting to some readers and unfathomable to others who seek a straightforward, consistent interpretation of a text. Learners must be nimble, flexibly moving between different formats of texts and also actively and continually refining their interpretation.

Metacognition, Text Evidence, and Close Reading

Our goal is for learners to be actively involved during the reading process. Glassy-eyed, drooping heads are a sign that mental engagement is nowhere to be found. To gain meaning from text, a reader must be both actively thinking *and* aware of his thinking. Harvey and Goudvis (2013) describe this metacognitive process as "thinking about reading in ways that enhance learning and understanding" (p. 433). A strategic reader has a plan of action and knows when, where, and how to use strategies, or thinking tools, in a deliberate way for gathering information to make sense of the world. The CCSS call for students to be "thoughtfully engaged" as "attentive" and "critical" readers (NGA & CCSSO, 2010).

Learning to synthesize, or stitch together bits of information into an "intricate mental tapestry" (Harvey & Goudvis, 2013, p. 433), develops from clear explanations, practice with text, and deep thinking. When children are young, their background experiences may be limited or may have gaps. In addition, inexperienced readers may draw conclusions from what they read based on their own thoughts and ideas, rather than on details from the text. An effective synthesis creates a link between text details and our own interpretation. For instance, one third-grade collaborative group, when working on an inquiry project about a hero, chose Martin Luther King, Jr. because he was African American rather than relying on evidence from the text to support King as a hero. The teacher encouraged the group to return to their print and online sources to find words or deeds that made Dr. King a hero rather than relying only on his ethnicity. The students returned later with a collection of information to support their choice of Martin Luther King, Jr. as a hero.

When reading online, young children also tend to focus on the surface cues of a website (e.g., headings, capitalization, boldface) rather than digging more deeply into the details of the text, images, or multimedia. Such attention to the superficial makes it challenging to create a synthesis of information. On the other hand, more experienced readers typically have stronger comprehension skills and can balance surface cues with deep semantic cues collected by determining important ideas and making inferences (Rouet et al., 2011). As children gain more experiences with comprehension, they become more adept at processing information, monitoring their understanding, anticipating hurdles, and solving problems (Harvey & Goudvis, 2013).

> A synthesis is the sum of information from the text, other relevant texts, and the reader's background knowledge, ideas, and opinions, produced in an original way. —Keene (2008, p. 252)

Creating a synthesis relies on a reader's skillfulness at continually shifting between identifying, processing, summarizing, and monitoring. Such cognitive breadth and depth is not easy, even for more experienced readers. With modeling, guided practice, and feedback, learners come to recognize the power of their own thinking and use this power to synthesize information and transform it into a format they can share with others. In the book *Notice and Note: Strategies for Close Reading* (Beers & Probst, 2013), the authors discuss the importance of giving close attention to the interaction of these elements: the text, a reader's relevant experiences, and a reader's responses and interpretation. This process, also known as close reading, relies on readers' noticing and noting the details of the text and their own thinking in order to effectively move across, down, and within the text. A text's complexity may stymie some readers in this movement. The complexity of ideas, structure, vocabulary, sentence patterns, and writing style combine forces to create a text that may be complex to different readers in different ways (Figure 8.2).

Synthesis and Reading on the Web

Web readers face additional complexities when trying to pull together ideas from various sources within a website or among several websites. The wide variety of text features and structures encountered in Web text are part of this complexity (see Chapter 3). "The Internet introduces additional challenges to coordinate and synthesize vast amounts of information presented in multiple media formats, from a nearly unlimited and disparate set of sources" (Leu et al., 2011, p. 7). Even before readers can apply their knowledge of synthesis, they must be skilled at navigating or deciding the path to follow in their Internet reading, based on knowledge of navigational tools and an evolving understanding of the text. There is so much information available on the Web that it is difficult to know where to focus one's attention. Yet, in some ways, the Web provides us with supports for synthesizing. Search engines make it easier for readers to locate information, thus "the subsequent reduction in cognitive energy needed to accomplish these activities allows for more time to engage in higher order thinking" (DeSchryver, 2015,

FIGURE 8.2. A synthesis is a unique representation of an individual's thought processes.

p. 388). In Chapter 3, we described the process readers use during their transactions with online text. Skilled Web readers demonstrate a complex weaving of navigation and reading strategies as they make decisions about where to read, what to read, and how carefully to read (Coiro & Dobler, 2007).

Skilled Web readers recognize the need to readjust their rate and the ways they access information, as their online reading experience may require adeptly moving among information presented in various formats. With each click of the mouse or tap of the finger, experienced online readers know they must reorient themselves, looking for headings and access points to guide their reading. They understand that synthesizing information from the Internet relies heavily on skimming and scanning, as well as navigating among various electronic formats such as web pages, wikis, blogs, podcasts, interactive diagrams, videos, and images. Proficient Web readers understand that finding the key idea in a blog entry is quite different from finding the key idea in an interactive diagram, and they must adapt the application of their strategy knowledge in a flexible way. Adapting the use of strategies between types of text is not a new expectation; it also occurs when students gather information from print text. The difference is that students working on a research project with print text typically collect information from vetted print sources with fairly similar structures and formats, whereas Web readers must be able to collect and synthesize ideas from resources that present information in quite different ways.

 Library Media Standard: **Make sense of information gathered from diverse sources by identifying misconceptions, main and supporting ideas, conflicting information, and point of view or bias.**

In order to teach synthesis with Web texts, we must slow down the reading process and help students consider and practice each component (Figure 8.3). Putting comprehension into slow motion can be a challenge because the strategies used to synthesize occur simultaneously, intertwining with each other while a reader is actively making meaning. Activating prior knowledge and determining important ideas are two strategies that form a symbiotic relationship. We determine what is important in a text, in part, based on what we know and what we need to know. "Supporting readers to connect their prior knowledge to new information is at the core of learning and understanding" (Harvey & Goudvis, 2013, p. 437), and activating prior knowledge before reading Web texts lets a reader consider what he knows about the topic, as well as what he knows about using search engines, navigating, and reading within and among websites. These various types of prior knowledge are crucial for readers in making connections between what they read and what they know and in using these connections to develop a deeper understanding of online text (Coiro & Dobler, 2007).

 Teacher: How do you know when you find good information for your inquiry project?

Student: When it's something you wouldn't usually know.

Determining important ideas entails getting the gist, or main idea, and recognizing that important points in online text may be found not only in the text but also in the images (e.g., icons, charts, diagrams, photographs) and multimedia. Some of the cognitive skills involved in reading, including making inferences and visualizing, "may be enhanced by opportunities for explicit, metacognitive practice with the use of video, film, or other nonprint media" (Hobbs & Frost, 2003, p. 333). Giving students

FIGURE 8.3. Teaching synthesis entails slowing down the reading process.

experiences with media literacy activities, such as synthesizing a video or identifying the author's message from an infographic, may help students develop comprehension and writing skills beyond what is gained from traditional literacy activities (Fisher et al., 2012). Images and multimedia can serve as primary sources of information that may be a better match for some students' learning style and needs. Determining what is important in nonprint media requires:

- Identifying a purpose (what will hopefully be gained from the multimedia).
- Activating prior knowledge about the topic depicted in the multimedia resource.
- Viewing (or listening to) the entire piece without stopping, focusing on a general impression of the meaning.
- Watching or listening again, this time pausing several times to stop, think, and write about the important ideas.
- Summarizing important ideas and making a connection to other things read, seen, or heard (May & Downey, 2009).

Once a synthesis has been formed, or a connection made with these ideas, the learner's new way of looking at the synthesized idea is typically shared in a written or oral format. In the past, a synthesis was often shared through a research report, mural, poster, or other art media. Now, a synthesis of ideas gathered electronically often involves the use of technology to communicate ideas through the creation of a web page, slide show, video, word cloud, or digital book. To create a synthesis "outside the head," not only must the student be able to plan, locate, evaluate, and synthesize information, but he must also be able to understand the various electronic formats for presenting this information. In this way, the complexities of synthesizing Web-based information continue to grow.

> We believe it is the interaction, the transaction, between the reader and the text that creates not only meaning but creates the reason to read.
> —Beers and Probst (2013, p. 3)

Demonstrating the Process of Synthesis

The following studies illustrate the ways in which learners synthesize when reading on the Web. In the first example, a group of 11 sixth-grade students were given the task of finding the answer to the question "What is the difference between a landfill and a dump?" (Coiro & Dobler, 2007). All of the learners demonstrated a need for the development of stronger reading and navigating skills in order to locate useful information efficiently, but some were closer to reaching this goal than others. One student explained her process of locating information by first looking for information about landfills and then returning to the search engine to look for information about dumps. She joined together the ideas she had collected to describe a landfill as a modern dump. As is ideal, this student synthesized her ideas into a new perspective.

Learners who appeared to be less skilled with Internet inquiry began the search with a limited understanding of how to pull ideas together from various websites to create a synthesis. It was clear that some students were searching for a one-stop website with all the information in one place. These readers typically skimmed the web page for an answer to their question, often hoping to find the *exact* answer. Not surprisingly, these learners simply wanted to find the information and be finished with the task, following the principle of least effort discussed in Chapter 1. Several readers bypassed useful information by scanning and skimming too quickly. For instance, one boy spent about 3 seconds on each web page, hoping that the information he was looking for would jump out at him—it never did. Luckily, his persistence kept him going, and after little success, he began to slow down and read more carefully. In contrast, another student was a slow, careful reader. She read every word on each web page because this was the same process she used for reading a book. As a result, her search for the similarities between a landfill and a dump was quite time-consuming. Web readers typically do not have time to give such careful attention to every web page encountered, nor is this attention necessary.

> Coordinating among the many processes of navigation, selection, evaluation, connection, and monitoring increases the need for self-regulation skills.
> —Goldman, Braasch, Wiley, Graesser, and Bradowinska (2012, p. 357)

In the second example, pairs of high school students were asked to write a joint argumentative essay in response to the question "Should Internet censorship be tightened?" (Kiili, Laurinen, Marttunen, & Leu, 2012). The activity began with a brief discussion about the topic in order to activate prior knowledge. Then each pair was given 30 minutes to search on the Internet and 45 minutes to compose the essay, using a single computer. Their discussions were recorded and analyzed as their essays were evaluated. The study revealed that, *when working in pairs*, students spent 23% of their time locating information, 65% of their time processing content, and 12% of their time evaluating information, monitoring comprehension, and being off-task. Working in pairs enabled these learners to find information more efficiently, thus freeing up time and cognitive energy for deeper thinking. It appears that reading and discussing different points of view together promoted each pair's co-construction of meaning during online reading and possibly led to a stronger piece of writing. In contrast, students working individually often spend "most of their time on searching and scanning and only a small amount of time on processing and organizing information" (Walraven et al., 2009, p. 244).

Based on these studies and similar research, we know that skilled Web readers are: (1) persistent; (2) flexible; (3) aware when information is not accurate or making sense; and (4) confident in their ability to find information (Coiro, 2012). We know that many learners struggle with the depth of thinking that synthesis requires, which makes it imperative that educators provide explicit instruction, modeling, and guided practice opportunities in the classroom and library.

 Science and Technical Standard: Integrate quantitative or technical information expressed in words in a text with a version of that information expressed visually (e.g., in a flowchart, diagram, model, graph, or table).

How Do We Teach Synthesis Strategies?

Of all the steps in the QUEST, Synthesizing may be one of the most challenging to teach, because it's difficult to explain exactly how a synthesis is formed within our own minds or in the minds of others. How do we explain such complex thinking to a reader? How do we describe something that occurs in the mind? One place to begin is to focus on building a strong foundation in reading comprehension strategies, as described in Chapter 3. In this section we highlight two models of instruction, teacher think-aloud and gradual release of responsibility (described in Chapter 2), and present two classroom examples of synthesis in action.

Teacher Think-Aloud

We have intentionally highlighted teacher think-alouds throughout this text. We cannot emphasize enough the importance of making visible the thoughts that run inside a person's head during a reading task. Thinking aloud is especially important for teaching the strategy of synthesis because of its mental complexity. As mentioned previously, creating a synthesis occurs in the mind. There is no concrete way to demonstrate this strategy, nor can learners easily grasp the concept simply by watching someone else. As the lead learner in the classroom or library, the instructor has the potential to turn on the lightbulb for a student in the dark when it comes to thinking deeply about texts. For creating a synthesis when reading on the Web, a think-aloud is as much about the process of reading, listening, and viewing as it is about the process of making decisions about which website to select or where to read on the web page, both of which are integral parts of the Web reading process.

When we say "think-aloud," we don't mean just saying things like "First, I looked at the search results and then I selected the third link." Simply describing your sequence of actions does not get at the deeper question of *why*, which is crucial for novice Web readers. An effective think-aloud is more like a dramatization of the reading process. For the experienced reader, this process occurs in a split second. The teacher's job is to zoom in and stretch out that split second, much like a slow motion instant replay in sports. You are like the player after the game providing commentary about what he did and why he did it—except that you are doing it in the moment. Use phrases such as "Right now I'm thinking . . ." or "I was going to do this but I changed my mind because . . ." Be clear and specific. As with other forms of teacher modeling, think-alouds are most effective when the strategy explanation is explicit, leaving few opportunities for the reader to guess at the process (see Fisher, Frey, & Lapp, 2009; Raphael, Wonnacott, & Pearson, 1983).

Gradual Release of Responsibility

Another concept that we have purposefully included throughout this text is the gradual release of responsibility. As learners move from listening and watching to demonstrating and doing, they become more skilled at creating syntheses on their own (Pearson & Gallagher, 1983). Early in the instructional sequence, a teacher breaks down the synthesis strategy into smaller steps, describes each step, models each step, and gives students the opportunity for repeated practice until readers are able to create syntheses independently.

Because readers vary in skill and experience levels, different amounts of support and practice may be needed at different stages along the way. Students who struggle with decoding may need to begin practicing synthesis by using text to speech, as described in Chapter 4. These tools and apps reduce the cognitive load of decoding so that readers can focus on developing synthesis strategies through listening comprehension.

> The accumulation of many small and large differences of frequency, degree, and speed has indeed produced a qualitative change and a new kind of cognitive challenge for comprehending online.   —Hartman, Morsink, and Zhang (2010, p. 132)

In our work with less skilled Internet readers, we notice that if students get stuck at one step of a synthesis process, they typically stop reading. If they cannot find useful information or find a website that connects to their prior knowledge, they never harvest enough information to create a synthesis. Young readers tend to struggle with the step of determining important ideas. When asked to create a summary of what they have read, some readers say too much because everything seems as important as everything else. Alternately, they focus on the interesting and exotic ideas rather than the essential ideas. At other times, readers struggle with obtaining enough important information to create a summary. Still other readers are skilled at determining important ideas but are unsure of what to do with this information and how to make it their own. They may lack the prior knowledge and experiences needed for developing personal connections to the text. Another group of readers may prefer to stick with the literal, hoping to go right to a single paragraph or web page, find the information, and be finished reading, seeming to lack the inner drive of inquiry that encourages them to keep searching and pulling together ideas from various websites in order to create a synthesis. By explaining, modeling, and guiding, a teacher can gradually set students on the path toward independence equipped with strategies and expectations of what it takes to find and understand information.

Clearly, the process of the synthesis is fraught with possible difficulties. Synthesis can be characterized as mental aerobics, stretching our brains in different directions as we learn new ideas. For the rest of this chapter, we focus on ways to help students become more strategic about synthesizing.

Synthesis in Action: Inquiry Projects

Every year, Scott Ritter's third graders work through the inquiry process as a part of their district reading and language arts curriculum, completing seven inquiry projects a year. Students use these questions to guide their inquiry projects:

"What do you wonder about?
"What do you do to seek answers?"
"How do you share what you have learned with others?"

Early in the school year, Scott and the students work through the inquiry process together, as Scott explains, models, and provides guided practice on a class collaborative project. For the next and subsequent projects, students work in teams of four, with Scott providing less support for each project (Figure 8.4).

One team created the inquiry question, "How was the earth formed?" The group made a plan for answering their question by reading books and online resources, then coming together at the end of each inquiry session to discuss an information summary. Part way through the project, the team began to synthesize their ideas into an electronic slide show. Throughout this process, Scott continually reminds students of their inquiry question and the importance of locating, reading, and summarizing information relevant to this question. Final projects representing the students' synthesis of ideas are shared with the class (Figure 8.5). Scott uses rubrics from the district-adopted reading series to assess the inquiry process, products, and speaking and listening skills.

FIGURE 8.4. An inquiry project conference.

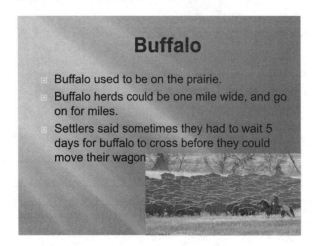

Buffalo

- Buffalo used to be on the prairie.
- Buffalo herds could be one mile wide, and go on for miles.
- Settlers said sometimes they had to wait 5 days for buffalo to cross before they could move their wagon

FIGURE 8.5. A group project represents a collaborative synthesis.

Synthesis in Action: Scaffolded Inquiry

Sue Bowman scaffolds her fifth graders as they use the inquiry process to answer the question, "How will giving animals prosthetic limbs benefit humans?" To begin, Sue and the students read an article about artificial limbs for animals from a print classroom magazine. The article piques the students' interest and inspires a lively class discussion. Next, the students gain additional information by watching a related video and reading an article from the online children's newspaper *DOGOnews* (*dogonews.com*). Students summarize the information from each of the three sources onto a graphic organizer and synthesize that information to write a persuasive essay answering the guiding question. Sue pauses periodically to remind students of the steps of the inquiry process. These gentle nudges are much like a horseback rider using the reins to guide a horse along the trail.

Synthesis in Action: 30-Minute Expert

Ginger Lewman's seventh- and eighth-grade social studies students learn about Haiti through the 30-minute expert activity. Students work in groups of three or four, selecting a broad topic (geography, culture, economy, government, climate), searching online for information, and synthesizing it into a paragraph, which is added to an online collaborative document on Google Docs. This fast-paced activity is like calisthenics when training for a big race, serving as a quick practice before a full-fledged inquiry project. Students move through the process of generating an inquiry question, searching, making inferences, summarizing, and reaching consensus on a synthesis of information presented as a written paragraph, all within 30 minutes. To facilitate the creation of a group synthesis, Ginger encourages the students to share "oh, I didn't know that" moments experienced during their reading.

Activities to Promote Synthesis

An introduction to synthesis should utilize print and digital texts with familiar vocabulary and text structures so instruction can focus on the strategy rather than the other challenges a reader may face with the text. Some students may prefer to practice synthesizing with images or media rather than text, depending on their learning styles. Two key activities to teach students about synthesizing the big ideas from informational text include (1) explicit instruction about synthesis and (2) think-aloud mini-sessions (Cummins & Stallmeyer-Gerard, 2011). A teacher should model how he thinks while determining the key idea in a text and creating a line of thinking that is his own. As students become more skilled, text complexity can be increased, and more responsibility can be passed on to the students until they are able to form a synthesis on their own. This process will likely take time and practice, because synthesizing is a higher level thinking skill.

The Text Map (Handout S-8.1) helps students identify the features of a website that point out important information. The SQ3R Strategy (Handout S-8.2), which has assisted readers of print text for years, is adapted for Internet text. Before, During, and After (Handout S-8.3) is a great way to assist students in planning ways to collect information throughout the reading process. Because determining and summarizing important ideas from a website can be difficult, we offer the handout Determining Important Ideas (Handout S-8.4). Skills for synthesizing visuals and multimedia can be developed with Worth a Thousand Words (Handout S-8.5) and What You See and Hear (Handout S-8.6). The Key

> [Synthesis] should go on throughout the process of reading—not just at the end. In a way it's a matter of bringing together different ideas and facts, from the text and from the reader's experience, and weaving them together into a tapestry, something larger, more complete than all the threads.
> —Keene and Zimmerman (1997, p. 173)

Idea Synthesis Chart (Handout S-8.7) not only helps students identify important ideas but also asks them to justify their choices. The Synthesis Map (Handout S-8.8) provides a structure for pulling together ideas from several websites to form a synthesis, along with the Two-Column Web Journal (Handout S-8.9). The Evidence For and Against (Handout S-8.10) provides practice with synthesizing persuasive arguments. The Synthesis Self-Checker (Handout S-8.11) provides a format for evaluating the quality of a written synthesis. Students are encouraged to reflect on their own synthesizing abilities with the Synthesis Self-Reflection (Handout S-8.12). Finally, we offer a Synthesizing Lesson Plan (Handouts S-8.13 and S-8.14) for the elementary level and the middle level.

SUMMARY ●

Synthesis facilitates the process of understanding what we see, hear, and read by creating a link between a collection of facts and ideas. At the heart of synthesis is determining what is important. Titles, headings, and visuals provide the Web reader with hints at important ideas, but valuable information can also be gained from a careful reading of longer texts, viewing a video, or listening to a sound clip. Once these important ideas are gathered and summarized, a reader forms a mental thread linking the ideas together. He makes the information his own through the creation of a personal interpretation or understanding.

After Synthesis, the next step in an Internet QUEST often involves the Transforming of this newfound knowledge into a format that can be shared with others through the creation of a final product. Chapter 9 is devoted to the idea of transformation, how it occurs, and ways to help students become more strategic when making notes, organizing information, citing sources, creating final products, and presenting what they've learned.

Handouts

All of the handouts listed in the following chart can be used with both print and Internet texts; in fact, you may want to have students practice using some of them on easy informational texts before trying them with web pages, which are more complex owing to all the additional cueing systems (see Chapter 3). As with all of our handouts, choose a few that look promising and save the rest for another time.

Number	Name of handout	Purpose
S-8.1	Text Map	Identify features of a website
S-8.2	SQ3R Strategy	Record the main points on a page
S-8.3	Before, During, and After	Engage in active reading strategies
S-8.4	Determining Important Ideas	Summarize important ideas
S-8.5	Worth a Thousand Words	Synthesize visuals
S-8.6	What You See and Hear	Synthesize multimedia
S-8.7	Key Idea Synthesis Chart	Identify ideas and justify choices
S-8.8	Synthesis Map	Synthesize from multiple sites
S-8.9	Two-Column Web Journal	Compare facts and responses
S-8.10	Evidence For and Against	Synthesize persuasive arguments
S-8.11	Synthesis Self-Checker	Check your synthesis
S-8.12	Synthesis Self-Reflection	Assess a synthesis
S-8.13	Synthesizing Lesson Plan—Elementary Level	Process of creating a synthesis from print and online sources
S-8.14	Synthesizing Lesson Plan—Middle Level	Process of creating a synthesis from print and online sources

HANDOUT S-8.1. Text Map

Name _____ Class _____ Date _____

Directions: *Choose a website and list/describe the features that that highlight important information.*

URL: _____

Headings:	Subheadings:

Bolded or Italicized Words:	Graphics (pictures, icons, charts, maps, etc.). Describe:

Multimedia (audio, video, etc.). Describe:	Based on this information, what are the main ideas of this website?

HANDOUT S-8.2. SQ3R Strategy

Name _____ Class _____ Date _____

Directions: *Use the SQ3R Strategy to practice summarizing web page information.*

S̲URVEY—Q̲UESTION—R̲EAD—R̲ECITE—R̲EVIEW

URL: _____

SURVEY: Skim over the web page, glancing at all the features (text, images, links, etc.) What do you think this page is going to cover?

QUESTION: Turn the titles and headings into questions. For example, if the site says "Panda Habitat" at the top, write the question, "What is the panda's habitat?"

READ: Read one section at a time. Write answers to the questions you wrote above.

RECITE: Summarize the main points without looking back at the web page.

REVIEW: Reread your summary, checking the web page for any main points you may have missed. Write any missing points here.

HANDOUT S-8.3. Before, During, and After

Name _____ Class _____ Date _____

Directions: *Pick a website for your topic that you want to read closely and ask yourself the following questions.*

URL: _____

BEFORE READING

1. What do I already know about this topic?

2. Why am I reading this?

3. How is this website organized?

DURING READING

1. What will the web page talk about next? Use clues from text, links, and media.

2. What does it mean? (If you find something hard to understand.)

3. How does it connect with what I already know?

AFTER READING

1. What did I learn?

2. What did I miss? Reread to see if you missed anything important.

3. How can I use this information?

HANDOUT S-8.4. Determining Important Ideas

Name _____ Class _____ Date _____

Directions: *Pick a website and use this chart to identify important ideas.*

URL: _____

	Write your answers in this column
1. Skim the web page. What is it about?	
2. Scan for five keywords from the web page.	
3. Sketch or describe an illustration, icon, or chart on the web page.	
4. What is the most important idea on the web page?	
5. I know this idea is important because . . .	

HANDOUT S-8.5. Worth a Thousand Words

Name _____ Class _____ Date _____

Directions: *Choose one visual from a website to analyze. Valuable information can be gained from the visuals on a website (photos, drawings, charts, graphs, maps, etc.).*

URL: _____

Sketch the visual here:

(1) OVERVIEW: Look over the whole visual. What does it make you think about? What does it make you wonder?

(2) FOCUS: What are three details you notice about the labels, captions, or description? What is one question you have?

(3) CONNECT: Build connections between the parts and the whole. How do the parts help you understand the visual?

HANDOUT S-8.6. What You See and Hear

Name _____ Class _____ Date _____

Directions: *Follow these steps to understand information that is provided on a website in multimedia form rather than text.*

URL: _____

Circle the type of media: VIDEO   AUDIO   ANIMATION

____ Step 1: Identify your purpose. Think about why you are listening or watching. What do you hope to learn?

____ Step 2: Think about what you know. Before you begin listening or watching, write down three or four things that you already know about the subject.

____ Step 3: Watch or listen to the media clip straight through with no interruptions. What is your general impression?

(continued)

____ Step 4: Watch or listen again. This time, pause three times while listening or watching. When you pause, think about what you have seen or heard. Write down two or three key ideas you want to remember. Then return to finish watching or listening.

Pause #1: What do you want to remember?

Pause #2: What do you want to remember?

Pause #3: What do you want to remember?

____ Step 5: Summarize. Write a sentence or two explaining the most important idea about what you saw or heard.

HANDOUT S-8.7. Key Idea Synthesis Chart

Name _____ Class _____ Date _____

Directions: *Identify five of the most important ideas related to your inquiry question. Use at least two different websites to locate information about these ideas. Think about how you would explain the most important ideas to someone who had not read these websites.*

Key Idea with URL	Put the Idea in Your Own Words	Explain Why the Idea Is Important
1.		
2.		
3.		
4.		
5.		

HANDOUT S-8.8. Synthesis Map

Name _____ Class _____ Date _____

Directions: Find information on your topic from three different websites, summarize the information, then create a synthesis of all three.

URL #1 _____

Summary

URL #2 _____

Summary

URL #3 _____

Summary

Synthesis

HANDOUT S-8.9. Two-Column Web Journal

Name _____ Class _____ Date _____

Directions: *Use this journal to record facts and your thinking as you read various websites. Feel free to use these sentence starters for your personal responses.*l

- I wonder . . .
- I can't believe . . .
- I didn't realize . . .
- Now I think . . .

- I am curious about . . .
- I doubt . . .
- This reminds me of . . .
- I still want to know . . .

URL #1: _____

Facts from the Website	Personal Response

URL #2: _____

Facts from the Website	Personal Response

URL #3: _____

Facts from the Website	Personal Response

HANDOUT S-8.10. Evidence For and Against

Name _____ Class _____ Date _____

Directions: *Identify two websites that display opposite views on an issue. Use this chart to list the evidence for and against the issue, then explain your personal opinion.*

What's the issue? _____

URL #1: Evidence For
URL #2: Evidence Against
My Personal Opinion

HANDOUT S-8.11. Synthesis Self-Checker

Name _____ Class _____ Date _____

Directions: *Synthesize information on your topic from two sites and use the self-checker to see how you did.*

URL #1: _____

URL #2: _____

My Synthesis

- ☐ Is my synthesis short?
- ☐ Is my synthesis accurate?
- ☐ Is it in my own words?
- ☐ Does it include the most important ideas and information?
- ☐ Does it include some supporting details?
- ☐ Is there anything missing?
- ☐ Does the order make sense?

HANDOUT S-8.12. Synthesis Self-Reflection (use with Lesson Plan Handout S-14)

Name _____ Class _____ Date _____

Directions: *Think about the following questions as they relate to your synthesis activity.*

1. How would I rate the quality of my activity between 1 (low) and 5 (high) _____
   Why did I give it this rating?

2. What is the best part of my synthesis activity?

3. What do I wish I had done differently during this activity?

4. How well did my partner and I work together? If you worked alone, write N/A.

5. What did I learn about creating a synthesis?

HANDOUT S-8.13. Synthesizing Lesson Plan—Elementary Level

Objectives

1. To determine important ideas from text and websites.
2. To create a synthesis of important ideas.

Time

Three or four class periods

Materials

1. QUEST Inquiry Model (Handout P-4.11)
2. Synthesis Self-Checker (Handout S-8.11)
2. Locate two grade-level-appropriate websites related to a topic of study in science or social studies. The search engine KidsClick (*www.kidsclick.org*) is a useful resource for locating informational websites appropriate for children.

Assessment Options

1. Checklist on Synthesis Self-Checker (Handout S-8.11)

Introduction

1. Tell students you will be teaching them a strategy for synthesizing that many other students have found useful. Contextualize the lesson, using the QUEST Inquiry Model (Handout P-4.11), by pointing out that they are in the **S** phase of the QUEST, which includes synthesizing information.
2. Explain that a synthesis is a way to bring together the ideas you learn from reading books, magazines, and websites. Say, "We can take these ideas and explain them to someone else, such as a teacher, other students, and parents, by writing a synthesis."
3. Activate prior knowledge about the topic of the websites by creating a group list of facts.
4. Display the suggested websites on a projector. Together, read sections of the text. If helpful, a paper copy of the web text can be provided to students who may need to see the text more closely or may need to return to the text to create a synthesis.

Modeling

1. Pause at strategic points in the text to think aloud about your comprehension process.
2. Model for students how you will determine an important idea and how you will put this idea into your own words.

Practice

1. Invite a few students to orally share an idea pulled from the text that is in their own words. If students have a paper copy, ask them to turn the copy over and not to peek.
2. After working through the reading process with both websites, ask students to complete the Synthesis Self-Checker (Handout S-8.11).
3. Ask students to self-assess their completed syntheses. Talk through each item on the checklist, explaining terminology and expectations, encouraging students to give honest reflections about their own syntheses.

Scaffolding

1. Allow weaker writers to dictate ideas to stronger writers.

Feedback

1. Look over the students' Synthesis Self-Checker and provide feedback about the match between their syntheses and their perception of their syntheses.

Ticket Out the Door

Have students name one positive quality of their syntheses.

HANDOUT S-8.14. Synthesizing Lesson Plan—Middle Level

Objectives

1. To determine important ideas from text and websites.
2. To create a synthesis of important ideas.

Time

Three or four class periods

Materials

1. QUEST Inquiry Model (Handout P-4.11)
2. Access to a variety of print and online resources related to a topic of study in the grade-level science or social studies curriculum
3. A paper copy of a page of informational text from two websites related to the topic
4. Synthesis Self-Checker (Handout S-8.11)

Assessment Options

1. Self-assessment checklist on Synthesis Self-Checker (Handout S-8.11)

Introduction

1. Tell students you will be teaching them a strategy for synthesizing that many other students have found useful. Contextualize the lesson, using the QUEST Inquiry Model (Handout P-4.11), by pointing out that they are in the **S** phase of the QUEST, which includes synthesizing information.
2. Explain that a synthesis occurs when we bring together information found in various sources and then present it to others in a new way. Have students brainstorm why synthesizing is useful in this class, in other classes, and outside of school. This can be done in pairs, in small groups, or as a whole class.
3. Activate prior knowledge about the topic of study.
4. Have students locate resources from the library or in the classroom with information about the topic and do background reading.

Modeling

1. Demonstrate locating informational websites related to the topic of study by using the search engine KidsClick (*www.kidsclick.org*). Think aloud the considerations you give when selecting which website to read from the list of search results. Select one website for modeling.
2. Think aloud while reading from a selected website.
3. Model for students how you will determine an important idea, utilizing highlighting, underlining, arrows, or some other visual guide to important information. Be sure to explain why you do not select some information as important.
4. Model writing a synthesis, thinking aloud as you write your ideas. Then think through the self-assessment checklist (Handout S-8.11) aloud, also inviting students to give you feedback.

(continued)

Practice

1. Have students read their paper copies of web texts with partners and identify three important ideas for each. Mark these on the paper and encourage discussion of the reasons for selecting this important information.
2. Have the students work individually to write a synthesis from the two websites. Encourage students to keep their paper copies turned over, so they are not tempted to copy word for word.
3. Next, ask students to read over their syntheses and consider the points in the checklist to evaluate the quality of their syntheses. Then have students read their syntheses to their partners and have the pairs discuss the elements on the checklist for each other's synthesis.

Scaffolding

1. If anyone is struggling to decode their text, have a proficient reader read it aloud.
2. Allow weaker writers to dictate ideas to stronger writers.

Feedback

1. Have students provide feedback to each other when sharing their syntheses, using the self-assessment checklist as a guide.

Ticket Out the Door

Have students name one quality of an effective synthesis.

⑨ Transforming

Questioning
What do I
want to know?

Transforming
What will I do
with it?

QUEST

Understanding
Resources
How will I
find out?

Synthesizing
What does
this mean?

Evaluating
Is this what
I need?

KEY IDEAS ●

- Information by itself is not knowledge. Because many students struggle with Transforming information into knowledge, we must provide instruction and scaffolding in this important skill.

- The key question that guides the T phase of the inquiry process is "What will I do with this information?"

- Because a large majority of learners do not know how to make notes in their own words, they need to be taught specific strategies for notemaking and annotating, whether it be from printed or online resources.

- Citing sources has traditionally been an area of challenge for students, and the ease of copying information and media from the Internet has made this task even more challenging.

- It's important to offer students choices in how they demonstrate the knowledge gained during an inquiry project.

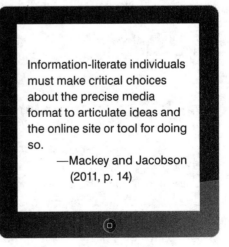

Information-literate individuals must make critical choices about the precise media format to articulate ideas and the online site or tool for doing so.

—Mackey and Jacobson (2011, p. 14)

A collection of information is only useful if it is internalized as knowledge. It is even more useful when transformed into something new and shared with others. In this chapter, we draw from years of classroom-based research to investigate the strategies involved in Transforming information into knowledge. For all types of information transformation, learners seek to express their own voices, to feel like their ideas matter, to solve problems, and to persuade others. Successful Transformation necessitates that students have strategies for notemaking, organizing information, citing sources, creating a product, and presenting final products to others.

Why Is It Important to Transform Information?

As with writing, in which not all rough drafts are selected for a final polish, not all inquiries lead to a final product. For example, a simple search for an isolated fact on the Internet may satisfy a practical information need, such as accessing the day's weather forecast. However, full-scale classroom inquiry often requires transforming various pieces of information into an original product. Information by itself is not power; rather, knowledge is power (Perkins, 1986). Students who can convert information into useful knowledge, perhaps even derive solutions to real problems, and then share it with others are well on their way to success in school and in life (Leu et al., 2013).

Regrettably, many students are not able to transform information into knowledge. Often, students' final projects simply mirror what they happen to find on the Web, with no real synthesis or formation of a new idea, as described in Chapter 8. For example, one student found a bulleted list on a website, so she copied it into a digital slide show covering the exact same information. Students' final projects are often a simple recall of facts rather than a synthesized, compelling perspective on a topic. Students need guidance on appropriate use of media formats, such as captioning images and using large fonts with minimal text on slide show presentations. They must resist the temptation to become so enamored with multimedia features that their products lack substantive content.

Teachers and librarians with whom we've worked have remarked that although a few of their students are facile at *finding* information, most lack strategies for *doing* something with it. Students also have difficulty knowing when they have "enough" information to begin constructing a final product. These skills do not come naturally to all learners, so they must be taught, modeled, and practiced.

When Do We Transform Information?

We transform information in our daily lives every time we have an "aha!" moment, when seemingly random pieces of information suddenly meld into a coherent whole. Transformation can also happen more intentionally, as when a teacher looks over a few different lesson plan ideas and then creates her own plan to suit her objectives and the needs of her students. Transformation occurs every time we write, draw, make up a song or dance, invent a recipe, or use an original metaphor to explain an abstract concept.

Transformation is at the core of a constructivist philosophy of learning (see Chapter 2). In classrooms where creativity and originality are celebrated (as opposed to environments that promote rote memorization and correct answers), transformation takes place all the time. It is impressive to observe what happens when students are given freedom to express themselves using any format they wish and to participate in determining how they will be assessed. With proper scaffolding, most students thrive when given the freedom to create. These are the times when kids forget they are learning and beg to be given extra time during recess, lunch, and after school to work on projects. Most students are especially motivated when designing multimedia projects (Frey et al., 2010; Yang & Wu, 2012) because they feel empowered by the notion of "leaving digital footprints for other people to find" (November, 2012, p. 85). Creating their own messages, whether through multimedia or traditional forms, lets learners experience the power of authorship (Hobbs, 2011), transforming their learning and themselves.

> When there is an authentic audience and one that provides feedback, students produce incredible work.   —Frey, Fisher, and Gonzalez (2010, p. 102)

What Characterizes Information Transformation?

Information transformation is analogous to the concept of transmediation. Transmediation means taking content from one form of representation (such as print) and recreating it in another (such as art). In the context of Internet inquiry, transformation means synthesizing content from various sources and creating something original based on a personally meaningful research question. To be successful with the Transformation phase of the QUEST, students must have strategies for notemaking, organizing information, citing sources, designing a product, and presenting it to others, topics that we address in turn.

Notemaking

Many students have a naïve understanding of their ability to hold extensive amounts of information in their heads (Fisher & Frey, 2013). Making notes is crucial to information transformation, because it is impossible to remember everything that is encountered in the course of an Internet QUEST. We *take* notes when we're viewing or listening to something once with no opportunity to replay; in contrast, we *make* notes when we can return to the source and check our notes again (Fisher et al., 2012). The process of notemaking goes beyond recording information for later retrieval; it provides an opportunity for learners to "translate and integrate that information into the student's own knowledge and schema" (Beach, Campano, Edmiston, & Borgmann, 2010, p. 122). Unfortunately, very few students make notes in their own words. For instance, one eighth grader admitted, "I don't take down notes, I just print and highlight, that's how I get my info."

The CCSS call for students to determine central ideas, notice how smaller and larger parts of the text relate, and integrate knowledge across diverse media (NGA &

CCSSO, 2010). This is complex brain work. When gathering and interpreting information in the vast world of the Web, learners face additional challenges in making notes. Even the seemingly simple action of scrolling can add to the cognitive load of online reading and complicate the process of notemaking (Kauffman, Zhao, & Yang, 2011). Learners often respond to these complexities by using what they think are shortcuts. The most common is making heavy use of copy/paste and print, which results in final projects that contain large volumes of plagiarized information. Even though students can parrot back a definition of *plagiarism* at a young age, most don't know how to avoid it and don't appear to realize when they've done it. The vast majority of students who plagiarize do so because they lack the training and experience to do otherwise (Frey et al., 2010). Figure 9.1 shows one seventh grader's final text as compared to the website text from which she got the information. Do you notice any similarities? Not only did the student submit the text unaltered, but she did not even understand what it meant. When she presented her project to the class and the teacher asked for clarification on the "dun factor" information, the student was unable to define it, much less expand on the concept.

 Reading Standard: **Gather relevant information from multiple print and digital sources, assess the credibility and accuracy of each source, and integrate the information while avoiding plagiarism.**

Guinee and Eagleton (2006) found that when eighth graders were required to make notes during online inquiry, they used four types of notemaking strategies: (1) copying and pasting large chunks; (2) copying small chunks; (3) paraphrasing; and (4) making notes to themselves. On average, students saved only *five* notes during an Internet inquiry project in which 2 weeks were devoted to searching and notemaking. This raises the question, "How did they complete final products based on only five notes?" Only 16% of these eighth graders' notes were paraphrased; in contrast, nearly 77% of their notes were copied verbatim. Most of these verbatim notes were then included in final projects without substantial changes.

Copying and Pasting Large Chunks

In the same study, 45% of the students' notes involved highlighting gigantic portions of web pages and copying the unfiltered contents into word processing documents, a

Website Text	Student's Final Text
A description of the Kiger Mustang would begin with their coloration which is known as the "dun factor." The dun factor colours are dun (which resembles a buckskin but is genetically different), red dun, grulla and claybank. There are also a few bays, blacks, and sorrels present in the Kiger Mustang herds.	A description of the Kiger Mustang would begin with their coloration which is known as the "dun factor." The dun factor colours are dun (which resembles a buckskin but is genetically different), red dun, grulla and claybank. There are also a few bays, blacks, and sorrels present in the Kiger Mustang herds.

FIGURE 9.1. Information without transformation.

strategy we call copying large text chunks (Guinee & Eagleton, 2006). Some students pasted more than 1,000 words of text, and although this can save time up front, it simply postpones the inevitable chore of extracting key information. The challenge for teachers is to make sure students eventually do evaluate and synthesize this material.

Copying Small Chunks

Copying small chunks means copying less than four lines of text, or about 50 words. Unlike the previous approach, this strategy requires the reader to selectively identify target information for copying. In this Guinee and Eagleton study (2006), students copied small chunks for an average of 32% of their notemaking. For example, in addition to collecting short quotations by Martin Luther King, Jr., one student copied the following information on his family life:

> **Students need to learn how to use note-taking to critically synthesize and reformulate texts or presentations in their own words related to their own purposes.**
> **—Beach, Campano, Edmiston, and Borgmann (2010, p. 122)**

> Four children were born to Dr. and Mrs. King: Yolanda Denise (November 17, 1955, Montgomery, Alabama) Martin Luther III (October 23, 1957, Montgomery, Alabama) Dexter Scott (January 30, 1961, Atlanta, Georgia) Bernice Albertine (March 28, 1963, Atlanta, Georgia).

Paraphrasing

Paraphrasing key ideas is the optimal notemaking strategy from an educator's perspective. One learner described it thus: "I look at a certain paragraph and pick out whatever useful it has and put it down in my own words." In his search for information on Vivaldi's family, this student's notes read, "Vivaldi had four brothers and four sisters, He and his father were the two musisions [sic] of the family." Similarly, in an investigation of George Harrison's personality, one girl wrote, "George was the easy going on [one] in the beatles group." Unfortunately, only 16% of the notes saved by these students fell into this category (Guinee & Eagleton, 2006).

Making Notes to Oneself

The strategy of writing a metacognitive note to oneself was evidenced in only 4% of the notes analyzed in the previously described study and can be attributed to only two students; however, this strategy is worthy of mention. Examples of (unedited) metacognitive notes are as follows:

> Gotta come here again!!!!!!!!!!!!!!!! I mean it!!!!!!!!!!!!!! This is and exelent site!!!!!

> Keep in mind. This is a really informative site, one that should be used as a good resorce.

> Need this for future ref.

The relatively few notes collected by the eighth graders and the lack of synthesis present in their notes led researcher Kathleen Guinee to look more closely at notemaking practices in the upper elementary level. In a fifth-grade class, she observed that during the short Web-based research assignments, the students tended not to make *any* notes, with only a third of the fifth graders reporting that they made notes during their research task. When asked, the students explained that they didn't make notes because they didn't feel the need. Typical reasons included "because I could keep the info in my mind" and because the information source and writing tool were both on the computer. The CHoMP notemaking strategy described next accentuates that making notes is useful for more than simply helping students remember what they've read.

> **TEACHER: What have you learned about inquiry?**
>
> **STUDENT: I have learned if you set your mind to something that you may learn something that you didn't know before.**

CHoMP Notemaking Strategy

Clearly, students are in serious need of notemaking strategies. Notemaking is useful not only during Web inquiries but also when writing down directions, studying textbooks, conducting interviews, and listening to lectures. Based on a compilation of the literature on summarization (e.g., Brown & Day, 1983; Hare & Borchardt, 1984; Winograd, 1984), Maya developed an original strategy for notemaking called "CHoMP" (Guinee & Eagleton, 2006). The verb *chomp* serves as an effective metaphor for the concept that notemaking involves selectively biting off small pieces of information. With CHoMP, students learn to:

- **C**ross out small words, such as prepositions and conjunctions.
- **H**ighlight important information in the remaining text.
- o (placeholder).
- **M**ake notes based on the highlighted information by abbreviating, truncating, making lists, using symbols, and drawing instead of writing full sentences.
- **P**ut the notes in their own words.

The CHoMP strategy not only stresses the importance of making notes but also helps students to create useful paraphrased notes for transforming information they've gathered into their own words. Before teaching CHoMP, we recommend administering a pretest of students' existing notemaking strategies. Using a one-page expository text, such as an Informal Reading Inventory for your grade level, instruct students to "show how you normally make notes." Ask them to make notes using pens and highlighters and then write a summary based on their notes. In our experiences during this pretest, students highlight far too much information, write verbatim notes, and generate a mostly verbatim summary. Use this same procedure for a posttest after the instructional unit to observe changes in your students' notemaking. We've observed dramatic change by our students, even those with learning disabilities who struggle with print.

Introduce CHoMP as a generalizable strategy for notemaking that will help students not only in your class but also in other classes and in the future. It is advisable to have students brainstorm the uses of notemaking to ensure they understand the purpose of the lesson and increase the potential for transfer. After discussing the purpose, model the first step of CHoMP (Cross out) on the overhead with a single paragraph, such as the one shown in Figure 9.2. It is especially powerful to use sample sentences and paragraphs from websites that students have actually encountered in mini-inquiries prior to a notemaking unit. Provide additional paragraphs for guided and independent practice and for homework, if desired. Most students find this first step easy; in fact, Figure 9.2 was produced by a seventh grader with severe learning disabilities.

For CHoMP Step 2 (Highlight), repeat the modeling, guided practice, and independent practice procedure used with Step 1. This time, demonstrate the process of highlighting important information. This is generally the most difficult step for students, because it's hard for many of them to discern what is *important* versus merely interesting or unusual. We found it extremely helpful to model this decision-making process using a teacher think-aloud at the overhead. Figure 9.3 shows a different student's highlighted text.

In preparation for CHoMP Step 3 (Make notes), model a variety of notemaking methods, such as abbreviating, truncating, making lists, using symbols, and drawing. Then return to the texts with which the students have been working to model and practice making notes. Figures 9.4 and 9.5 show two students' different approaches to making notes about the Siberian tiger text.

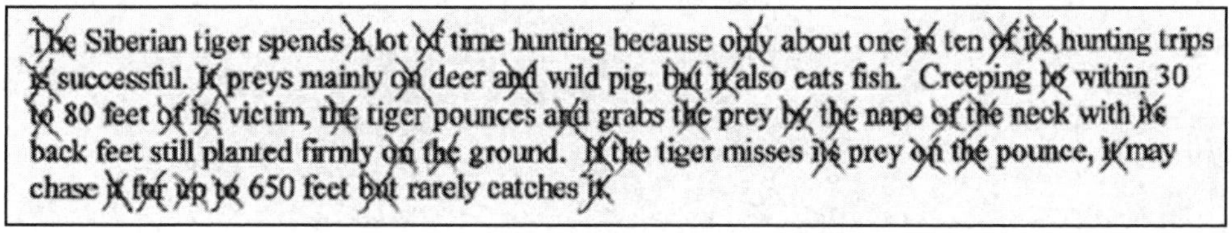

FIGURE 9.2. CHoMP Step 1: Cross out.

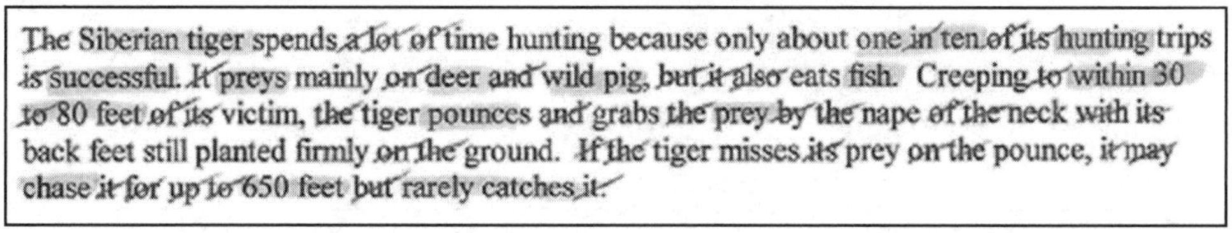

FIGURE 9.3. CHoMP Step 2: Highlight.

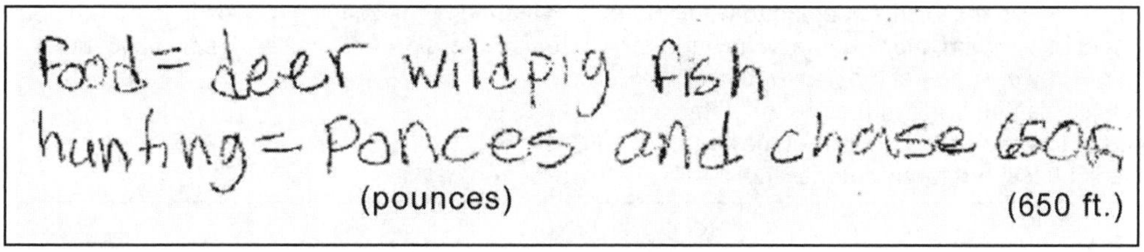

FIGURE 9.4. CHoMP Step 3: Make notes (using truncation and lists).

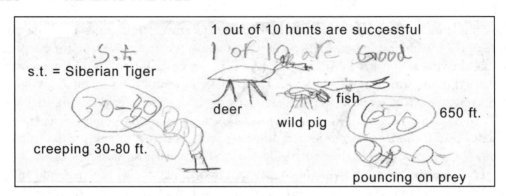

FIGURE 9.5. CHoMP Step 3: Make notes (abbreviating and drawing).

Finally, for CHoMP Step 4 (Put in your own words), have the students use their notes to write an original summary. This step is most effective when students do not refer to the original text. Figure 9.6 shows one student's final notes, which were creatively and accurately paraphrased from the original text. As evidence of CHoMP's promise as a notemaking strategy, this summary was produced by the same student whose verbatim notes were shown earlier in Figure 9.1.

Once students have transformed texts using CHoMP, the likelihood of plagiarism is greatly diminished, and students are in a much better position to construct their own knowledge. We share lesson plans and handouts for teaching the CHoMP notemaking strategy at the end of this chapter.

Annotating

Although the process for making notes can be a critical part of getting information into a learner's own words, there are also times when a quick note serves as a metacognitive reminder of one's thinking during the inquiry process. An annotation is a brief note or comment added to a text. Annotating is like the tracks one leaves when walking in the snow or on the beach, providing evidence of a reader's thought process or a visual arrow pointing to ideas worth remembering. Often accompanied by highlighting and underlining, annotations might be handwritten on a sticky note or typed on a digital

Original Text	Final Text Using CHoMP
The Siberian tiger spends a lot of time hunting because only about one in ten of its hunting trips are successful. It preys mainly on deer and wild pig, but it also eats fish. Creeping to within 30 to 80 feet of its victim, the tiger pounces and grabs the prey by the nape of the neck with its back feet still planted firmly in the ground. If the tiger misses its prey on the pounce, it may chase it for up to 650 feet but rarely catches it.	The Siberian tiger can hunt very well, here is how it hunts. The tiger awaits its prey 30 or 80 feet away and ponces [*sic*] on its prey with feet clenched in the soil. If it misses it, it will run 650 feet or more. But otherwise, it's bye-bye lunch.

FIGURE 9.6. CHoMP Step 4: Put it into your own words.

TABLE 9.1. Examples of Digital Annotation and Notemaking Tools

Annotation and notemaking tools	Format	Features
Diigo (*diigo.com*)	website and app	Users can save websites and use tags to organize sites into categories. A webpage can be highlighted and sticky notes attached. These annotations can be kept private or shared.
Evernote (*evernote.com*)	website and app	A note can be a text file, a webpage, a voice memo, or an image. Each can be stored in searchable folders, annotated, and tagged.
Notability	app	This app lets users sketch an idea, add notes to a pdf, create an outline, or type a list.
Thinglink (*thinglink.com*)	website and app	Comments can be embedded within an image, along with links, to other websites and multimedia.
Video Notes (*videonot.es*)	website	When streaming a video from YouTube, users can crop, slow down, and add timed annotations. Video Notes can be integrated with Google Drive.

note. Chapter 4, Preparing for the QUEST, discussed the topic of digital curation, and annotations can play an important role in helping learners to organize their online information. When using digital annotation tools (see Table 9.1), the user can collect the annotations together into one electronic document. In many cases, these annotations can be shared with others.

Organizing Information

After asking dozens of students to describe their strategies for organizing information, we've come to the conclusion that organizing information is not an area of strength for many elementary and middle school students. We have all witnessed the hapless student with a binder stuffed full of wrinkled papers from all her classes, the inevitable dropping of the binder, the hasty restuffing, and well, you know the rest. Then there's the daily frantic search for homework in the backpack or desk full of who-knows-what. Add these images to classic excuses such as "my dog ate it," and you have a fairly accurate picture of the level of organization on which many students operate.

Figure 9.7 shows typical responses by students in grades 5–8 to the question, "How do you usually organize the information you find about a research topic?" sorted by the headings No Strategies, Weak Strategies, Somewhat Strong Strategies, and Strong Strategies. Note that there was only *one* student in this sample who was able to articulate a strong organizational strategy.

One of the most striking aspects of these students' responses is the way in which technology can both help and hinder the organizational process. Technology can help

	TYPICAL STUDENT RESPONSES
No Strategies	• I don't have a strategy. • Well, since I usually do it on the last day, my mom helps me look at stuff, so I don't need to keep it. [*laughter*] • Usually you try to save it, at least that's what the teachers tell you to do.
Weak Strategies	• I usually write it down on a scrap paper. • I just copy it, I mean just print it. Yeah. • I print 'em and put them in a folder. • I usually copy and paste it to Word. And after that I print it and read it over. Or I just print it from the webpage. • I usually cut and paste to a file so that I could just have all my stuff together and then after that I would print.
Somewhat Strong Strategies	• I'd print it out and lay it out in a stack. Maybe put one pack of paper sideways, to keep track of each section. • I'd organize it and collect the useful information out of it and then probably trash the rest. • I'll copy it and put it on a word processor because then I could just copy that sentence or two that I think would really go good with my topic.
Strong Strategies	• On the same computer I open up Word and I minimize it and then when I find important information then I type it into my Word document and I paraphrase it.

FIGURE 9.7. Students' typical organizational strategies.

when students are taught to create separate digital folders for each research project and to create separate files to save notes for each research question and/or focus area. Technology can also be helpful in reducing the volume of "scrap paper" notes that are easily lost. However, technology devices can also hinder the organizational process because students may forget where they saved files, lose thumb drives, forget passwords to online storage sites, or may simply copy, paste, and print without any clear plan for what to do with all the unprocessed information.

Helping students learn stronger organizational strategies is beneficial in school and in life. For some learners, reordering information on a screen is too visually and cognitively demanding, especially if scrolling is involved. The age-old 3″ × 5″ notecard method is still viable. Despite all the conveniences of modern technology, we often find ourselves suggesting to students that they sort notecards or print out their notes, cut them up with scissors, and physically rearrange them on a large, flat surface (Figure 9.8). One teacher has students write their paraphrased notes on a work table with a dry erase marker, emphasizing the fluidity of the process (Figure 9.9).

Another effective strategy for organizing information and ideas is the creation of concept maps (i.e., mind maps, thinking maps; see Figure 9.10), visually displaying and linking ideas to show connections between ideas (see Moline, 2012, for ideas). Visual mapping can enhance the recognition of visual, verbal, and spatial patterns, an important component of synthesizing and transforming information (Hyerle & Alper, 2013). Digital mind mapping tools provide opportunities for learners to collaborate and share (see Table 9.2). Deep thinking is promoted during map creation by defining ideas in context, describing qualities of a concept, comparing and contrasting, classifying, sequencing, and identifying cause and effect.

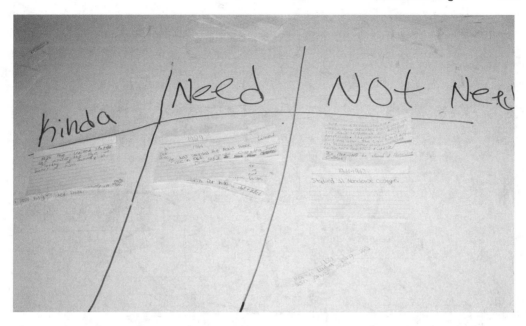

FIGURE 9.8. Sorting inquiry notes.

An evidence chart is another way to scaffold students' organizational skills during inquiry (Hobbs, 2011). To complete this chart, students identify 5–10 different information sources and rank them in order from highly credible to less trustworthy. For each source, a brief summary, a paraphrase, or a direct quote is added to the chart, along with a correctly formatted citation. Students then must provide an explanation for their ranking of

> Organizing and curating can be likened to a neatly arranged spice cabinet. It is like a medley of resources made available within easy reach and situated in a digital array that is both visually pleasing and cognitively intuitive.
> —Summey (2013, p. 17)

FIGURE 9.9. Notes can be easily revised with a marker and whiteboard table.

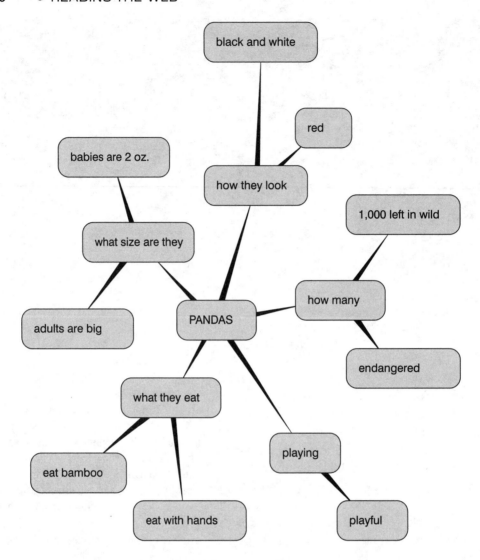

FIGURE 9.10. Fourth grader's concept map.

each source, thus giving them the chance to carefully consider the characteristics of a reliable source.

Another approach is to provide students with a matrix containing headings that give clues to the type of information they should be seeking. For example, a fourth-grade teacher provided the headings of *location, landforms, weather,* and *industry* for an inquiry project on the regions of the United States. Organizing the information into a visual display increases the likelihood that students will learn and remember the information (Kauffman et al., 2011). Organizational skills developed in the elementary and middle school years can be useful through one's time in school and beyond. We have both worked with undergraduate *and* graduate students who could benefit from improving their strategies for organizing information.

TABLE 9.2. Examples of Digital Mind-Mapping Tools

Mind-mapping tool	Format	Description
Coggle (*coggle.it*)	website	Visual displays of information can be created collaboratively and shared with others.
Dipity (*dipity.com*)	website	Information is displayed in a timeline and can include multimedia.
Bubbl.us (*bubbl.us*)	website and app	Create an interactive concept map showing relationships between text and images.
InstaGrok (*instagrok.com*)	website and app	Search for, create, and share an interactive concept map showing concepts and relationships between text and multimedia.
Popplet (*popplet.com*)	website and app	This tool lets users capture ideas and share them by creating a visual diagram.

Citing Sources

To produce responsible research products and show readers the path of your learning, it is necessary to cite sources. Citing sources poses particular challenges for Web readers because new

 Library Media Standard: **Respect copyright/intellectual property rights of creators and producers.**

ways to digitally share, remix, and "borrow" content are continually emerging. Students must be taught about information ethics so they are knowledgeable about issues of copyright, fair use, and attribution. Many online readers jump from website to website so quickly that they can't remember from which ones their information was gleaned. We need to teach younger students and retrain older students to *slow down* on the information highway. Probably every one of us, at one time or another, has forgotten where we found something really cool on the Internet, so just imagine how hard it must be for our students.

To help with remembering and citing sources, a handy browser feature is the "history" button, which tracks all the websites you've visited recently. Another strategy is to use the "bookmark" or "favorites" feature in the web browser to save sites for return visits. Before students get too deep into an inquiry project, they should get in the habit of copying and pasting URLs (web addresses) into their notes, so they'll have a permanent record of where information was obtained and can easily return to sites. This has the added benefit of reminding students that we expect them to make notes rather than try to hold all the information in their heads.

 Plagiarism Categories

1. **Those who don't know how to properly cite.**
2. **Those who don't know when to properly cite.**
3. **Those who don't know enough about the topic.**
4. **Those who waited too long to get started on an assignment and panicked.**
   —**Frey, Fisher, and Gonzalez (2010, p. 19)**

Social bookmarking websites and apps, such as Diigo (*diigo.com*) and Delicious (*delicious.com*), also provide a way for students to collect and organize useful websites for later retrieval. Online citation sites, such Zotero (*zotero.org*), let users store resource information and organize by project, also providing correct citation format, although we recommend students check to make sure the citation format matches school expectations. Google Docs (*docs.google.com*) has a feature that lets users open the search feature and access search results while working within a document. A direct link and citation for a website can be easily added to the document.

When it comes to locating and citing images, videos, and sound files, we recommend that learners begin their search at Creative Commons (*creativecommons.org*), a nonprofit organization that provides users with a means to legally modify a copyrighted work. Searchers can look for multimedia that can be modified, republished, or used commercially, depending on the creator's designation and the searcher's purpose. Creative Commons searches sites such as Flickr, Google Images, and YouTube, only displaying results that meet the searcher's purpose. Creative Commons does not negate the need for citing sources, but it connects learners with legally modifiable work.

Creating a Product

As discussed in Chapter 5, some students have difficulty envisioning a final project for their inquiries and often create final projects that don't do justice to the knowledge that

 Library Media Standard: **Create products that apply to authentic, real-world contexts.**

was gained. Some begin their final project before they have even started gathering and synthesizing information. In some cases, students don't plan their time well and are rushed when they get to the final product. In other cases, students don't actually have enough information to make an adequate final product. Many students simply don't know how to represent knowledge, especially in formats other than a traditional research report. We try to encourage them to be creative without losing sight of the goal of answering their original research question(s) (Figure 9.11).

An effective approach for keeping students on track toward a final project is to invite them to codevelop benchmarks for each part of the process. For example, we

FIGURE 9.11. The process of creating a project gives students the opportunity to show what they know.

always require rough drafts of notes and products before polished drafts. When feasible, we read students' Reflection Logs daily so that we can address issues immediately. It's always a good idea to have a bulletin board or teacher mailbox where students can place their questions and concerns. We give frequent assessments and use rubrics to ensure that students understand our instructional objectives and so that we can provide timely feedback. We reserve time for students to share their ideas, strategies, and processes with each other while engaged in inquiry, rather than at the end when it is too late to change course.

Anchor projects, or examples of former students' work (both weak and strong), are great models for creating a final product. Teacher-designed templates can also help scaffold learners who need guidance. One teacher we know requires students to create the same type of project for two inquiry units in a row, so students begin to master the format (e.g., poster, digital slide show, time line, play, web page) before trying a new format. When working on an inquiry team, students might complete one part of a larger project, possibly on a wiki (*wikispaces.com*) or a document-sharing site, such as Google Docs (*docs.google.com*). In this case, the process of collaboration becomes as important as, if not more valuable than, the completed project.

> The act of communicating a concept to another person helps us learn it better. When we communicate, we are forced to organize and clarify our thoughts into coherent sentences before we speak. —Zwiers (2004, p. 10)

To promote the development of quality projects, focus on giving students clear criteria and a sequential list of steps that lead up to project creation. Both of these elements help students learn the value of process *and* product. Here are some common pitfalls with respect to inquiry projects:

- Large chunks of information that are copied straight from a source.
- Multimedia products that have more glitz than content.
- Posters that don't include captions or any other descriptive text.
- Artistic projects that don't include any actual information.
- Poems, crossword puzzles, and acrostics that don't contain sufficient information.
- Any product that doesn't show evidence of research and transformation.

Digital Sharing

The atmosphere of collaboration that is prolific on the Web makes the digital sharing of an inquiry project a natural next step. Teachers may find that students put forth more effort and give more attention to editing when their work can be seen by family, friends, and potentially anyone else on the Web (Frey et al., 2010; November, 2012). Digital comments posted by viewers give learners authentic feedback and a powerful means to interact with a real audience. The decision about whether and where to post a project online may need to come early in the creation process so a student can plan for the various components to be included. Most digital sharing options entail the creation of written text and perhaps images, videos, or podcasts. These resources can be collected in a digital folder until ready to actually publish as a wiki, blog, website, ebook, video, or other format.

When selecting an online tool, consider one that matches the type of content created, the ease of use, and the intended audience. For example, Glogster (*edu.glogster.*

com), a digital poster site or app, is useful for combining images, sound, and art for a visual presentation. Voki (*voki.com*) lets users record their voices or enter their texts and create an avatar to deliver their presentation. Wikispaces (*wikispaces.com*) allows students to collaboratively create a project to be displayed online. Ideas, content, and media can be linked within the wiki. A blog posted on a site such as Blogster (*blogster. com*) can serve as an online space to post student work, including text and images. Websites can be created fairly simply with tools such as Weebly (*weebly.com*) or WiX(*wix. com*). Both present a polished layout of information. For these, and many other digital tools, students can select the level of privacy, limiting the people who can access their work and/or leave comments.

 When our choices and actions, as both authors and audiences, match up to our values, we become humane, responsible, and effective communicators.
—Hobbs (2011, p. 139)

Orally Presenting

Regardless of whether student work is shared digitally, the final step in the QUEST process often involves an oral presentation. The CCSS (NGA & CCSSO, 2010) require students to present information in a clear and organized way and to strategically use digital media and visual displays of ideas. Students need to gain experience and comfort with presenting in front of peers, teachers, school staff, parents, and the community.

Writing Standard: Introduce a topic clearly; organize ideas, concepts, and information into broader categories as appropriate; include formatting, graphics, and multimedia when useful to aiding comprehension.

Even shy students feel pride in presenting inquiry projects because it is exciting to share their passions and creations with others and even more thrilling if the audience actually learns something valuable. Students who like to ham it up really shine during oral presentations, as did one learner who surprised everyone by wearing a white T-shirt for his presentation and standing directly in front of the projector so that his website on Humvees appeared on his shirt instead of on the screen (Figure 9.12). He was animated and extremely funny, evidencing none of the print literacy challenges that had hampered him throughout the project.

However, unlike our Humvee enthusiast, many students have weak oral presentation skills. For example, in one classroom, although the teacher required an introduction and a conclusion to each oral presentation, many of her students neglected to mention key contextual information or state why they had selected their topics. The teacher later reflected:

"A student presented this morning on Jackie Robinson. She had a fabulous bubble map that she used to talk about his family. She had a digital slide show that traced his career, and she had a fabulous skit in two scenes, which showed Jackie Robinson attempting to get a meal at a restaurant and being denied because of his color. However, in the introduction she didn't tell the class that he was the first African American baseball player and it was before the Civil Rights Act in 1964, so he encountered a lot of discrimination."

FIGURE 9.12. Creative presentation technique.

While we expect students to demonstrate effective oral presentation skills, we must ask ourselves, "Are we specifically teaching speaking skills?" Modeling, thinking aloud, and guided practice are effective instructional approaches for promoting strong oral presentation skills. Educators should share or codevelop assessment criteria with students before presentations so they know the important behaviors to practice. Rubrics and checklists can be useful informal assessment tools. One teacher we know digitally records presentations so students can self-reflect on the process (and share with caregivers not in attendance). Immediately following the presentation, the teacher and students complete a rating form with written feedback for the presenter.

Besides expecting students to share accurate and complete information as presenters, we also expect certain behavior of those students receiving the information. In the area of listening, the CCSS (NGA & CCSSO, 2010) set out the expectation that students integrate information presented in various media formats and evaluate the quality of the information and the speaker's message. These high-level listening skills can only occur if students are taught and have opportunities to practice specific listening behaviors. Being an effective presenter and being a respectful audience member go hand in hand. Encourage presenters to be aware of posture, voice, and content of their presentations. Ask audience members to be considerate and polite. Students will often rise to our expectations.

How Do We Teach Transformation Strategies?

As with all the other QUEST strategies, we recommend the teaching approach described in Chapter 2 that includes modeling, scaffolding, practice, and feedback. If you have been conducting inquiry alongside your students, talk through how you intend to go about transforming the information you've gathered into something original that demonstrates what you've learned. Moving from a collection of notes to a polished finished product is not an easy process for students, so they need expert modeling and scaffolding.

Notemaking

Prior to starting a unit focused on notemaking, we recommend that you administer a pretest in order to assess your students' current notemaking strategies with informational text. Short passages from informal reading inventories or basal readers are good sources for this purpose. Give each student a passage that best matches her independent reading level and have her follow the instructions on the Notemaking Assessment (Handout T-9.1). Encourage the use of highlighters or pens so you can compare how your students perform on the posttest at the end of the unit. After the pretest, have students share their notemaking strategies and record similarities and differences. Have students look for the following characteristics of effective notemaking strategies:

- Highlighting key ideas.
- Highlighting words and phrases instead of whole sentences.
- Notes that are not in full sentences.
- Notes that use abbreviations, symbols, lists, and pictures.
- Summaries that are shorter than the original passages.
- Summaries that are primarily in students' own words.

We have had great success teaching the four-step CHoMP notemaking strategy (discussed earlier) by teaching each step individually. You may wish to print out the CHoMP Notemaking Poster (Handout T-9.2). Although your lessons may be more effective if you use text that is familiar to the students (perhaps drawn from their textbooks or websites that they've visited during mini-inquiries), we provide practice activities for Two-Step Notemaking (Handout T-9.3), Three-Step Notemaking (Handout T-9.4), and Four-Step Notemaking (Handout T-9.5). Each has several passages to use for guided practice, independent practice, and homework, with the passages increasing in length for each additional step of the process. Because notemaking can be arduous for some learners, continue to emphasize the value of notemaking strategies in and out of school. You can also have students work together on notemaking exercises (Figure 9.13). Once students have demonstrated the ability to make notes without plagiarizing, it is helpful to provide scaffolds such as the Two-Column Notemaking Template (Handout T-9.6) and Sample Two-Column Notes (Handout T-9.7).

Inquiry Projects

As reiterated throughout this text, we like to offer as much student choice as possible when conducting inquiry projects. Not only is it critical to allow students to choose their own topics, but also most students will devote additional effort if they are also given some latitude to demonstrate what they've learned in a format of their own

FIGURE 9.13. Notemaking collaboration.

choosing. However, because many students do not know how to effectively show what they've learned, they need to be taught strategies for creating a variety of inquiry products. If you don't have prior student projects to use as models, we provide samples and criteria for common formats at the end of this chapter (Handouts T-9.8–T-9.17).

To support students with presentations and group work, you can use or adapt the Oral Presentation Guidelines (Handout T-9.18), the Inquiry Project Presentation Rubric (Handout T-9.19), or the Inquiry Project Teamwork Rubric (Handout T-9.20). To support students with cit-

 Social Studies Standard: **Integrate visual information (e.g., in charts, graphs, photographs, videos, or maps) with other information in print and digital texts.**

ing sources, use the APA Citation Format (Handout T-9.21) or search for whatever format your school prefers; for example, <MLA citation format kids>. See the Notemaking Lesson Plans for Elementary and Middle School Levels (Handouts T-9.22 and T-9.23) for ideas on how to begin.

SUMMARY ●

This chapter on Transforming provided research and classroom examples of the process of transforming information into knowledge. We discussed strategies for notemaking, annotating, organizing information, citing sources, creating a product, digital sharing, and presenting final products to others.

The final chapter of this book briefly presents some thoughts and ideas for reflecting on the QUEST. Although students are expected to self-reflect during inquiry, it is also advisable to set aside some time to debrief the experience at the end. In addition to being evaluated by traditional measures such as posttests and interviews, students can evaluate their progress by rereading their Reflection Logs and by reenacting the inquiry process. Teachers can also engage in self-reflection and share their insights with the class.

Handouts

The following chart lists the activities and templates that were discussed in this chapter on Transforming. Because notemaking is such a crucial skill for gathering, synthesizing, and transforming information into something original, we offer quite a few handouts that can be used in a unit focused on transformation. Similarly, because many students, from the early grades through high school, struggle with envisioning and designing final formats that showcase their knowledge of an inquiry topic, we've included sample formats along with the criteria that were determined by the class in advance. These examples are genuine student artifacts that can serve as reasonable models for students in grades 3–8.

Number	Name of handout	Purpose
T-9.1	Notemaking Assessment	Assess notemaking strategies
T-9.2	CHoMP Notemaking Poster	Poster for wall or overhead
T-9.3	Two-Step Notemaking	Teach CHoMP strategy
T-9.4	Three-Step Notemaking	Teach CHoMP strategy
T-9.5	Four-Step Notemaking	Teach CHoMP strategy
T-9.6	Two-Column Notemaking Template	Scaffold notemaking
T-9.7	Sample Two-Column Notes	Scaffold notemaking
T-9.8	Sample Web Page	Sample final format
T-9.9	Sample Website	Sample final format
T-9.10	Sample Slide Show—Elementary Level	Sample final format
T-9.11	Sample Slide Show—Middle School Level	Sample final format
T-9.12	Sample Interactive Presentation	Sample final format
T-9.13	Sample News Article	Sample final format
T-9.14	Sample Acrostic Poem	Sample final format
T-9.15	Sample Curated Collection	Sample final format
T-9.16	Sample Flier	Sample final format
T-9.17	Sample Q & A	Sample final format
T-9.18	Oral Presentation Guidelines	Scaffold presentation
T-9.19	Inquiry Project Presentation Rubric	Assess inquiry presentations
T-9.20	Inquiry Project Teamwork Rubric	Assess inquiry teamwork
T-9.21	APA Citation Format	Template for citations
T-9.22	Notemaking Lesson Plan—Elementary Level	Teach notemaking strategies
T-9.23	Notemaking Lesson Plan—Middle Level	Teach notemaking strategies

HANDOUT T-9.1. Notemaking Assessment

Name _____ Class _____ Date _____

☐ Pretest   ☐ Posttest

Directions: *Please show your best notemaking strategies. You have 15 minutes to complete the test after the passage is read aloud to you.*

DIRECTIONS:

1. Review the passage.
2. Use a highlighter pen and/or pencil to make marks on the passage.
3. Make notes on this page.
4. Write a summary, based on your notes, on the next page.

MY NOTES: _____

_____

_____

_____

_____

_____

_____

_____

_____

_____

_____

_____

_____

_____

_____

_____

_____

(continued)

MY SUMMARY: _____

QUEST

Name _____ Class _____ Date _____

STEP 1: Cross out small words.

STEP 2: Highlight important information.

o

STEP 3: Make notes (shorten, change words, make lists, use symbols, draw).

STEP 4: Put in your own words.

HANDOUT T-9.3. Two-Step Notemaking

Name _____ Class _____ Date _____

Directions: *Read each sentence, then practice notemaking by doing these two steps.*

STEP 1: Cross out small words.

STEP 2: Highlight important information.

I. GUIDED PRACTICE

 1. Boa constrictors have poor vision, so they have to sense their prey by smelling the air with their tongues.

 2. Peacocks are among the easiest birds to raise, but they must be kept in pens so they don't run away.

 3. Guinea pigs communicate with each other using lots of different sounds, which shows how important their hearing is to them.

 4. One reason Siberian tigers are endangered is that some people believe that almost every part of the tiger can be used for medicine or to cure diseases.

II. INDEPENDENT PRACTICE

 5. Rockhopper penguins live in rocky areas with high grasses, where they make burrows and nests.

 6. The Kiger mustang is more than just another wild horse on the range of the American West; it is a descendant of horses brought to the New World by the Spaniards.

 7. Fat bears in winter coats overheat quickly and may run slower than 30 mph, whereas slim bears can run faster than 30 mph.

 8. The platypus's large front feet can be used as powerful paddles for swimming as well as for digging a burrow in a riverbank.

HANDOUT T-9.4. Three-Step Notemaking

Name _____ Class _____ Date _____

I. GUIDED PRACTICE

Directions: *Read each paragraph, then practice notemaking by doing these three steps.*

STEP 1: Cross out small words.
STEP 2: Highlight important information.
STEP 3: Make notes (shorten, change words, make lists, use symbols, draw).

---

1. Siberian tigers are among the most endangered animals in the world. Fewer than 200 are believed to still live in the wild. Their range includes eastern Russia, northern Korea, and northeastern China.

2. The platypus is a small egg-laying mammal with webbed feet, a tail like a beaver's, and a horny beak resembling the bill of a duck. It has a thick covering of waterproof hair. The bill is a blue-gray, blackish color, and the lower bill is smaller than the upper bill.

3. Boas' sharp teeth help them to get a good grip on their prey, but unlike some snakes, they do not have fangs or venom. Instead, the boa constrictor kills its prey by suffocating it. The boa tightens its coils each time the prey exhales until the animal can no longer breathe in.

(continued)

II. INDEPENDENT PRACTICE

STEP 1: Cross out small words.
STEP 2: Highlight important information.
    o
STEP 3: Make notes (shorten, change words, make lists, use symbols, draw).

---

4. Grizzly bears are found in river valleys, mountain forests, and open meadows all over the world. They range in North America, Western and Central Europe, some parts of Japan, and Russia, and can be found as far north as the tundra region.

5. The Kiger mustang is smaller than some of today's breeds of horses, averaging 14–15 hands and 800–1,000 pounds. They are of medium size with heavy shoulders and necks. Their feet are small and black. Their legs are long and have rounded bones.

6. Rockhopper penguins gather in very large, noisy colonies when they breed, all gabbling away at once. The male sits on the egg for 4 months until it hatches. When trying to attract a mate, a Rockhopper shakes its head back and forth, tossing and showing off its yellow feathers.

Name _____ Class _____ Date _____

Directions: *Read each paragraph, then practice notemaking by doing these four steps.*

I. GUIDED PRACTICE

STEP 1: Cross out small words.
STEP 2: Highlight important information.
        o
STEP 3: Make notes (shorten, change words, make lists, use symbols, draw).
STEP 4: Put in your own words.

---

1. Boa constrictors are snakes that can grow to 3–14 feet long and can weigh over 100 pounds. Their bodies can have different patterns, such as oval, diamond, or bat-shaped, in colors of reddish brown outlined in black, on a background of cream, pale tan, or gray.

MY NOTES:

MY SUMMARY: _____

_____

_____

_____

_____

_____

(continued)

I. GUIDED PRACTICE

STEP 1: Cross out small words.
STEP 2: Highlight important information.
     o
STEP 3: Make notes (shorten, change words, make lists, use symbols, draw).
STEP 4: Put in your own words.

---

 2. The grizzly bear is one type of brown bear. The bears' color ranges from light brown (almost blonde) to black. They have a sturdy, stocky build and a noticeable hump behind the head. They get their name from the silver color that appears on the tips of their fur as they get older.

MY NOTES:

MY SUMMARY: _____

_____

_____

_____

_____

_____

(continued)

II. INDEPENDENT PRACTICE

STEP 1: Cross out small words.

STEP 2: Highlight important information.

      o

STEP 3: Make notes (shorten, change words, make lists, use symbols, draw).

STEP 4: Put in your own words.

---

 3. Even though it is a strange-looking creature, the platypus is an excellent underwater hunter. It catches crayfish and worms on the bottoms of muddy rivers where visibility is low. It is able to search for food in darkness using its special, beak-like snout, which is filled with sensors and can detect any movement in the murky water.

MY NOTES:

MY SUMMARY: _____

_____

_____

_____

_____

_____

(continued)

II. INDEPENDENT PRACTICE

STEP 1: Cross out small words.
STEP 2: Highlight important information.
          o
STEP 3: Make notes (shorten, change words, make lists, use symbols, draw).
STEP 4: Put in your own words.

 4. No other horse in America is quite like the Kiger mustang found on Steens Mountain in Central Oregon. The Spanish mustang was a part of early American history, having roots in Native American culture, and is the horse that helped settle the West. At one time, it was thought to be extinct in the wild. Since the Kiger mustangs might be the best remaining examples of the Spanish mustang, it is very important to preserve them.

MY NOTES:

MY SUMMARY: _____

_____

_____

_____

_____

_____

HANDOUT T-9.6. Two-Column Notemaking Template

Name _____ Class _____ Date _____

Directions: *Write or type your theme, topic, inquiry question, and at least two focus areas. There is also a section at the end for interesting facts that might not fit with your focus areas. When you find a good website, write or paste the URL. Make notes in your own words in the column on the left and record your thoughts about each note on the right.*

Theme:
Topic:
Question:

Sentence Starters for Thoughts: I wonder . . . I can't believe . . . I didn't realize . . . Now I think . . . I am curious about . . . I doubt . . . This reminds me of . . . I still want to know . . .

FOCUS AREA #1: _____

URL:	
NOTES	THOUGHTS

URL:	
NOTES	THOUGHTS

URL:	
NOTES	THOUGHTS

(continued)

FOCUS AREA #2: _____

URL:	
NOTES	THOUGHTS

URL:	
NOTES	THOUGHTS

URL:	
NOTES	THOUGHTS

INTERESTING FACTS NOT RELATED TO FOCUS AREAS:

URL:	
NOTES	THOUGHTS

URL:	
NOTES	THOUGHTS

250

HANDOUT T-9.7. Sample Two-Column Notes

Theme: Insects

Topic: Honey Bees

Question: How do honey bees communicate?

FOCUS AREA #1: *Communication*

Keywords: <honey bees + communicate>

URL: http://www.dogonews.com/2009/1/29/can-bees-count	
NOTES	**THOUGHTS**
Honey bees do the waggle dance to tell other bees when they find a new food source.	What is the waggle dance?
According to a study in Australia, honey bees can count up to the number 4.	Really? How did they test this theory? I want to know more.

URL: http://www.dummies.com/how-to/content/how-honey-bees-communicate.html	
NOTES	**THOUGHTS**
Honey bees communicate in two ways: pheromones and choreography.	pheromones = scent choreography = dance movement
Two common dances are the round dance and the waggle dance. The round dance says that the food source is near the hive (within 10–80 yards).	I've never heard of the round dance.
The waggle dance tells about a food source farther from the hive. The bee flies in a figure eight while doing a side-to-side motion with its belly.	I'd like to see a video of this dance.
The intensity of the waggle, the number of times it's repeated, the direction of the dance, and the sound the bee makes gives info about the location of the food.	Now I'm interested in the different types of sounds they make.
Dancing bees stop during the dance to let other bees taste the food. This gives more info about where the food is and what type of flower it's from.	How do the other bees get a taste of the food?

URL: http://cals.arizona.edu/pubs/insects/ahb/inf7.html	
NOTES	**THOUGHTS**
Bees communicate when it's time to find a new colony. When the scouts come back, the swarm chooses a location and they all fly to it.	How does the swarm "decide" where to go?? How do they know it's time to find a new colony?

(continued)

FOCUS AREA #1: *Honey Bee Waggle Dance*

Keywords: <bee waggle dance video>

URL: http://www.youtube.com/watch?v=-7ijl-g4jHg (55 seconds)	
NOTES	THOUGHTS
Shows how the waggle dance uses angles from the sun to show where the food is.	I thought the dance was in the air, not on the honeycomb itself.

URL: http://video.pbs.org/video/2300846183 (3:25)	
NOTES	THOUGHTS
A scientist wiggles his behind to show the bee dance.	Are all the scouts female? What do the males do?

URL: http://video.nationalgeographic.com/video/animals/bugs-animals/bees-and-wasps/weirdest-bees-dance (1:50 + 15 second ad)	
NOTES	THOUGHTS
Shows how the pollen sacs communicate the smell of the new food.	How do the bees who aren't scouts eat?

URL: http://www.youtube.com/watch?v=Vaszh2bY3mc (2:42)	
NOTES	THOUGHTS
Lots of great info! Typical hive is 30,000 bees. Queen lays 150,000 eggs per day. All worker bees are female. Usually only 100 males (drones). Worker bees feed the drones. Shows a bee hatching.	Are all worker bees scouts or are there other "jobs" for worker bees?

Name _____ Class _____ Date _____

Arnold Shwarzenegger

"I'm Gonna Pump You Up!"

Childhood

Arnold was born July 30, 1947 in Graz, Austria. He grew up in a small village. When he was 15, he started weightlifting. When he was 20, he won the Mr. Universe title because he was the strongest man in the world. He made 13 bodybuilding records. He became a U.S. citizen in 1983. He went to the University of Wisconsin and got his Bachelor's degree in Business and Economics.

Career

Arnold is an actor, a writer, and a politician. He has been in Terminator and Batman. He fights the bad guys in movies, like an action hero. He wrote a book called "The New Encyclopedia of Modern Bodybuilding." Now he is the Governer of California.

Webliography

http://www.actorarchives.com/arnold/biography.html

http://www.facts1.com/general/recent.htm

http://www.fasbnet.com/T3/arnold1.htm

Web page Criteria:
- Theme: Famous person
- Topic: Arnold Schwarzenegger
- Focus areas: Childhood and career
- Number of images: At least 2
- Sources: At least 3
- Digital Tool: Dreamweaver

Name _____ Class _____ Date _____

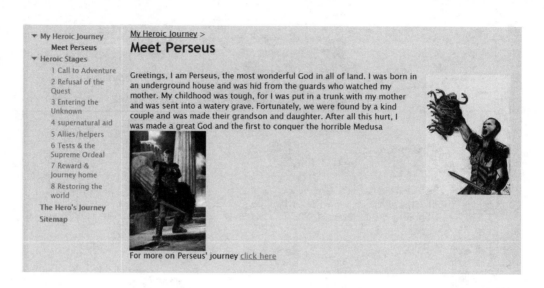

Website Criteria:

- Theme: Greek Gods
- Topic: Perseus
- Focus area: The Hero's Journey
- Number of images: At least 2 per webpage
- Sources: At least 3
- Digital Tool: Google Webmaster

Name _____ Class _____ Date _____

Do you like llamas?

well you can buy one!

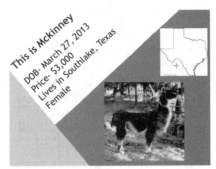

This is Mckinney
DOB- March 27, 2013
Price- $3,000
Lives in Southlake, Texas
Female

Ms. Gwen

DOB- July 25, 2014
Price is $1,200
Southlake, Texas
Female

OBERON!
DOB- February 18, 2012
Price- $1,500
Southlake, Texas
Male

LLAMAS TELL THEIR STORY

Click here for
YouTube Video

THANKS FOR WATCHING!

`@llama`
`llove`

Slide Show Criteria:
- Theme: Student Choice
- Topic: Llamas
- Focus area: Buying a llama
- Number of slides: Minimum of 4
- Images: Minimum of 4
- Digital Tool: Microsoft PowerPoint

Name _____ Class _____ Date _____

Slide Show Criteria:

- Theme: Hero
- Topic: Princess Diana
- Focus area: Family
- Number of slides: Minimum of 6
- Images: Minimum of 6
- Sources: Minimum of 3
- Digital Tool: Microsoft PowerPoint

HANDOUT T-9.12. Sample Interactive Presentation

Name _____ Class _____ Date _____

Interactive Presentation Criteria:

- Theme: Literature
- Topic: Harry Potter
- Focus area: History of Characters
- Number of nodes: Minimum of 4
- Images: Minimum of 4
- Sources: Minimum of 3
- Digital Tool: Prezi

Name _____ Class _____ Date _____

Princess Diana

Date: 1/12/2002

Diana, Princess of Wales, Makes Many Contributions to Society

Princess Diana Contributes to society

She helps:

Breast cancer

HIV/AIDS

Domestic abuse

Drug addiction

The banning of land mines

Princess Diana supported many charities throughout her career. At one time, she supported as many as 110. These charities included HIV/AIDS, domestic abuse, drug addiction, breast cancer, and the banning of land mines.

After her separation and divorce, she cut back to supporting only six charities. Her schedule was hectic, including travel and public appearances. She traveled thousands of miles a year to support her favorite charities. She often took her sons with her to visit hospitals and homeless shelters.

In June 1997 she auctioned off seventy-nine of her evening gowns. This was part of an event held at Christie's in New York. This event raised more than $5.7 million for AIDS and Cancer funds.

In 1997, she received the Nobel Peace Prize. She worked to increase public awareness about the dangers of land mines. She traveled to far off areas such as Angela and the former Yugoslavia. She represented the International Campaign to ban Land mines.

Had Princess Diana's life not been cut short by the tragic car accident on August 31, 1997. She would have continued her charity work. During her short lived career, she made many contribution to society.

Diana with Mother Teresa during a visit at a convent in the Bronx borough of New York on June 18, 1997

News Article Criteria:
- Theme: Royalty
- Topic: Princess Diana
- Focus area: Contributions to society
- Images: Minimum of 2
- Sources: Minimum of 3
- Digital Tool: Microsoft Publisher

Name _____ Class _____ Date _____

Little Women was the title of one of her most popular books

On November 29, 1832, Louisa was born.

Under her father's supervision, Louisa was taught everything she needed to know.

It was in concord, MA, that Louisa was mainly raised.

She read a lot of books and even tutored a girl named Ellen.

At the age of twelve, Louisa got a job to support her family.

May, Elizabeth, and Anna, were Louisa's sisters.

Amos Bronson Alcott was Louisa's Dad.

Years of writing helped to improve every one of her books.

Abigail May was Louisa's Mom.

Louisa died after working in a hospital and catching Typhoid Fever.

Contrast between the storyline of Little Women and her family, was very similar.

Often trying to help her family with finances, Louisa was inspired to write many thrillers.

To Louisa's horror, her sister Elizabeth died in 1858.

The whole family supported many causes like women's rights and the abolition of slavery.

Acrostic Poem Criteria:
- Theme: Authors
- Topic: Louisa May Alcott
- Focus area: Family life
- Sources: Minimum of 3
- Digital Tool: Microsoft Word

Name _____ Class _____ Date _____

Curated Collection Criteria:

- Theme: Useful Resources
- Topic: Student Choice
- Focus area: Teaching
- Sources: Minimum of 12
- Digital Tool: Pinterest

Name _____ Class _____ Date _____

BACK TO THE MAT

FREESTYLE WRESTLING

Summer Camp for Beginners

Lowest Price Camp Anywhere, only $17 for one week!

Featuring **Live Demos** by Famous Wrestlers, such as:

Bobby Douglas	Daniel Lgali	John Goodbody
Head coach for Iowa	2nd World Cup 1998	Bouncer in the meanest bar

You will learn these basic moves in **Only One Week!**

- Takedown: Getting the opponent from standing position down to the mat. You have to have control to get a point for a takedown.
- Breakdown: Getting the opponent from hand and knees to flat on the mat.
- Crotch Lift: From flat on his face, put arm around his leg and lift! Then flip him over.
- Gut Wrench: When you have him flat on the mat face down, lock arms around his waist. Lift and roll him onto his back.
- Pin: When opponent's shoulders are flat on the mat and you in control for 3 seconds.
- Headlock: Get the back of his head into the crook of your arm, lift his head up so he can't bridge. Wait for ref to call a pin!
- Arm Bar: Thread your forearm behind his elbow and over his back then apply the pressure!
- Half Nelson: Put arm under opponent's armpit, wrap hand behind his head, make a fist, drive fist downward toward the mat.
- Cradle: Wrap one arm around opponent's head and one arm around the back of his knee, lock hands together take him to his back.

We're located at 321 North Pole Drive 12938

We're open from 1:00 pm to 8:00 pm

Call now to register!

677-766-7667

Flier Criteria:

- Theme: Sports
- Topic: Wrestling
- Focus area: Wrestling techniques
- Images: Minimum of 2
- Digital Tool: Microsoft Word

Name _____ Class _____ Date _____

History of the Stanley Cup

- Q: When was the Stanley Cup introduced?
- A: Lord Stanley and his seven sons from England came to Canada in March 1892 because Lord Stanley was going to become the governer general of Canada. It was originally called the Dominion Hockey Challenge Cup.

- Q: How much did the original cup cost?
- A: Lord Stanley sent his assistant to buy the cup for ten Guineas, which was about $50 bucks back then.

- Q: Does the Stanley Cup look the same today?
- A: No, the Stanley cup now is bigger and it is all silver with the names of the teams who won the Stanley Cup game and the dates when they won it. The original cup is now in a museum because it got too big.

- Q: What is the meaning of the rings around the cup?
- A: On the old Cup they added a new ring for every year that a team won. The new Stanley Cup has rings, but they don't keep adding rings, now they just carve the teams names.

- Q: Does the winning team get to keep the cup?
- A: They get to keep the cup until the next season begins. One time one of the teams go so drunk they threw the Stanley Cup into a river. It was a deep river and the Cup sank to the bottom, so someone had to go get it.

- Q: Why was hockey created?
- A: Because the people who played an Irish field game called Hurley, which as like hockey, but it was played on grass. The thought in the winter, why not try to play it on ice. Hockey was originally called ice hurley.

- Q: Why is the Stanley Cup a cup?
- A: That one is still a mystery!

Original Dominion Challenge Cup	Modern Day Stanley Cup
http://www.canada.com/entertainment/ Gallery+April/1499001/story.html	http://en.wikipedia.org/wiki/Stanley_Cup

Q&A Criteria:

- Theme: Sports
- Topic: Hockey/Stanley Cup
- Focus area: History
- Images: Minimum of 2
- Digital Tool: Microsoft Word

HANDOUT T-9.18. Oral Presentation Guidelines

Name _____ Class _____ Date _____

Directions: *Use this outline for your oral presentation.*

1. Hello, my name is _____

2. I did my inquiry project on the _____ and _____
   (focus area 1)   **(focus area 2)**

   of _____ **(topic)**.

3. I chose these focus areas because _____

   _____

   _____

4. Some interesting facts about this topic are _____

   _____

   _____

5. I will show you what I've learned by presenting my _____
   (formats)

   _____

6. SHOW PROJECT NOW

7. Some things I've learned about this topic are _____

   _____

   _____

   _____

8. Some things I've learned about _____ are _____
   (instructional focus of unit)

   _____

   _____

   _____

9. I hope you enjoyed my presentation. Are there any questions?

HANDOUT T-9.19. Inquiry Project Presentation Rubric

Name _____ Class _____ Date _____

I am evaluating _____

(names of peers)

presentation on _____

(topic)

	4	3	2	1	Student Score	Teacher Score
Speaking	The speakers were very easy to hear and understand.	The speakers were a little bit hard to hear and understand.	The speakers were hard to hear and understand.	The speakers were very hard to hear and understand.		
Length	The presentation was neither too long nor too short.	The presentation was a little too long or a little too short.	The presentation was too long or too short.	The presentation was way too long or way too short.		
Teamwork	Everyone was involved in an important way.	Most of the group was involved in an important way.	Some of the group was involved in an important way.	Only one or two people were involved in an important way.		
Information	The presentation had lots of new information.	The presentation had some new information.	The presentation had very little new information.	The presentation had no new information.		
Presentation	The presentation was very clear and interesting.	The presentation was somewhat clear and interesting.	The presentation was a little bit unclear and not very interesting.	The presentation was unclear and not interesting at all.		

TOTAL POINTS out of 20

Bonus Points

Percent/Grade

HANDOUT T-9.20. Inquiry Project Teamwork Rubric

My Name _____

Team Names _____

Class _____ Date _____

	4	3	2	1	Student Score	Teacher Score
Personal Effort	I did a lot of work on the project.	I did some work on the project.	I did a little work on the project.	I barely did anything on this project.		
Teamwork	Our team always worked together well.	Our team sometimes worked together well.	Our team rarely worked together well.	Our team did not work together well at all.		
Group Effort	We always used our time wisely.	We sometimes used our time wisely.	We rarely used our time wisely.	We did not use our time wisely.		
Final Product	Our product has lots of information.	Our product has some information.	Our product has very little information.	Our product has no information.		
Presentation	Our presentation was very clear and interesting.	Our presentation was somewhat clear and interesting.	Our presentation was a little bit unclear not very interesting.	Our presentation was unclear and not interesting at all.		
				TOTAL POINTS out of 20		
				Bonus Points		
				Percent/Grade		

Name _____ Class _____ Date _____

Note: Always put citations in alphabetical order by author's last name.

PRINT

Allman, T. (2004). *Killer bees (animals attack)*. Farmington Hills, MI: Kidhaven Press.

Owings, L. (2013). *Killer bees (nature's deadliest)*. Minneapolis, MN: Bellwether Media.

Woodward, S. L., & Quinn, J. A. (2011). Africanized honey bees. *Encyclopedia of Invasive Species*. Westport, CT: Greenwood Press.

WEBSITE

CBS News (2013, July 29). *What makes killer bees so deadly?* Retrieved from *http://www.cbsnews.com/ news/what-makes-killer-bees-so-deadly*

Wikipedia (2014, August 20). *Africanized bee*. Retrieved from *http://en.wikipedia.org/wiki/Africanized_bee*

BLOG

Bee-Magic Chronicles. (2010, January 10). *What are killer bees?* [Web log post]. Retrieved from *http:// bee-magic.blogspot.com/2010/01/what-are-killer-bees.html*

IMAGES

Suzuki-Martinez, S. (n.d.) *Killer bee colony*. Retrieved from *https://www.flickr.com/search/?q=killer%20 bee*

VIDEO

National Geographic (2014). *Killer bees*. Retrieved from *http://video.nationalgeographic.com/video/ killer_bee*

HANDOUT T-9.22. Notemaking Lesson Plan—Elementary Level

Objective

Students will learn an effective strategy for notemaking, which involves crossing out little words and highlighting important words.

Time

One or two class periods

Materials

1. QUEST Inquiry Model (Handout P-4.11)
2. CHoMP Notemaking Poster (Handout T-9.2)
3. Two-Step Notemaking (Handout T-9.3)
3. Highlighter pen and pencil for each student

Assessment Options

Notemaking Assessment (Handout T-9.1), along with short passages that students can easily decode.

Introduction

1. Share notemaking strategies from the Notemaking Assessment (Handout T-9.1) as a group.
2. Tell students you will be teaching them a strategy for notemaking that many other students have found useful. Contextualize the lesson, using the QUEST Inquiry Model (Handout P-4.11), by pointing out that they are in the **T** phase of the QUEST, which includes putting information in their own words.
3. Have students brainstorm reasons that notemaking can be useful in your class, in other classes, and outside of school (examples: doing research, taking down directions, making shopping lists, writing in calendars). This can be done in pairs, in small groups, or as a whole class.
4. Generate excitement and get student buy-in on the purpose of the lesson before proceeding. Tell students that effective notemaking strategies will help them now and in the future when they get into middle school and beyond.

Modeling

1. Tell the class you are going to teach them an easy notemaking strategy called "CHoMP" and that today's lesson will focus on the first two steps.
2. Model crossing out and highlighting on the overhead while thinking aloud about your choices.

Practice

1. Pass out Two-Step Notemaking (Handout T-9.3) and highlighters.
2. Read each passage aloud before having anyone start crossing out or highlighting.
3. Conduct guided practice on CHoMP Steps 1 and 2 (crossing out and highlighting).
4. Have students carry out independent practice and/or homework activities.

(continued)

Scaffolding

1. Create a new handout with easier text for weaker readers.
2. Reduce the number of passages for younger children and struggling learners.
3. Do more guided practice and less independent practice and homework for students who are having difficulty.
4. Increase font size for students with visual impairments.

Feedback

1. Go over independent practice passages with the class. Compare strategies.
2. Look over the homework to see who gets the idea and who needs additional practice.
3. Let students know how they are doing. If they're struggling, try to isolate the problem—are they having trouble decoding or comprehending the passages, or are they having trouble with one of the first two steps of the CHoMP strategy?

Ticket Out the Door

Have each student tell you what the *C* and the *H* stand for in *CHoMP*.

HANDOUT T-9.23. Notemaking Lesson Plan—Middle Level

Objective

Students will learn an effective strategy for notemaking, which involves eliminating unnecessary information, identifying important information, and making short notes.

Time

One or two class periods

Materials

1. QUEST Inquiry Model (Handout P-4.11)
2. CHoMP Notemaking Poster (Handout T-9.2)
3. Three-Step Notemaking (Handout T-9.4)
4. Pencil and highlighter pen for each student

Assessment Options

Notemaking Assessment (Handout T-9.1), along with short passages that students can easily decode.

Introduction

1. Share notemaking strategies from the Notemaking Assessment (Handout T-9.1) as a group.
2. Tell students you will be teaching them a transferable strategy for notemaking that many other students have found useful. Contextualize the lesson, using the QUEST Inquiry Model (Handout P-4.11), by pointing out that they are in the **T** phase of the QUEST, which includes making notes without plagiarizing. Ask students to define plagiarizing and the reasons why it's a problem.
3. Have students brainstorm reasons that notemaking is useful in this class, in other classes, and outside of school (examples: doing research, taking down directions, making shopping lists, writing in calendars, taking notes from textbooks or lectures). This can be done in pairs, in small groups, or as a whole class.
4. Generate excitement and get student buy-in on the purpose of the lesson before proceeding. Tell them that effective notemaking strategies will help them now and in the future when they get into high school and college.

Modeling

1. Tell the class you are going to teach them an easy notemaking strategy called "CHoMP" and that today's lesson will focus on the first three steps.
2. Emphasize that notes are NOT complete sentences; rather, they are a type of shorthand. Describe and model five notemaking styles:
   a. shortening (abbreviating)
   b. changing words (converting "big" words into small words)
   c. making lists (items that go together)
   d. using symbols (=, +, ?)
   e. drawing

(continued)

Practice

1. Pass out Three-Step Notemaking (Handout T-9.4) and highlighters.
2. Read each passage aloud.
3. Conduct guided practice on CHoMP Steps 1 through 3 (crossing out, highlighting, and making notes).
4. Have students carry out independent practice and/or homework activities.

Scaffolding

1. Create a new handout with easier text for weaker readers.
2. Reduce the number of passages for struggling learners.
3. Do more guided practice and less independent practice and homework for students who are having difficulty.
4. Increase font size for students with visual impairments.

Feedback

1. Go over independent practice passages with the class. Compare strategies.
2. Look over the homework to see who gets the idea and who needs additional practice.
3. Let students know how they are doing. If they're struggling, try to isolate the problem—are they having trouble decoding or comprehending the passages, or are they having trouble with some aspect(s) of CHoMP: crossing out, highlighting important info, or making notes?

Ticket Out the Door

Have each student tell you what the three letters *C, H*, and *M* stand for in *CHoMP*.

10 Reflecting on the QUEST

KEY IDEAS •

- Although students should engage in self-reflection throughout an Internet inquiry QUEST, it is also valuable to reflect on the process at the end.

- Student progress can be measured with posttests, interviews, surveys, and self-reflection.

- Reenacting an inquiry project can be an effective method of solidifying the QUEST process for students.

- When teachers engage in self-reflection, it is beneficial for them to share their discoveries with their students.

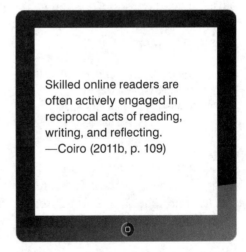

Skilled online readers are often actively engaged in reciprocal acts of reading, writing, and reflecting.
—Coiro (2011b, p. 109)

In this chapter we take a look at various ways that teachers can promote self-reflection among ourselves and our students. A first step in our own self-reflection is to call to mind the information we have gained that influences our learning. In Chapter 1 of this book, we focused on the opportunities and challenges in developing Web literacy. In Chapters 2 and 3, we provided a foundation for effective instructional practices in learning and reading. Chapters 4–9 presented the QUEST model as a systematic way to teach the inquiry process, emphasizing essential literacy strategies that our students need in order to be successful in school and in life. This final chapter is written with the goal of bringing together ideas into a cohesive view of learning, reading, the Web, and the QUEST model. We conclude with our own self-reflections as authors of this book.

Reflecting: What Have I Learned as a Teacher?

Master teachers engage in ongoing self-reflection. These teachers recognize the importance of checking one's progress toward a goal, in much the same way we check the progress of our students. As we reach the end of our journey together in this text, we encourage you to ask yourself what new knowledge and strategies *you* have gained and how these will be used to adjust your teaching. We hope you will share these insights with your students. Students appreciate when we present ourselves as lifelong learners rather than all-knowing dispensers of information. If you are relatively new to technology, you've probably come a long way in your understanding of the Internet inquiry process. If you are new to literacy, then you've probably made headway in both areas. If you are trying out an inquiry-based curriculum for the first time, we hope you've found a comfortable place at the intersection of technology, literacy, and inquiry, which is the heart and soul of this book.

Figure 10.1 contrasts two remarks from Deborah, who, as a seventh-grade special educator, had a strong grasp of literacy instruction but was less experienced with inquiry and technology before she worked with us. She, like the other teachers with whom we have collaborated, valued being mentored during Internet inquiry instruction. Because we cannot visit all your classrooms, our intent is that this text will serve as a guide and model for your teaching.

 Library Media Standard: **Conclude an inquiry-based research process by sharing new understandings and reflecting on the learning.**

We sincerely hope that, like Deborah, you have gained confidence in your ability to navigate the Internet and use it as a tool for your own learning and that of your students. The QUEST model provides a framework to support and encourage both teachers and students to gather information and transform this information into new ideas. We hope you have recognized the important and valuable Web literacy skills needed to locate, understand, and use information from the Internet and the strong need our students have to be literate in many different ways.

BEFORE QUEST	AFTER QUEST
"In all the years I've taught I've always dreaded doing research projects with my students because I'm terrified to do it! You end up doing all the work for the kids, and they're frustrated and you're frustrated, and it's a nightmare boat that you're all rowing down the same river."	"I gained the satisfaction of knowing that research projects don't have to be a big dinosaur—that big scary thing that is overwhelming because no one can do it. That fear's been diminished for me because now I know how to break down the process and teach it to my students."

FIGURE 10.1. Teacher reflection-before and after.

What Have My Students Learned?

Formal assessments are not the only means of evaluating student learning. You will also want to provide opportunities for your students to engage in frequent self-reflection. If your students have been keeping Reflection Logs during inquiry projects, provide opportunities for them to reread their logs, comparing their entries at the beginning, middle, and end. Sample Reflection Log prompts follow.

- This is how things are going with my research project:
- Today, we learned:
- My project would be going so much better if:
- Today, I was working on these parts of my project:
- This is how I feel about what I've done so far:
- Something new I've learned about finding information on the Web is:
- Something I am still having trouble with is:
- Things I want to remember to work on tomorrow are:
- These things were easy that I did today:
- These things were hard that I did today:
- Some things I still want to know about searching on the Web are:
- I think a good topic for a mini-lesson would be:
- Some things I learned about the inquiry/working on an inquiry team are:
- Some things I learned about choosing research topics (research questions, focus areas, keywords) are:

Students can also be asked to reflect orally. One teacher does an oral reflection activity in which he plays music while students walk briskly around the classroom. When the music stops, each student finds a partner. The teacher

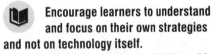

Encourage learners to understand and focus on their own strategies and not on technology itself.
—Tabatabai and Shore (2005, p. 238)

gives the class a reflection prompt and 30 seconds to think. Then each pair takes turns sharing. When asked what advice they would give to a younger student learning about inquiry, one student said, "Keep on going. Don't give up. If you get frustrated trying to find something, go back later. If you get mad at the computer, then find another one."

There are many other activities you can do to promote self-reflection (see Beach et al., 2010, for more ideas). One is to have the students prepare a Help Manual for another class or for next year's students. Another is to have students create a brief video tutorial about one or all of the QUEST steps. They can share the video on the school website or elsewhere. Students can also teach someone at home how to be a more effective Internet QUESTer and then report back to you. Some schools hold evening Internet inquiry workshops, inviting families for one-to-one tutoring sessions from students. It is empowering for students to take on the role of teacher, especially students who are traditionally "at the margins" of the peer group (Hall et al., 2012).

TEACHER: What advice would you give to other students about inquiry?

STUDENT: Work as a team. Stick with your question. Be prepared.

A powerful method of self-reflection is to have students reenact the inquiry process from beginning to end. This can be done in less than one class period. Figure 10.2 shows a reenactment by a group of fourth- and fifth-grade students of their cartoon inquiry project, with photos and captions to illustrate each step of the process. You can imagine how effective this activity is in solidifying students' understanding of what the process of inquiry entails. To illustrate the lasting impression of inquiry-based projects: Maya bumped into one of the fourth-grade girls from the cartoon project *five years later* when she was in high school, whereupon the teen instantly recognized Maya and recalled the cartoon inquiry project with great enthusiasm and nostalgia.

To determine whether your students have internalized new strategies for reading and learning on the Web, be on the lookout for evidence of generalization and transfer. In other words, do your students independently and automatically apply the skills and strategies they've been learning in their next inquiry project? In their next reading project? In their next writing project? Do they apply synthesis and transformation strategies while studying for a test or when working across the content areas? If so, this is how you know that real learning has taken place.

 Language Arts Standard: **Draw evidence from literary or informational texts to support analysis, reflection, and research.**

Deep learning takes time. Be patient while your students learn the skills and strategies needed to effectively locate, understand, and use information. As one student said about the inquiry process, "It takes time. You don't have to get it all done in one day." Please don't feel disappointed if your students don't demonstrate an immediate shift in their approaches to inquiry. Keep your eye out for small gains. Look for indicators of

First, we brainstormed the topic. We agreed on cartoons.

Then, we got cartoon books from the library.

We wrote cartoon scripts in two teams.

We interviewed adults and kids about cartoons.

We organized our information on note cards.

Then we typed our information on the laptop and created a website.

Ta-ta-ta-daaaaah! Th-th-th-that's all folks!

FIGURE 10.2. Inquiry project reenactment.

growth in areas such as "make a plan before you start searching," "use <topic focus> keywords," "decide whether this website has the information you need," or "make notes in your own words." These small but significant improvements are cause for great joy on your part. You may even notice improvements in students' dispositions toward learning (e.g., curiosity, persistence, flexibility, attention to detail).

Keep in mind that trial, error, and failure are important aspects of learning. When describing the inquiry process, one student reflected, "I've learned if you set your mind to something, that you may learn something that you did not know before." Opportunities abound for all of us to learn something new every day. As one teacher commented to his class after an inquiry presentation, "I know something that I didn't know when I woke up this morning. Thank you."

What Have We Learned as Authors?

Our work with Internet readers and their teachers is both enlightening and heartening. Students amaze us with their insights and creativity. When given focused instruction and choices about their learning, students usually rise to our high expectations. We know teachers and library media specialists who have made Internet inquiry a priority in their teaching because they recognize the value of information literacy in students' in-school and out-of-school lives. We have talked with teachers and library media specialists who have worked tirelessly to convince administrators and colleagues of the dire need to prepare students to be effective information users. These dedicated educators inspire and challenge us to continue this important work.

We have also been impressed by teachers and library media specialists who take risks and choose to be learners alongside their students. Teacher sometimes find themselves out of their comfort zone when working with technology but continue to return day after day, ready to tackle the next step of the process. Though it is a cliché, we feel that we have learned as much, if not more, from the students and teachers with whom we've worked as they have from us. We hope that we have painted a true picture of these learners and that they have inspired you as much as they inspire us.

> **Continuity between the curriculum within the school and the child's experiences outside the school promotes sustained, meaningful learning.**
> —Kuhlthau, Maniotes, and Caspari (2007, p. 26)

Final Thoughts

Throughout this text, we have set out to convey the urgent need to teach students to be information literate and to capture the essence of Internet inquiry by describing the process through the QUEST model. We have included detailed explanations, vivid descriptions, and illustrative graphics with the intent of bringing the inquiry process to life. We have built on what we as educators already know about learning, reading, and the quest for finding and making use of information.

When you encourage your students to ask deep questions, to critically evaluate information, and to transform ideas, you are embarking on a learning adventure for both yourself and your students. As teachers, we are asking students to generate questions that matter, to think deeply about topics and ideas, to see themselves as not just information consumers but also information creators. No lesson plan, teacher's guide, or professional development workshop can truly prepare you for the unexpected things that may occur. Our best advice is to keep your focus on the inquiry *process* through the QUEST model and go with the flow. The process of learning is more important than the end product, and students will watch for your cues about what is important and how to proceed.

This book has described authentic teaching and learning and presents the process of inquiry our students will face in their future as working professionals in the real world. Being a lifelong learner is about asking the questions burning in our hearts and having the strategies needed to find and use the answers. We are preparing students to internalize those habits. In doing so, we are letting go of some control by stepping aside to be a mentor or guide rather than a person who delivers information. This change may feel uncomfortable at first and may cause us to question whether to continue down this path, but on we must go. The convergence of literacy and technology is ubiquitous in the world of work, in our personal inquiries, and in the lives of our students. We would be doing students a disservice by not preparing them to apply the inquiry process to the world's most massive source of information, one that will affect their future daily lives in ways we cannot even imagine. We don't take this responsibility lightly. In fact, wanting to help educators become more comfortable with locating, using, and understanding information from the Web is the sole purpose of this text. When we approach Internet inquiry as both teachers and learners, we join our students on the journey of inquiry—and what an adventure it will be!

REFERENCES

Afflerbach, P., Cho, B. Y., Kim, J. K., Crassas, M. E., & Doyle, B. (2013). Reading: What else matters besides strategies and skills? *Reading Teacher, 66*(6), 440–448.

Afflerbach, P. P. (2002). Teaching reading self-assessment strategies. In C. C. Block & M. Pressley (Eds.), *Comprehension instruction: Research-based best practices* (pp. 96–111). New York: Guilford Press.

Afflerbach, P. P., & Cho, B. Y. (2010). Determining and describing reading strategies: Internet and traditional forms of reading. In H. S. Waters & W. Schneider (Eds.), *Metacognition, strategy use, and instruction* (pp. 201–255). New York: Guilford Press.

Afflerbach, P. P., & Johnston, P. H. (1986). What do experts do when the main idea is not explicit? In J. F. Bauman (Ed.), *Teaching main idea comprehension* (pp. 49–72). Newark, DE: International Reading Association.

Alvermann, D. E. (2008). Why bother theorizing adolescents' online literacies for classroom practice and research? *Journal of Adolescent and Adult Literacy, 52*(1), 8–19.

Alvermann, D. E., Hutchins, R. J., & McDevitt, R. (2012). Adolescents' engagement with Web 2.0 and social media: Research, theory, and practice. *Research in the Schools, 19*(1), 33–44.

American Association of School Librarians. (2007). Standards for 21st century learners. Retrieved from *www.ala.org/aasl/sites/ala.org.aasl/files/content/guidelinesandstandards/learningstandards/AASL_LearningStandards.pdf*.

Armstrong, T. (2000). *Information transformation: Teaching strategies for authentic research, projects, and activities*. Markham, Ontario, Canada: Pembroke.

Australian Curriculum Assessment and Reporting Authority. (2012). The Australian curriculum. Retrieved from *www.australiancurriculum.edu.au*.

Bartlett, J., & Miller, C. (2011). Truth, lies and the Internet: A report into young people's digital fluency. Retrieved from *www.demos.co.uk/files/Truth_-_web.pdf*.

Beach, R. (2012). Use of digital tools and literacies in the English language arts classroom. *Research in the Schools, 19*(1), 45–59.

Beach, R., Campano, G., Edmiston, B., & Borgmann, M. (2010). *Literacy tools in the classroom: Teaching through critical inquiry, grades 5–12*. New York: Teachers College Press.

Beck, I. L., McKeown, M. G., & Kucan, L. (2013). *Bringing words to life: Robust vocabulary instruction* (2nd ed.). New York: Guilford Press.

Beers, K., & Probst, R. E. (2013). *Notice and note: Strategies for close reading*. Portsmouth, NH: Heinemann.

Bingimlas, K. A. (2009). Barriers to the successful integration of ICT in teaching and learning environments: A review of the literature. *Eurasia Journal of Mathematics, Science and Technology Education, 5*(3), 235–245.

Blachowicz, C. L., & Fisher, P. J. (2003). Best practices in vocabulary instruction: What effective teachers do. In L. M. Morrow, L. B. Gambrell, & M. Pressley (Eds.), *Best practices in literacy instruction* (2nd ed., pp. 87–110). New York: Guilford Press.

Block, C. C., & Pressley, M. (Eds.). (2002). *Comprehension instruction: Research-based best practices*. New York: Guilford Press.

Branch-Mueller, J., & deGroot, J. (2011). The power of Web 2.0: Teacher-librarians become school technology leaders. *School Libraries Worldwide, 17*(2), 25–40.

Brown, A. L., & Day, J. (1983). Macrorules for summarizing texts: The development of expertise. *Journal of Verbal Learning and Verbal Behavior, 22*, 1–15.

Bruce, B. C., & Casey, L. (2012). The practice of inquiry: A pedagogical "sweet spot" for digital literacy? *Computers in the Schools, 29*(1–2), 191–206.

Bruner, J. (1986). *Actual minds, possible worlds*. Cambridge, MA: Harvard University Press.

Burn, A., Buckingham, D., Parry, B., & Powell, M. (2010). Minding the gaps: Teachers' cultures, students' cultures. In D. E. Alvermann (Ed.), *Adolescents' online literacies: Connecting classrooms, digital media, and popular culture* (pp. 183–202). New York: Lang.

Calkins, L. (1994). *The art of teaching writing*. Portsmouth, NH: Heinemann.

Carr, N. (2008, July). Is Google making us stupid?: What the Internet is doing to our brains. *Atlantic Monthly*. Retrieved from *www.theatlantic.com/magazine/archive/2008/07/is-google-making-us-stupid/306868*.

Cascio, J. (2009, July). Get smarter. *Atlantic Monthly*. Retrieved from *www.theatlantic.com/magazine/archive/2009/07/get-smarter/307548*.

Castek, J. (2012). If you want students to evaluate online resources and other new media—teach them how. In D. Lapp & B. Moss (Eds.), *Exemplary instruction in the middle grades: Teaching that supports engagement and rigorous learning* (pp. 105–123). New York: Guilford Press.

Castek, J., Zawilinski, L., McVerry, G., O'Byrne, W. I., & Leu, D. J. (2011). The new literacies of online reading comprehension: New opportunities and challenges for students with learning disabilities. In C. Wyatt-Smith, J. Elkins, S. Zawilinski, L. McVerry, O'Byrne, W. I., & Leu Gunn (Eds.), *Multiple perspectives on difficulties in learning literacy and numeracy* (pp. 91–110). New York: Springer.

Chandler-Olcott, K., & Lewis, E. (2010). "I think they're being wired differently": Secondary teachers' cultural models of adolescents and their online literacies. In D. E. Alvermann (Ed.), *Adolescents' online literacies: Connecting classrooms, digital media, and popular culture* (pp. 163–182). New York: Lang.

Cho, B.-Y., & Afflerbach, P. (2015). Reading on the Internet: Realizing and constructing potential texts. *Journal of Adolescent and Adult Literacy, 58*(6), 504–517.

Clay, M. (1991). *Becoming literate: The construction of inner control*. Portsmouth, NH: Heinemann.

Coiro, J. (2011a). Predicting reading comprehension on the Internet: Contributions of offline reading skills, online reading skills, and prior knowledge. *Journal of Literacy Research, 43*(4), 352–392.

Coiro, J. (2011b). Talking about reading as thinking: Modeling the hidden complexities of online reading comprehension. *Theory into Practice, 50*, 107–115.

Coiro, J. (2012). Understanding dispositions toward reading on the Internet. *Journal of Adolescent and Adult Literacy, 55*(7), 645–648.

Coiro, J. (2014). *Online reading comprehension: Challenges and opportunities*. Virtual paper presented to the annual meeting of the XI Encontro Virtual de Documentação em Software Livre (EVIDOSOL) e VIII Congresso Internacional de Linguagem e Tecnologia online (CILTEC-online). Retrieved from *www.periodicos.letras.ufmg.br/index.php/anais_linguagem_tecnologia/article/view/5859/5092*.

Coiro, J., & Dobler, E. (2007). Exploring the online reading comprehension strategies used by sixth-grade skilled readers to search for and locate information on the Internet. *Reading Research Quarterly, 42*(2), 214–257.

Coiro, J., & Fogleman, J. (2011). Using websites wisely. *Educational Leadership, 68*(5), 34–38.

Coiro, J., & Kennedy, C. (2011). The Online Reading Comprehension Assessment (ORCA) Project: Preparing students for Common Core standards and 21st-century literacies. Retrieved from *www.orca.uconn.edu/orca/assets/File/Research%20Reports/CCSS%20ORCA%20Alignment%20June%202011.pdf*.

Coiro, J., Knobel, M., Lankshear, C., & Leu, D. J. (2008). Central issues in new literacies and new literacies research. In J. Coiro, M. Knobel, C. Lankshear, & D. J. Leu (Eds.), *Handbook of research on new literacies* (pp. 1–22). Mahwah, NJ: Erlbaum.

Colwell, J., Hunt-Barron, S., & Reinking, D. (2013). Obstacles to developing digital literacy on the Internet in middle school science instruction. *Journal of Literacy Research, 45*(3), 1–30.

Crockett, L., Jukes, I., & Churches, A. (2011). *Literacy is "not" enough: 21st-century fluencies for the digital age.* Thousand Oaks, CA: Corwin.

Csíkszentmihalyi, M. (1998). *Finding flow: The psychology of engagement with everyday life.* New York: Basic Books.

Cummins, S., & Stallmeyer-Gerard, C. (2011). Teaching for synthesis of informational texts with read-alouds. *Reading Teacher, 64*(6), 394–405.

Dalton, B., & Proctor, C. P. (2008). The changing landscape of text and comprehension in the age of new literacies. In J. Coiro, C. Lankshear, M. Knobel, & D. J. Leu (Eds.), *Handbook of research on new literacies* (pp. 297–324). New York: Routledge.

DeSchryver, M. (2015). Web-mediated knowledge synthesis for educators. *Journal of Adolescent and Adult Literacy, 58*(5), 388–396.

DeStefano, D., & LeFevre, J. (2007). Cognitive load in hypertext reading: A review. *Computers in Human Behavior, 23*, 1616–1641.

Dewey, J. (1938). *Experience and education.* New York: Macmillan.

Dobler, E. (2015). e-Textbooks: Personalized learning experience or digital distraction? *Journal of Adolescent and Adult Literacy, 58*(6), 482–491.

Dole, J. A., Duffy, G. G., Roehler, L. R., & Pearson, P. D. (1991). Moving from the old to the new: Research on reading comprehension. *Review of Educational Research, 61*, 239–264.

Dresang, E. T. (2005). The information-seeking behavior of youth in the digital environment. *Library Trends, 54*(2), 178–195.

Drew, S. V. (2012). Open up the ceiling on the Common Core State Standards: Preparing students for 21st-century literacy—NOW. *Journal of Adolescent and Adult Literacy, 56*(4), 321–330.

Duke, N. K., & Pearson, P. D. (2002). Effective practices for developing reading comprehension. In A. E. Farstrup & S. J. Samuels (Eds.), *What research has to say about reading instruction* (pp. 205–242). Newark, DE: International Reading Association.

Dwyer, B., & Harrison, C. (2008). There's no rabbits on the Internet: Scaffolding the development of effective search strategies for struggling readers during Internet inquiry. In Y. Kim, V. Risko, D. Compton, D. Dickinson, M. Hundley, R. Jimenez, et al. (Eds.), *57th annual yearbook of the National Reading Conference* (pp. 187–202). Oak Creek, WI: National Reading Conference.

Eagleton, M. B., & Dobler, E. (2007). *Reading the Web: Strategies for Internet inquiry.* New York: Guilford Press.

Eagleton, M. B., & Guinee, K. (2002). Strategies for supporting student Internet inquiry. *New England Reading Association Journal, 38*(2), 39–47.

Eagleton, M. B., Guinee, K., & Langlais, K. (2003). Teaching Internet literacy strategies: The hero inquiry project. *Voices from the Middle, 10*(3), 28–35.

Educational Testing Service. (2014). The iSkills Assessment. Retrieved from *www.ets.org/iskills.*

Eisenberg, M., & Berkowitz, B. (2001). Big6: An information problem-solving process. Retrieved from *http://big6.com.*

Eisenberg, M. B. (2008). Information literacy: Essential skills for the information age. *Journal of Library and Information Technology, 28*(2), 39–47.

Eisner, E. W. (1994). *Cognition and curriculum reconsidered.* New York: Teachers College Press.

Fabos, B. (2004). *Wrong turn on the information superhighway: Education and the commercialization of the Internet.* New York: Teachers College Press.

Fabos, B. (2008). The price of information: Critical literacy, education and today's Internet. In J. Coiro, C. Lankshear, M. Knobel, & D. J. Leu (Eds.), *Handbook of research on new literacies* (pp. 839–870). New York: Routledge.

Fielding, L. G., & Pearson, P. D. (1994). Synthesis of research: Reading comprehension that works. *Educational Leadership, 51*(5), 62–67.

Fisher, D., & Frey, N. (2013). Engaging the adolescent reader: Note-taking and note-making for academic success. Newark, DE: International Reading Association. Retrieved from *www.reading.org/general/ Publications/e-ssentials/e8014.*

Fisher, D., Frey, N., & Lapp, D. (2009). *In a reading state of mind: Brain research, teacher modeling, and comprehension instruction.* Newark, DE: International Reading Association.

Fisher, D., Frey, N., & Lapp, D. (2012). *Teaching students to read like detectives: Comprehending, analyzing, and discussing text.* Bloomington, IN: Solution Tree.

Frey, N., Fisher, D., & Gonzalez, A. (2010). *Literacy 2.0: Reading and writing in 21st-century classrooms.* Bloomington, IN: Solution Tree.

Gardner, H. (1983). *Frames of mind: The theory of multiple intelligences.* New York: Basic Books.

Gardner, H., & Davis, K. (2013). *The app generation: How today's youth navigate identity, intimacy, and imagination in a digital world.* New Haven, CT: Yale University Press.

Garner, R., & Gillingham, M. G. (1998). The Internet in the classroom: Is it the end of transmission-oriented pedagogy? In D. Reinking, M. McKenna, L. Labbo, & R. Keiffer (Eds.), *Handbook of literacy and technology: Transformations in a post-typographic world* (pp. 221–231). Mahwah, NJ: Erlbaum.

Goldman, S. R., Braasch, J. L. G., Wiley, J., Graesser, A. C., & Brodowinska, K. (2012). Comprehending and learning from Internet sources: Processing patterns of better and poorer learners. *Reading Research Quarterly, 47*(4), 356–381.

Goodman, K. S. (1982). *Language and literacy: The selected writings of Kenneth S. Goodman* (G. V. Gollasch, Ed.). Boston: Routledge & Kegan Paul.

Goodman, K. S. (1994). Reading, writing and written texts: A transactional sociopsycholinguistic view. In R. B. Ruddell, M. R. Ruddell, & H. Singer (Eds.), *Theoretical models and processes of reading* (4th ed., pp. 1093–1130). Newark, DE: International Reading Association.

Goodman, K. S. (1996). *On reading.* Portsmouth, NH: Heinemann.

Gordon, D., Proctor, C. P., & Dalton, B. (2012). Reading strategy instruction: Universal Design for Learning and digital texts: Examples of an integrated approach. In T. E. Hall, A. Meyer, & D. H. Rose (Eds.), *Universal Design for Learning: Practical applications* (pp. 25–37). New York: Guilford Press.

Graves, D. (1983). *Writing: Teacher and children at work.* Portsmouth, NH: Heinemann.

Grisham, D. L. (2001, April). Technology and media literacy: What do teachers need to know? *Reading Online, 4*(9). Retrieved from *www.readingonline.org/editorial/edit_index.asp?HREF=/editorial/ april2001/index.html.*

Gross, M., & Latham, D. (2012). What's skill got to do with it?: Information literacy skills and self-views of ability among first-year college students. *Journal of the American Society for Information Science and Technology, 63*(3), 574–583.

Guccione, L. M. (2011). Integrating literacy and inquiry for English learners. *Reading Teacher, 94*(8), 567–577.

Guinee, K. (2007). *The little searcher that could: Middle-school students' search string construction during Web-based research.* Unpublished doctoral dissertation, Harvard Graduate School of Education, Cambridge, MA.

Guinee, K. (2012). E-learning behaviors in middle school. In Z. Yan (Ed.), *The encyclopedia of cyber behavior* (pp. 1–20). Hershey, PA: IGI.

Guinee, K., & Eagleton, M. B. (2006). Spinning straw into gold: Transforming information into knowledge during Web-based research. *English Journal, 95*(4), 46–52.

Guinee, K., Eagleton, M., & Hall, T. E. (2003). Adolescents' Internet search strategies: Drawing upon familiar cognitive paradigms when accessing electronic information sources. *Journal of Educational Computing Research, 29*(3), 363–374.

Hall, T. E., Meyer, A., & Rose, D. H. (2012). An introduction to Universal Design for Learning: Questions and answers. In T. E. Hall, A. Meyer, & D. H. Rose (Eds.), *Universal Design for Learning: Practical applications* (pp. 1–8). New York: Guilford Press.

Hare, V. C., & Borchardt, K. M. (1984). Direct instruction of summarization skills. *Reading Research Quarterly, 20,* 62–78.

Hargittai, E., Neuman, W. R., & Curry, O. (2012). Taming the information tide: Perceptions of information overload in the American home. *Information Society, 28,* 161–173.

Harrison, C. (2011). Literacy, technology and the Internet: What are the challenges and opportunities for learners with reading difficulties, and how do we support them in meeting those challenges and grasping those opportunities? In C. Wyatt-Smith, J. Elkins, & S. Gunn (Eds.), *Multiple perspectives on difficulties in learning literacy and numeracy* (pp. 111–131). New York: Springer.

Harrison, C., Dwyer, B., & Castek, J. (2014). *Using technology to improve reading and learning.* Huntington Beach, CA: Shell Education.

Harste, J. C. (1994). Literacy as curricular conversations about knowledge, inquiry and morality. In R. B. Ruddell, M. R. Ruddell, & H. Singer (Eds.), *Theoretical models and processes of reading* (4th ed., pp. 1220–1242). Newark, DE: International Reading Association.

Hartman, D. K., Morsink, P. M., & Zheng, J. (2010). From print to pixels: The evolution of cognitive conceptions of reading comprehension. In E. A. Baker (Ed.), *The new literacies: Multiple perspectives on research and practice* (pp. 131–164). New York: Guilford Press.

Harvey, S., & Goudvis, A. (2007). *Strategies that work: Teaching comprehension for understanding and engagement* (2nd ed.). Portland, ME: Stenhouse.

Harvey, S., & Goudvis, A. (2013). Comprehension at the CORE. *Reading Teacher, 66*(6), 432–439.

Head, A. J. (2013, April). *Project information literacy: What can be learned about the information-seeking behavior of today's college students?* Paper presented at the 74th annual conference of the Association of College and Research Libraries, Indianapolis, IN. Retrieved from *www.ala.org/acrl/sites/ala. org.acrl/files/content/conferences/confsandpreconfs/2013/papers/Head_Project.pdf.*

Henry, L. (2006). SEARCHing for an answer: The critical role of new literacies while reading on the Internet. *Reading Teacher, 59*(7), 614–627.

Henry, L. H., Castek, J., O'Byrne, W. I., & Zawilinski, L. (2012). Using peer collaboration to support online reading, writing, and communication: An empowerment model for struggling readers, *Reading and Writing Quarterly, 28*(3), 279–306.

Hobbs, R. (2006). Multiple visions of multimedia literacy: Emerging areas of synthesis. In M. McKenna, L. D. Labbo, R. D. Kieffer, & D. Reinking (Eds.), *International handbook of literacy and technology* (pp. 15–28). Mahwah, NJ: Erlbaum.

Hobbs, R. (2011). *Digital and media literacy: Connecting culture and classroom.* Thousand Oaks, CA: Corwin.

Hobbs, R., & Frost, R. (2003). Measuring the acquisition of media-literacy skills. *Reading Research Quarterly, 38*(3), 330–355.

Hyerle, D., & Alper. L. (2013). Thinking maps for meetings of the mind. In A. Costa & P. O'Leary (Eds.), *The power of the social brain: Teaching, learning, and interdependent thinking* (pp. 102–114). New York: Teachers College Press.

Kajder, S. B. (2003). *The tech-savvy English classroom.* Portland, ME: Stenhouse.

Kauffman, D. F., Zhao, R., & Yang, Y. (2011). Effects of online note-taking formats and self-monitoring prompts on learning from online text: Using technology to enhance self-regulated learning. *Contemporary Educational Psychology, 36*(4), 313–322.

Keene, E. O. (2008). *To understand: New horizons in reading comprehension.* Portsmouth, NH: Heinemann.

Keene, E. O., & Zimmermann, S. (1997). *Mosaic of thought: Teaching comprehension in a reader's workshop.* Portsmouth, NH: Heinemann.

Keene, E. O., & Zimmermann, S. (2007). *Mosaic of thought: The power of comprehension strategy instruction.* Portsmouth, NH: Heinemann.

Kent State University Libraries. (2014). TRAILS: Tool for Real-time Assessment of Information Literacy Skills. Retrieved from *www.trails-9.org.*

Kiili, C., Laurinen, L., & Marttunen, M. (2008). Students evaluating Internet sources: From versatile evaluators to uncritical readers. *Journal of Educational Computing Research, 39*(1), 75–95.

Kiili, C., Laurinen, L., Marttunen, M., & Leu, D. J. (2012). Working on understanding during collaborative online reading. *Journal of Literacy Research, 44*(4), 448–483.

Kolowich, S. (2011, August 22). What students don't know. *Inside Higher Ed.* Retrieved from *www.*

insidehighered.com/news/2011/08/22/erial_study_of_student_research_habits_at_illinois_university_libraries_reveals_alarmingly_poor_information_literacy_and_skills.

Kozma, R. B. (1991). Learning with media. *Review of Educational Research, 61*(2), 179–211.

Kuhlthau, C. C. (2010). Guided inquiry: School libraries in the 21st century. *School Libraries Worldwide, 16*(1), 17–28.

Kuhlthau, C. C., Maniotes, L. K., & Caspari, A. K. (2007). *Guided inquiry: Learning in the 21st century.* Westport, CT: Libraries Unlimited.

Kuiper, E., & Volman, M. (2008). The Web as a source of information for students in K–12 education. In J. Coiro, C. Lankshear, M. Knobel, & D. J. Leu (Eds.), *Handbook of research on new literacies* (pp. 241–266). New York: Routledge.

Kymes, A. (2005). Teaching online comprehension strategies using think-alouds. *Journal of Adolescent and Adult Literacy, 48*(6), 492–500.

Labbo, L. D. (1996). A semiotic analysis of young children's symbol making in a classroom computer center. *Reading Research Quarterly, 31*(4), 356–383.

Ladbrook, J., & Probert, E. (2011). Information skills and critical literacy: Where are our digikids at with online searching and are their teachers helping? *Australasian Journal of Educational Technology, 27*(1), 105–121.

Langford, L. (2001). A building block: Towards the information-literate school community. *Teacher Librarian, 28*(5), 18–21.

Lapinski, S., Gravel, J. W., & Rose, D. H. (2012). Tools for practice: The Universal Design for Learning guidelines. In T. E. Hall, A. Meyer, & D. H. Rose (Eds.), *Universal Design for Learning: Practical applications* (pp. 9–24). New York: Guilford Press.

Leander, K. M. (2010). Afterword. In D. E. Alvermann (Ed.), *Adolescents' online literacies: Connecting classrooms, digital media, and popular culture* (pp. 203–208). New York: Lang.

Lehman, C. (2012). *Energize research reading and writing: Fresh strategies to spark interest, develop independence, and meet key Common Core standards.* Portsmouth, NH: Heinemann.

Leu, D. J., & Forzani, E. (2012). New literacies in a Web 2.0, 3.0, 4.0, . . . ∞ world. *Research in the Schools, 19*(1), 75–81.

Leu, D. J., Forzani, E., Burlingame, C., Kulikowich, J., Sendransk, N., Coiro, J., et al. (2013). The new literacies of online research and comprehension: Assessing and preparing students for the 21st century with Common Core State Standards. In S. B. Neuman & L. B. Gambrell (Eds.), *Quality reading instruction in the age of Common Core Standards* (pp. 219–236). Newark, DE: International Reading Association.

Leu, D. J., Kinzer, C. K., Coiro, J., Castek, J., & Henry, L. A. (2013). New literacies: A dual-level theory of the changing nature of literacy, instruction, and assessment. In D. E. Alvermann, N. J. Unrau, & R. B. Ruddell (Eds.), *Theoretical models and processes of reading* (6th ed., pp. 1150–1181). Newark, DE: International Reading Association.

Leu, D. J., Kulikowich, J., Sedransk, N., & Coiro, J. (n.d.). Online reading comprehension assessments. Retrieved from *www.orca.uconn.edu.*

Leu, D. J., McVerry, J. G., O'Byrne, W. I., Kiili, C., Zawilinski, L., Everett-Cacopardo, H., et al. (2011). The new literacies of online reading comprehension: Expanding the literacy and learning curriculum. *Journal of Adolescent and Adult Literacy, 55*(1), 5–14.

Leu, D. J., Zawilinski, L., Forzani, E., & Timbrell, N. (2014). Best practices in new literacies and the new literacies of online research and comprehension. In L. M. Morrow & L. B. Gambrell (Eds.), *Best practices in literacy instruction* (5th ed., pp. 343–364). New York: Guilford Press.

Lewis, C., & Fabos, B. (2005). Instant messaging, literacies, and social identities. *Reading Research Quarterly, 40*(4), 470–501.

Macedo-Rouet, M., Braasch, J. L., Britt, M. A., & Rouet, J.-F. (2013). Teaching fourth and fifth graders to evaluate information sources during text comprehension. *Cognition and Instruction, 31*(2), 204–226.

Mackey, M. (2003). Researching new forms of literacy. *Reading Research Quarterly, 38*(3), 403–407.

Mackey, T. P., & Jacobson, T. E. (2011). Reframing information literacy as metaliteracy. *College Research Libraries, 72*(1), 62–78.

May, F. A., & Downey, A. (2009). Problem-based learning meets Web 2.0: Using a YouTube video to teach information literacy in a problem-based learning format. *Library Orientation Exchange.* Retrieved from *http://commons.emich.edu/cgi/viewcontent.cgi?article=1016&context=loexconf2009.*

McEneaney, J. E. (2011). Web 3.0, Litbots, and TPWSGWTAU. *Journal of Adolescent and Adult Literacy, 54*(5), 376–378.

McEneaney, J. E., Li, L., Allen, K., & Guzniczak, L. (2009). Stance, navigation, and reader response in expository hypertext. *Journal of Literacy Research, 41,* 1–45.

McKenzie, J. (1999). The research cycle. *From Now On: The Educational Technology Journal, 9*(4). Retrieved from *http://questioning.org/rcycle.html.*

Meyer, A., & Rose, D. H. (1998). *Learning to read in the computer age.* Cambridge, MA: Brookline Books.

Meyer, A., Rose, D. H., & Gordon, D. (2014). *Universal Design for Learning: Theory and practice.* Wakefield, MA: CAST.

Miller, C., & Bartlett, J. (2012). "Digital fluency": Towards young people's critical use of the Internet. *Journal of Information Literacy, 6*(2), 35–55.

Moje, E., Ciechanowski, K., Kramer, K., Ellis, L., Carrillo, R., & Callazo, T. (2004). Working toward third space in content-area literacy: An examination of everyday funds of knowledge and discourse. *Reading Research Quarterly, 39*(1), 38–70.

Moje, E. B. (2009). A call for new research on new and multi-literacies. *Research in the Teaching of English, 43*(4), 348–362.

Moline, S. (2012). *I see what you mean: Visual literacy K–8.* Portland, ME: Stenhouse.

National Governors Association Center for Best Practices & Council of Chief State School Officers. (2010). *Common Core State Standards.* Washington, DC: Author.

NationMaster. (2014). Education: Schools connected to the Internet. Retrieved from *www.nationmaster.com/country-info/stats/Education/Schools-connected-to-the-Internet.*

New London Group. (1996). A pedagogy of multiliteracies: Designing social futures. *Harvard Educational Review, 66*(1), 60–92.

Next Generation Science Standards. (2011). The next generation science standards. Retrieved from *www.nextgenscience.org/next-generation-science-standards.*

Novak, K. (2014). *UDL now!: A teacher's Monday morning guide to implementing the Common Core Standards using Universal Design for Learning.* Wakefield, MA: CAST.

November, A. (2012). *Who owns the learning?: Preparing students for success in the digital age.* Bloomington, IN: Solution Tree.

Open Education Database. (2013, November 11). The ultimate guide to the invisible Web. Retrieved from *http://oedb.org/ilibrarian/invisible-web.*

Overturf, B. J., Montgomery, L. H., & Smith, M. H. (2013). *Word nerds: Teaching all students to learn and love vocabulary.* Portland, ME: Stenhouse.

Palincsar, A. S., & Brown, A. L. (1984). Reciprocal teaching of comprehension-fostering and comprehension-monitoring activities. *Cognition and Instruction, 1,* 117–175.

Pappas, M. L., & Tepe, A. E. (2002). *Pathways to knowledge and inquiry learning.* Santa Barbara, CA: Libraries Unlimited.

Paris, S. G., Lipson, M. Y., & Wixson, K. K. (1983). Becoming a strategic reader. *Contemporary Educational Psychology, 8,* 293–316.

Pariser, E. (2012). *The filter bubble: How the personalized web is changing what we read and how we think.* New York: Penguin Books.

Partnership for Assessment of Readiness for College and Careers. (2014). The PARCC assessment. Retrieved from *www.parcconline.org/assessment-system.*

Pearson, P. D., & Gallagher, M. C. (1983). The instruction of reading comprehension. *Contemporary Educational Psychology, 8,* 317–344.

Pearson, P. D., Roehler, L. R., Dole, J. A., & Duffy, G. G. (1992). Developing expertise in reading comprehension. In S. J. Samuels & A. E. Farstrup (Eds.), *What research has to say about reading instruction* (pp. 145–199). Newark, DE: International Reading Association.

Perkins, D. N. (1986). *Knowledge as design.* Hillsdale, NJ: Erlbaum.

Pew Research Center. (2013). *Teens and technology 2013.* Retrieved from *www.pewinternet.org/2013/03/13/teens-and-technology-2013.*

Pikulski, J. J., & Chard, D. J. (2005). Fluency: Bridge between decoding and reading comprehension. *Reading Teacher, 58*(6), 510–519.

Pink, D. H. (2009). *Drive: The surprising truth about what motivates us.* New York: Riverhead Press.

Pressley, M. (2002). Metacognition and self-regulated comprehension. In A. E. Farstrup & S. J. Samuels (Eds.), *What research has to say about reading instruction* (3rd ed., pp. 291–309). Newark, DE: International Reading Association.

Pressley, M., & Afflerbach, P. (1995). *Verbal protocols of reading: The nature of constructively responsive reading.* Hillsdale, NJ: Erlbaum.

Project SAILS. (2014). *Standardized Assessment of Information Literacy Skills.* Retrieved from *https://projectsails.org.*

RAND Reading Study Group. (2004). A research agenda for improving reading comprehension. In R. Ruddell & N. Unrau (Eds.), *Theoretical models and processes of reading* (5th ed., pp. 720–754). Newark, DE: International Reading Association.

Rankin, V. (1999). *The thoughtful researcher: Teaching the research process to middle school students.* Englewood, CO: Libraries Unlimited.

Raphael, T. E., & Pearson, P. D. (1985). Increasing students' awareness of sources of information for answering questions. *American Educational Research Journal, 22,* 217–236.

Raphael, T. E., Wonnacott, C. A., & Pearson, P. D. (1983). *Increasing students' sensitivity to sources of information: An instructional study in question-answer relationships* (Tech. Rep. No. 284). Urbana: University of Illinois Center for the Study of Reading.

Reinking, D. (1997). Me and my hypertext:) A multiple digression analysis of technology and literacy (sic). *Reading Teacher, 50*(8), 626–643.

Rose, D. H., Gravel, J. W., & Domings, Y. (2012). Universal Design for Learning "unplugged": Applications in low-tech settings. In T. E. Hall, A. Meyer, & D. H. Rose (Eds.), *Universal Design for Learning: Practical applications* (pp. 120–134). New York: Guilford Press.

Rosenblatt, L. R. (1985). Viewpoints: Transaction versus interaction—A terminological rescue operation. *Research in the Teaching of English, 19,* 96–107.

Rosenblatt, L. R. (1994). The transactional theory of reading and writing. In R. Ruddell, M. Ruddell, & H. Singer (Eds.), *Theoretical models and processes of reading* (4th ed., pp. 1057–1092). Newark, DE: International Reading Association.

Rosenshine, B., & Meister, C. (1994). Reciprocal teaching: A review of the research. *Review of Educational Research, 64*(4), 479–530.

Rothstein, D., & Santana, L. (2011). *Make just one change: Teach students to ask their own questions.* Cambridge, MA: Harvard Education Press.

Rouet, J.-F., Ros, C., Goumi, A., Macedo-Rouet, M., & Dinet, J. (2011). The influence of surface and deep cues on primary and secondary school students' assessment of relevance in Web menus. *Learning and Instruction, 21,* 205–219.

Rowlands, I., & Nichols, D. (2008). Information behaviour of the researcher of the future: Executive summary. Retrieved from *www.jisc.ac.uk/media/documents/programmes/reppres/gg_final_keynote_11012008.pdf.*

Salomon, G. (1997). Of mind and media: How culture's symbolic forms affect learning and thinking. *Phi Delta Kappan, 78*(5), 375–380.

Schrock, K. (2014). Kathy Schrock's guide to everything. Retrieved from *www.schrockguide.net/literacy-in-the-digital-age.html.*

Serafini, F. (2012). Reading multimodal texts in the 21st century. *Research in the Schools, 19*(1), 26–32.

Shirky, C. (2010). *Cognitive surplus: Creativity and generosity in a connected age.* New York: Penguin Press.

Short, K. G. (2009). Inquiry as stance on curriculum. In S. Davidson & S. Carber (Eds.), *Taking the PYP forward: The future of the IB Primary Years Programme* (pp. 11–26). Woodbridge, UK: John Catt Educational.

Short, K. G., & Burke, C. (1991). *Creating curriculum: Teachers and students as a community of learners.* Portsmouth, NH: Heinemann.

Short, K. G., Schroeder, J., Laird, J., Kauffman, G., Ferguson, M., & Crawford, K. (1996). *Learning together through inquiry: From Columbus to integrated curriculum.* York, ME: Stenhouse.

Siegel, M. (1995). More than words: The generative power of transmediation for learning. *Canadian Journal of Education, 20*(4), 455–475.

Smarter Balanced Assessment Consortium. (2014). Smarter balanced assessment. Retrieved from *www.smarterbalanced.org*.

Spiranec, S., & Zorica, M. B. (2010). Information literacy 2.0: Hype or discourse refinement? *Journal of Documentation, 66*(1), 140–153.

Spiro, R. J. (2006). The "New Gutenberg Revolution": Radical new learning, thinking, teaching, and training with technology. *Educational Technology, 46*(1), 3–5.

Suhor, C. (1984). Towards a semiotics-based curriculum. *Journal of Curriculum Studies, 16*(3), 247–257.

Summey, D. C. (2013). *Developing digital literacies: A framework for professional learning.* Thousand Oaks, CA: Corwin.

Sutherland-Smith, W. (2002). Weaving the literacy web: Changes in reading from page to screen. *Reading Teacher, 55*, 662–669.

Tabatabai, D., & Shore, B. M. (2005). How experts and novices search the Web. *Library and Information Science Research, 27*, 222–248.

Thornburg, D. D. (2004). *Inquiry: The art of helping students ask good questions.* Barrington, IL: Thornburg Center. Retrieved from *www.tcpdpodcast.org/briefings/inquiry.pdf*.

Todd, R. J., & Gordon, C. A. (2011). School libraries, now more than ever: A position paper of the Center for International Scholarship in School Libraries. Retrieved from *www.livingston.org/cms/lib4/NJ01000562/Centricity/Domain/1324/Oct2012_CISSL.pdf*

Tovani, C. (2011). *So what do they really know?: Assessment that informs teaching and learning.* Portland, ME: Stenhouse.

Turkle, S. (2011). *Alone together: Why we expect more from technology and less from each other.* New York: Basic Books.

Vygotsky, L. (1978). *Mind in society: The development of higher psychological processes.* Cambridge, MA: Harvard University Press.

Walraven, A., Brand-Gruwel, S., & Boshuizen, H. P. (2009). How students evaluate information and sources when searching the World Wide Web for information. *Computers and Education, 52*, 234–246.

Winograd, P. N. (1984). Strategic difficulties in summarizing texts. *Reading Research Quarterly, 19*, 404–425.

Wyatt-Smith, C., & Elkins, J. (2008). Multimodal reading and comprehension in online environments. In J. Coiro, C. Lankshear, M. Knobel, & D. J. Leu (Eds.), *Handbook of research on new literacies* (pp. 899–940). New York: Routledge.

Yang, Y. C., & Wu, W. I. (2012). Digital storytelling for enhancing students' academic achievement, critical thinking, and learning motivation. *Computers and Education, 59*(2), 339–352.

Zhang, M. (2013). Prompts-based scaffolding for online inquiry: Design intentions and classroom realities. *Educational Technology and Society, 16*(3), 140–151.

Zhang, S., & Duke, N. (2008). Strategies for Internet reading with different reading purposes: A descriptive study of twelve good Internet readers. *Journal of Literacy Research, 40*, 128–162.

Zhang, S., Duke, N. K., & Jimenez, L. M. (2011). The WWWDOT approach to improving students' critical evaluation of websites. *Reading Teacher, 65*(2), 150–158.

Zimmerman, B. J. (2002). Becoming a self-regulated learner: An overview. *Theory into Practice, 41*(2), 64–70.

Zwiers, J. (2004). *Building reading comprehension habits in grades 6–12: A toolkit of classroom activities.* Newark, DE: International Reading Association.

INDEX